# The Evolution of Consciousness

**Also available from Bloomsbury**

*Advances in Experimental Philosophy of Mind*, edited by Justin Sytsma
*A Short Philosophical Guide to the Fallacies of Love*, by José A. Díez and
Andrea Iacona
*Great Philosophical Objections to Artificial Intelligence*, by Eric Dietrich, Chris
Fields, John P. Sullins, Bram Van Heuveln and Robin Zebrowski
*Philosophy in a Technological World*, by James Tartaglia
*The Philosophy and Science of Predictive Processing*, edited by Dina Mendonça,
Manuel Curado and Steven S. Gouveia

# The Evolution of Consciousness

## *Representing the Present Moment*

Paula Droege

BLOOMSBURY ACADEMIC
LONDON • NEW YORK • OXFORD • NEW DELHI • SYDNEY

BLOOMSBURY ACADEMIC
Bloomsbury Publishing Plc
50 Bedford Square, London, WC1B 3DP, UK
1385 Broadway, New York, NY 10018, USA
29 Earlsfort Terrace, Dublin 2, Ireland

BLOOMSBURY, BLOOMSBURY ACADEMIC and the Diana logo
are trademarks of Bloomsbury Publishing Plc

First published in Great Britain 2022
This paperback edition published 2023

Copyright © Paula Droege, 2022

Paula Droege has asserted her right under the Copyright, Designs
and Patents Act, 1988, to be identified as Author of this work.

For legal purposes the Acknowledgments on pp. xii–xiii constitute
an extension of this copyright page.

Cover design by Charlotte Daniels
Cover image: Jorge Juan Perez / EyeEm / Getty Images.

A catalogue record for this book is available from the British Library.

A catalog record for this book is available from the Library of Congress.

ISBN:    HB:    978-1-3501-6678-3
         PB:    978-1-3502-7808-0
         ePDF:  978-1-3501-6679-0
         eBook: 978-1-3501-6680-6

Typeset by Integra Software Services Pvt. Ltd.

To find out more about our authors and books visit www.bloomsbury.com
and sign up for our newsletters.

*For Kenneth Klein*

# Contents

# List of Figures

# List of Table

# Preface

Google "consciousness explanation" and you find something like this: Science can't explain consciousness. Most theories of consciousness are wrong. Philosophers deny the existence of consciousness rather than explain it.

Yet as a philosopher who has been doing research on consciousness since the resurgence of scientific interest in the field in the mid-1990s, the prospect of an explanation has never been more tangible to me. Consensus is developing around answers to many of the early questions about methodology and definition. Lots of debate and disagreement still is ongoing, along with some amount of confusion.

This book aims to present a clear and coherent theory that explains how consciousness evolved as a result of physical processes. It is an unusual book of philosophy by contemporary standards. Rather than engage in technical arguments, objections, and responses, I take an interdisciplinary and synoptic view to show how advances in neuroscience, cognitive psychology, and other fields can be integrated into a comprehensive picture of the conscious mind. My model is the marvelous work of Daniel Dennett, whose books capture the productive explanatory dynamics of intersecting ideas. Since few writers are as witty and lucid as Dennett, be advised that my efforts here are rather more prosaic.

My approach is to describe the elements necessary to explain consciousness. I will certainly give reasons for and against various positions that are under debate, but I do not claim to be comprehensive or always conclusive. Readers can find more in-depth arguments in my published papers on the positions I advocate. I deliberately chose not to simply collect those papers into a volume, because I wanted to write a book that would be accessible to nonprofessionals. There are few philosophy books on consciousness that can be read by undergraduate students or a reader without previous introduction to the terminology and history of the topic. Far more reader-friendly books are published in neuroscience and psychology.

This book offers entry into the philosophical issues by providing an explanation of how and why consciousness could possibly be produced by biological systems. The task of bridging the explanatory gap, discussed in the

Introduction, is a "how possibly" problem. Fundamental differences in how we think about our own consciousness, and how we think about brains and bodies, create conceptual obstacles to understanding their connection. Philosophy should be able to help bridge this gap; I hope to show how possibly it could be done.

# Acknowledgments

This book was written for all my smart friends, like you. You are intellectually curious, generous of spirit, critical of unsubstantiated or unclear or jargon-laden claims, and deeply engaged by the puzzle of how minds fit into the world. All of you have helped me frame the argument that is developed in these pages, both by discussing and debating the issues and also by serving as my imaginary interlocutors as I struggled to find the right words and to put them in the right order. Your company, in person and in thought, has been a resource without which I could not have completed this book.

Two groups of friends deserve special mention. First, the 2015–16 Fellows of the Wissenschaftskolleg zu Berlin (WiKo) were the most present participants in my community of inquiry during the critical early phase of drafting the book. Thanks to the generous funding of WiKo and the DAAD (German Academic Exchange Service), I was able to spend a year leave from my teaching duties at the Pennsylvania State University and join the multidisciplinary group of Fellows at WiKo. While there, I participated in the Pain Focus Group with Daniel Weary and the late Victoria Braithwaite. Our conversations and collaborative work helped me think through issues such as the role of emotion in pain and consciousness, the difficulty of constructing cross-species tests of consciousness, and the moral issues in experimentation on animals.

My debt to Victoria is especially deep as she introduced me to comparative research on animal cognition. Before meeting Victoria, I had no specific proposal for applying my views on consciousness to animals. Now that I have learned about the remarkable capacities of fish and other wee beasts, the question of animal consciousness has become far more important to me. The result of our work together appears in Chapter 4. I am particularly grateful to Victoria for her indefatigable engagement with my views, even when she disagreed with them. I miss her deeply.

Second, my Friday Night Dinner companions—Caitlin Osborne, John Austin, Laura and Mark Morrisson, Kathe and Ola Sodiende, Cricket and Dave Hunter—are a continual source of information, humor, and inspiration. Without them, my representations would constitute a far sadder, lonelier mind.

William Robinson graciously read and commented on the entire book. I have acknowledged his most significant contributions in footnotes, but he deserves credit for saving me from numerous errors and obfuscations. Anna Strasser provided insightful comments and conversation on several chapters. I am also grateful to Keya Maitra, Carlos Montemayor, and Georgia Bastos for comments on chapter drafts. Joe Julian has been an invigorating conversation partner about topics ranging from chaos and dynamic systems to memory and metaphysics. The discussion groups, Mechanisms of Mind and the Center for Brain, Behavior, and Cognition, have introduced me to the vast and diverse research of the Pennsylvania State University faculty. I am extremely lucky to have such distinguished colleagues to consult on questions about attention, robotics, or the relation between genes and behavior.

I am also grateful to Bloomsbury Press and my editor, Colleen Coalter, for taking a chance on a book that fails to fit into the usual academic categories. Interdisciplinary research will be necessary to solve the most difficult problems we currently face: climate change, global inequality, systemic racism, sexism, and colonialism. There need to be more publications open to boundary-crossing work, and I applaud Bloomsbury Press for showing the way.

My husband Jon Brockopp, though also a contributor to Friday Night dinners and a commenter, warrants a special category of appreciation. Without Jon's unwavering support and encouragement, I could never have sustained my commitment to the research for this book. Jon has weathered my storms of frustration and shared my rays of insight. It is a gift to go through life with someone who is equally happy discussing the nature of time as hiking through the woods in companionable silence.

Kenneth Klein, to whom this book is dedicated, has been a philosophical inspiration throughout my career. As my first philosophy professor, Ken introduced me to the great puzzles of thought and gave me tools to think through them. He demonstrated how a really good argument can be simultaneously delightful and vexing. Most important to me personally, Ken took my ideas seriously; he genuinely believed that a small-town Midwest girl might have something to contribute to philosophy. I hope one day to prove him right.

# Introduction: *A House of Cards*

Quick. What is consciousness? There are so many answers: awareness, being awake, sensing, thinking, decision-making, having a sense of self. If you struggled to articulate what consciousness is, exactly, you are not alone. Philosophers have also struggled, even though our profession is to clarify concepts through analysis and definition. There is growing consensus that the aspect of consciousness most difficult to explain is the way things appear to a conscious person or animal. This aspect, known as *phenomenal consciousness,* is often characterized as *what it's like* to be a subject of experience. To illustrate, what it's like to be me right now includes seeing words on a computer screen, thinking about how to describe my experiences, and feeling cold feet on a wooden floor. What is it like to be you now?

Though this characterization is terribly vague, it points to the overall difference between being conscious and being unconscious. Seeing, thinking, and feeling are ways of being conscious, yet sensations, thoughts, and emotions can be processed unconsciously too, as I will argue in Chapter 2. We will need to pay careful attention to our own conscious experiences in order to determine exactly what "consciousness" involves. As we move through this book, I will offer several opportunities for you to test my claims against your own experiences. These tests serve the dual purpose of identifying the phenomena to be explained and proposing a means for you to verify the phenomena for yourself.

A clear sense of the target of explanation is necessary to understand how consciousness could have evolved from physical processes. By teasing out several strands of the tangle of ideas associated with consciousness, we can focus on the thread that results from prior processes of selection and adaptation to see what function phenomenal consciousness performs. One of the central claims of this book is that a description of consciousness in terms of function is key to explanation.

Consciousness is one of the last great philosophical and scientific mysteries. Aside from the basic human quest to understand how things work, a physical explanation of consciousness is motivated by problems with the familiar alternative view, *Dualism*. According to Dualism, consciousness cannot be physical. The special qualities of conscious experience are too different from physical properties and processes to be explained by them. The experience of inner thoughts and feelings seems utterly incommensurate with the mushy gray brain tissue that is supposed to house them.[1]

Yet house them it must, because the brain, in its interactions with body and world, is the *sine qua non* of consciousness. In the absence of a brain, there is no evidence of consciousness. Alterations in the brain produce alterations in consciousness, and vice versa. The dualist might be able to accommodate these facts if there were a way to account for causal interaction between physical and nonphysical processes. There is not.[2] The more we learn about the brain's operations, the less room there is for occult forces to intervene. Within the skull, a complete accounting can be given of the energy flow from sensory input to motor output. According to the physical law of the conservation of energy, no energy can be gained or lost from a closed system. That means that any motor output, such as the keystrokes being made by my hands to generate this text, is fully caused by the energy of the brain and body. This is not to say that these keystrokes can be fully *explained* by the energy of the brain and body. For a full explanation of mind and consciousness, we will need to understand how the inner aspects of action, the thoughts and feelings that accompany and motivate the keystrokes, are related to the externally observable processes of neurons and their interactions. The mystery of how consciousness is related to physical processes is called the *explanatory gap*.

In the eighteenth century, the great mystery was life, the *élan vital* that drove a being toward its destiny. Vitalists couldn't imagine how a physical system could animate or organize itself until Darwin (among others) articulated the underlying principle of function: life is driven by survival and reproduction. In the twenty-first century, the solution to the mystery of consciousness requires a similar act of imagination. We need to see how the Darwinian principle of function can be applied to phenomenal consciousness. An ongoing challenge will be to get a better perspective on exactly what phenomenal consciousness is and how it functions.

Let's go back to what phenomenal consciousness is. Again, ask yourself: what is it like to be me now? Answering this question should be easy. It is a safe bet that you, dear Reader, are conscious right now. The tricky part of answering this question is to focus on consciousness without interference. Normal life is so busy that it is hard to find time for quiet reflection. When the mind clears for a moment, every thought and concern that had been put aside comes crashing in. Meditators call this squabbling of incessant thoughts a "monkey mind," because it has no direction or focus. Neuroscientists call it the "default mode," because brains exhibit a standard pattern during gaps in the testing phases of experiments measuring brain activity. Subjects are put in brain scanning machines and told to do various mental tasks like think about tables and faces. The objective of these experiments is to determine which brain areas are active during which sorts of tasks. The default mode is where the mind goes when it is not engaged in a task. Research by Rafael Malach and colleagues shows that the same pattern of brain activity shown in the default mode also appears during self-reflection. Moreover, that pattern disappears during conscious attention to the world when a fundamentally different set of brain areas is active (Golland et al. 2007; Harmelech, Friedman, and Malach 2015). This suggests that self-reflective conscious thought is the default mode for humans; however, this sort of consciousness is not the target of explanation for this book.[3] Phenomenal consciousness can be self-reflective, but it is not the most basic form of consciousness. Fundamentally, evolutionarily, consciousness is an awareness of the world. Or so I will argue.

## The Origin of an Explanation

The story of how I came to the evolutionary explanation for consciousness described in this book begins when I was working on my doctoral dissertation in Jerusalem. I would daily walk up to the Hebrew University library on Mt. Scopus to read from their excellent collection of books in philosophy of mind. Higher-order (HO) theories of consciousness were then and are still the main philosophical theories to account for the difference between unconscious and conscious states. On a HO view, an unconscious state becomes a conscious one when a person has a HO state—either a sensation or thought—about that lower-order state. To simply things, we can focus on David Rosenthal's *Higher-Order Thought (HOT) Theory* (Rosenthal 2005).[4]

According to the HOT Theory, as I am sitting here thinking about consciousness, I am having various unconscious sensations about my bodily position, the low hum of the computer, even some of my visual sensations may not be conscious—people disagree about exactly how *rich* my visual consciousness is.[5] All kinds of sensations a person has remain unconscious. In terms of our working definition of phenomenal consciousness, there is "nothing it's like" to hear the hum of the computer, even though the sound waves are vibrating my auditory canals, and that stimulation is processed at least through the temporal lobe and possibly even further.

The question for theories of consciousness is: how do unconscious sensations become conscious ones? Since I have been writing about the low hum of the computer, I have become conscious of that hum; there now *is* something it is like for me to hear that hum. What happened? What's the difference between unconsciously hearing the hum and consciously hearing it? According to HOT theorists, I become conscious of the hum sensation when I acquire a HO thought about it. I now have a thought to the effect that: I am now hearing a low hum. The hum sensation is conscious when I have a HOT about it.[6]

I have never liked HO theories. HO states just seem too indirect and too complex to account for simple conscious experiences. When I am going about my business in the world, getting groceries, walking to class, I seem to be conscious of the world, not of my own states. To paraphrase Fred Dretske (1993), I am not conscious *of* my sensations, I am conscious of the world by means of my sensations.[7] However, this objection only takes us so far. We still need a way to distinguish unconscious sensations from conscious ones. Dretske offered a brilliant critique of HO Theory but failed to provide an adequate alternative account of consciousness.

That left me in a quandary. I agreed with both Rosenthal and Dretske that the mental is essentially *representational*. That is, mental states like sensations represent, or stand for, things like the hum of the computer. I'll come back to this concept of representation later in the chapter, and it will figure prominently in the explanation to come. Back in Jerusalem, the critical piece of the explanation that I was missing, the critical piece of any explanation of consciousness, was an account of the difference between unconscious and conscious sensations. What could explain why there is something it is like to hear the hum of the computer when that representation is conscious, but there is nothing it is like to represent the same hum when the sensation is unconscious?

This was my puzzle as I walked up to the Mt. Scopus library in Jerusalem. My dissertation advisor, Austen Clark, kept pushing me to articulate what magical $X$ constitutes consciousness. I had been thinking a great deal about what features of consciousness are essential and had determined that conscious representations are *selective*—not all sensations and thoughts that I have at any given moment are conscious. Many remain unconscious, like my body position. I also realized that conscious representations are *coordinated*—all the sensations and thoughts that are conscious at any given moment are unified; they appear together as part of a single experience. I see these words on the page, hear the sound of Sonny

Rollins on the saxophone, taste the smooth bitterness of my coffee—all together as my conscious experience of the world.[8]

But, Austen continued to object, how do selected and coordinated *conscious* representations differ from the selected and coordinated *unconscious* ones? Most actions, like walking, require sensorimotor coordination that remains unconscious, and linguistic expression, like speaking, requires coordinating semantic and syntactic information into appropriate structures, all of which remains unconscious. (If you're still skeptical about the existence of unconscious processes, try attending to the process of walking or speaking and see how difficult they become.) Doesn't the same problem of distinguishing the magic $X$ recur for collections of sensations?

And that's when it hit me. The conscious collections have a content component that the unconscious ones lack: conscious states represent the present moment. Everything that I represent consciously, I represent as occurring *now*. Unconscious representations might be *occurring* now, but they are not part of what I *represent as* occurring now. They are not part of what it's like to be me now. This revelation was a huge relief because it resonated so beautifully with aspects of consciousness that are often noted without explanation: conscious states must be occurrent, their contents change serially and flow in one direction from past toward future.

## Building an Explanation

The aha moment of explanation happened in a flash, and then the work of putting together the components of a theory began. This book is a guide to the conceptual pieces necessary to see how defining consciousness in terms of a representation of the present moment can solve the mystery of consciousness. Think of the process of explanation as constructing a house of cards. Each component is essential to maintaining the fragile structure, yet each can be examined separately. Different people tend to be concerned about particular cards, but if any one of them is pulled away from its place, the house falls.

So my first request of the reader is to suspend judgment. As each card is put in its place, you will likely have questions and be particularly dubious about one or another card.[9] I will do my best to address the most significant concerns and confusions as I explain the role of each card in the house of explanation. Even so, the goal here is to construct a whole house, to see the way all the pieces might fit together to provide a better perspective on what phenomenal consciousness is and how it functions. To understand how life could be explained in terms of function, people needed to rethink fundamental concepts, such as mechanistic explanation, the definition of life, and the relation between inorganic and organic material. To understand how consciousness can be explained in terms of physical processes, fundamental concepts will also need to be reconsidered.

The five cards in the house of explanation to be built in this book all involve a shift in some familiar way of thinking about the mind and its relation to the world. Try to shift your thinking enough to see how each card fits in relation to the rest of the house. Even if you ultimately think the house cannot stand, that one or another card is insufficient to support the structure, you should be able to see how an explanation of consciousness is possible. This shift in perspective, a vision of how possibly consciousness might be explained in terms of physical processes, is my primary objective. I don't really expect to convince you that my explanation is correct—the puzzle of consciousness has been around a long time. What I would like to show is the way that an explanation could be possible. In other words, the specific conceptual shifts I recommend may not ultimately be correct, but *if* they are, consciousness would be explained. Once we can see a possible way forward, it becomes easier to see other ways forward.[10]

To facilitate the required shift in perspective, the second request I have for the reader is to practice attending to your own consciousness. As mentioned earlier, I will invite you to undertake exercises designed to point you toward aspects of your experience that you may not have noticed. Take a moment to do these exercises and compare your experiences with the descriptions of my experiences. Think about how your experiences line up (or not) with the explanations offered. Regularly ask yourself: What is it like to be me now?

If the house of explanation is successful, you will be able to see how your experiences relate to the physical processes that constitute them. The cards form a kind of argument, a structure of concepts that together result in an explanation. Let me start by telling you what concepts will be involved so you can glimpse the house to come. In the rest of the Introduction, I will describe each conceptual card in a bit more detail, and point to the full explanation later in the book.

The top Bridge Card, that makes the cards a structure, is a solution to the explanatory gap. A definition of consciousness in terms of its *function* is necessary to understand how a physical system becomes conscious. Placing this card is the goal and will involve a good deal of work to get to this point. Four cards are foundational cards, on which the explanation stands or falls. The first Mind Card has already briefly appeared: the mental is representational. To be a mental state, like a thought about a tree, is to represent something, like a tree. The Representation Card is the related claim that a mental state represents something, because its function is to represent that thing. Respectively, these two cards explain what it is to be a mental state and how physical states become mental states.

The remaining two foundational cards together form the original contribution of this book to research on consciousness. The most important Definition Card is a definition of consciousness as the representation of the present moment. To be a conscious representation, like the hum of the computer, is to be represented as happening now. As with the Mind Card, this one rests against another foundational card, the Function Card, that explains its representational capacity in terms of function. Consciousness represents the present moment in order to facilitate flexible action. The *Temporal Representation Theory* offers a new definition of consciousness in terms of its function. A representation of presence is necessary for a flexible response to multiple goals and actions in a situation. Consciousness evolved for flexibility.

## The Explanatory Gap

The five cards have now been laid on the table, and you may well be inclined to rip up one or two right away. Try to resist this impulse until the cards are in place. Beginning with the top Bridge Card, the reasons that motivate the explanatory gap show why a definition of consciousness in terms of its *function* is necessary to bridging it. Thomas Nagel, one of the most famous proponents of the gap, put the problem this way: "[W]e have at present no conception of what an explanation of the physical nature of a mental phenomenon would be. Without consciousness the mind-body problem would be much less interesting. With consciousness it seems hopeless" (Nagel 1974: 436).

Explanation is hopeless, according to Nagel, because consciousness is subjective. Only you experience your consciousness, and so only you can know what it is like. Nagel dramatized the point by comparing human and bat consciousness. If you were to try to imagine the experience of a bat, the best you could do would be to imagine your own experience as a being that hangs upside-down, hunts at night, navigates by echolocation, and so forth. To actually *have* bat experiences would require that you *become* a bat (438–9). And, if you were a bat, you would no longer know what it is like to be a human. We are each trapped in our own experience, incapable of escaping subjectivity.

This essential gap between subjective experience and the objective world is familiar and very striking. The problem of solipsism is the troubling possibility that your consciousness is the only thing that exists, because you can only be certain of your own mind. Everything else could be an illusion. Here, perhaps, is the most comforting message on offer: mental isolation is not inevitable; indeed, understanding of the minds of others involves fundamentally the same processes as understanding the nature of the physical world. The full force of this message will not be clear until the end of the book, but a quick thought experiment from Ludwig Wittgenstein (1953) gives us a start:

> 303. [You might say] "I can only believe that someone else is in pain, but I know it if I am."—Yes [Wittgenstein responds]: one can make the decision to say "I believe he is in pain" instead of "He is in pain." But that is all.—What looks like an explanation here, or like a statement about a mental process, is in truth an exchange of one expression for another which, while we are doing philosophy, seems the more appropriate one.
> Just try—in a real case—to doubt someone else's fear or pain.

Especially in the case of a crying child or a friend's grief, it is simply impossible to doubt the conscious feelings[11] of others. This conviction isn't just sloppy thinking, generalizing without warrant from one's own experience to all experience; we have good epistemic reasons to attribute consciousness to others, and in some cases we can even share their experiences (see Chapter 7). Moreover, careful thinking about the nature of consciousness can help us move beyond analogy with our own experience to determine criteria for consciousness in animals radically unlike humans, such as an ant or an octopus (see Chapter 4).

So the crowning achievement of our house of conceptual cards is a solution to the explanatory gap. I will come back to it after we have looked a bit at the cards it depends on, beginning with the question of what a mind is.

## On the Nature of a Mind

The first foundational card in our house of explanation, the Mind Card, is the claim that all mental states are representational. The term "mental state" is a shorthand way of talking about all of the states, events, and processes that form a mind. A thought about lunch, for example, is likely extended in time as you consider whether to have a tuna sandwich or a salad. The thought is probably constituted by numerous brain processes subserving concepts and motivation and perception and desire as you stand in front of the open refrigerator. For convenience, all this activity can be called a "mental state." Refinements will be introduced when necessary.

Why think that all mental states are representational? Franz Brentano (1838–1917) is credited with the basic idea that the mind represents or presents things to itself. This notion of presentation or appearance before the mind may be a more intuitive way of thinking of consciousness than representation, although there are reasons to favor the idea of representation, as we will see. Philosophers in the era previous to Brentano, such as René Descartes (1596–1650) and John Locke (1632–1704), greatly influenced current conceptions of the mind and consciousness in their observations of the way ideas and impressions appear to a self-reflective mind. Though their views were opposed to one another in many respects, Descartes and Locke shared the intuition that the world can be perceived only indirectly. The world causes sensations, they assumed, and we are conscious of the world by means of the presentation of sensations in the mind. As compelling as this picture may be, it raises a significant problem: How, exactly, are sensations "presented" to the mind? There is no screening room in the brain, and no inner eyes capable of viewing these presentations.

While Brentano also adopted an indirect view, he helped solve the problem of presentation by focusing on the relation between the mind and its objects. A mental state is directed toward or *about* some object (or other sort of thing). This idea, that mental states can be characterized by this *aboutness* relation, has been enormously useful in developing contemporary theories about the mind. Brentano called this aboutness relation "intentional," but that word suggests conscious purpose in directing attention toward the object. Since the project here is to explain consciousness, and maybe purpose as well, the more neutral (albeit contested) word "representation" is preferable.

To get a better grip on the value of thinking about mental states in terms of representation, reflect for a moment on the sorts of mental states you have. Start with the perception of something in front of you, for me it is my pen. To perceive my pen is to have a mental state *about* the pen. My visual system produces visual representations of the pen's shape and color; my kinesthetic system produces tactile and proprioceptive representations of the smoothness and octagonal edges of the pen as well as the feeling of pressure against my fingers as I write. Touch is a useful illustration of the way representations can be about features of my body as well as features of an object. In all these cases, the relation of representation involves a direct isomorphism between the state of the sensory system and the features represented. When I move my pen back and forth, my visual and kinesthetic system varies in relation to the changes in light reflectance, spatial location, pressure, weight, and so forth.[12]

Perhaps I am very anxious or excited about what I am writing, in which case there will also be bodily representations about those emotions. Chapter 1 will consider how emotions can be explained in terms of how the body is represented. For now simply notice the way your emotions feel to you. Characteristically, fear will send your heart racing, and your breath will become quicker. Sadness involves a lack of energy and a heaviness in the chest. Joy, in contrast, is light and animated. These are all descriptions of bodily states.[13] What needs further argument is the claim that emotions are *entirely* representations of bodily states.

Thought can be considered the paradigmatic case of representation. To think about my pen is to have or be in some state that represents or stands for the pen. Thoughts are paradigmatic representations because they can occur in the absence of the object they represent. The absence highlights the relation central to the power and mystery of representation. How can I manage to think about my pen when it is not in front of me? Something in me, presumably in my brain, is able to represent my pen, that very pen that is resting on my desk when I am elsewhere. In order to stand for that very pen, the representation must somehow be differentiated from representations about other pens on my desk and other pens that look and feel identical to it. The representation relation somehow picks out just that pen. Minds do this all the time.

Now that we have reason to think of mental states as representations, the second card in our house, the Representation Card, is an explanation of how physical states come to represent. The kernel of the theory, to be developed in Chapter 1, is that representations serve functions for living organisms. Representations of dangers and resources are needed for an organism to survive and reproduce; physical processes such as nerves and neurons evolved to represent.

A purely physical thing has no needs of its own, it has no homeostatic mechanisms for self-maintenance. Rocks become ground into sand, clouds condense into rain, fire consumes dead wood. These causal processes occur as part of a network of interactions originating from the Big Bang. They form fundamentally indeterminate yet consistent patterns of relations over time. No aspect of this physical system cares that these patterns occur one way or another. The cloud neither rejoices in nor regrets its transformation into rain.

Living things, on the other hand, have interests. Even a lowly single-celled organism needs nutrients and avoids toxins. These interests are the beginning forms of a mind. Of course, the way an amoeba represents its environment is vastly different from the way you represent your environment. Nonetheless, I think it is worthwhile to mark the basic difference between physical states that are mental and those that are nonmental at the same point as the difference between living and nonliving. As Evan Thompson puts it, "life and mind share a set of basic organizational properties, and the organizational properties distinctive of mind are an enriched version of those fundamental to life. Mind is life-like and life is mind-like" (Thompson 2007: 128).[14]

At this point let's move away from the amoeba and back to humans to get a personal perspective on the way representations function to aid survival. My ability to represent the pen in my hand is due to various mechanisms in my body and brain that process visual and tactile information about the pen. They function in the way they do, because they have been helpful in the past to get me to pens, indeed to get me to this very pen. Some of these mechanisms are sensory and convey details about color, shape, and feel. Some of these mechanisms are cognitive and facilitate object recognition and semantic evaluation. I see the pen as a *pen* and know to call it "pen."

Though it might seem a stretch to say that my ability to represent the pen in my hand aids my survival, it is important to think generally about the value of representational structures. The same structures used to represent pens are used to represent food and water, other people, threatening situations, and any other benefit or danger in my environment. In the next chapter I will suggest a continuum of representation types that become increasingly articulate as the mind is challenged to represent more complex interactions with the environment. At the simplest level, a specific stimulus elicits a specific response in a one-to-one relation. At the most complex level, stimuli are grouped into concepts and patterns related to an infinite number of possible responses.

In other words, my capacity to represent pens and other esoteric items like the average homeowner or transcendental deduction is a consequence of the evolved ability to represent immediately useful things and events (Dennett 2018). The continuum from simple to complex representational capacities based on functional requirements is one of the most important consequences of the Representation Card in the house of explanation. If human consciousness is a feature of evolved brains, as I maintain in this book, it must have appeared as the result of a series of mutations that were gradually selected for over the course of evolutionary history. So long as we see consciousness as fundamentally different from other evolved traits, in no way continuous with other mental and physical states, we will despair of finding an explanation.

In contrast, by thinking of mental states as serving a function, we can see why and how some physical states come to acquire that function and others do not.

For example, natural causal relations, sometimes called *natural signs*, are not representations. Smoke does not mean fire unless there is a mind to interpret that sign. Likewise, computers do not understand any of the words or images they process, they simply operate in a way that allows minds to interpret their output as representational. My laptop doesn't care what uses I have for it; it does not even care that it functions at all. Its functions are dependent on my needs and desires, because it has none of its own. Whether a computer, or a robot, or other form of artificial intelligence *could ever* have needs and desires of its own is a question that will be considered in Chapter 7.

## Vehicle and Content

In the previous section I suggested that the difference between mental and nonmental states can be understood in terms of representation. Mental states represent; nonmental states don't. On the face of it, however, this looks like Dualism. Mental states are one kind of thing, physical states are another. Indeed, Representational Theory is neutral about the sort of stuff that constitutes the mind. In principle, mental states could be made out of anything: brains, souls, chewing gum, whatever. Of course, the most plausible thing to constitute mental states is a brain, and the most plausible reason for mental states to exist is that they serve a biological function; they are somehow useful to aid an organism's survival.

This is the position of the first two cards in the house of explanation: mental states (a thought about a table or a taste of tea) are representations, and some physical states (nerves and neurons) have the function to be representations. One of the challenges is to understand how a physical state can also *be* a mental state even though brains seem so different from minds. A conceptual tool to help meet this challenge is the distinction between the *vehicle* of representation and its *content*.

Take a moment to enjoy the cartoon in Figure 0.1 before I ruin it with a philosophical analysis. The cartoon is funny because the boys are confusing a feature of the content of the cards, a high number value, with a feature of the cards themselves, greater weight. Since the bigger numbers are an aspect of content, they cannot make the physical cards heavier, contrary to what the boys suppose. A similar confusion between features of vehicle and content often happens when thinking about brains and minds. The neural systems that represent features of the object, like my pen, are the *vehicles* of representation. They are like the

**Figure 0.1** FOXTROT © 2005 Bill Amend. Reprinted with permission of ANDREWS MCMEEL SYNDICATION. All rights reserved.

cards on which the value is written. But their *content*, what they represent, is not a feature of the neural system. The content is the object in the world that the neurons have the function of representing.

Think about other representations, like the characters in a book or people in a photo. The book is made of paper and ink, yet it represents a teddy bear and a piglet, or a president negotiating a missile crisis. The content represented may or may not exist in the world, but in any case its features are not the same as the features of the vehicle. The people represented in the photo are not made of pixels, even though the pixels represent the people.

On photos, the pixels ideally match the colors of the items represented—the purple and gold of the sunset, the chartreuse of new leaves in spring. In brains, however, the neurons representing my pink and cylindrical pen are not themselves either pink or cylindrical. Nor does there need to be *anything* pink or cylindrical in my brain in order for the neurons to represent these features of the pen. Colors and other sensory qualities are complicated, because the quality spaces are determined by the physical relations of the sensory systems. Ultimately, I think color and other types of qualitative character can be explained in terms of sensory representation. We experience pink the way we do because our visual system has evolved to get us to pink things. Like some of the other sticky issues about representation, I'll save the details for later (see Chapter 1).

## Describing Consciousness

The foregoing discursus on representation was needed to make two points: (1) representation distinguishes mental from nonmental physical states (the point made in the last section); (2) representations can be either unconscious or conscious (the point this and the next section will make). This transition is a good time to return to the central question of what consciousness is: what is it like to be you now?

Have you been noticing your experience while reading these pages? Do you have a sense of how difficult it is to prevent stray worries and plans from interfering? Remember that the target is consciousness of the world rather than *self-consciousness*, a consciousness *of* sensations and thoughts.[15] Keep at it. As best you can, try to focus on *what* you are experiencing rather than on *how* you are experiencing, in order to foreground the conscious content and background the self-conscious mode.

As an example, here is how I would describe my own current experience:

A scribbled, white page is before me, on which one hand rests and the other furiously writes. Sounds of words appear in internal speech which are stifled by my attempt to write them down. As my attention shifts from the inner words to the sound of the clock ticking, my writing hand begins to move freely again. My other hand moves to the cup, followed by the feeling of warm, sweet tea flowing down my throat.

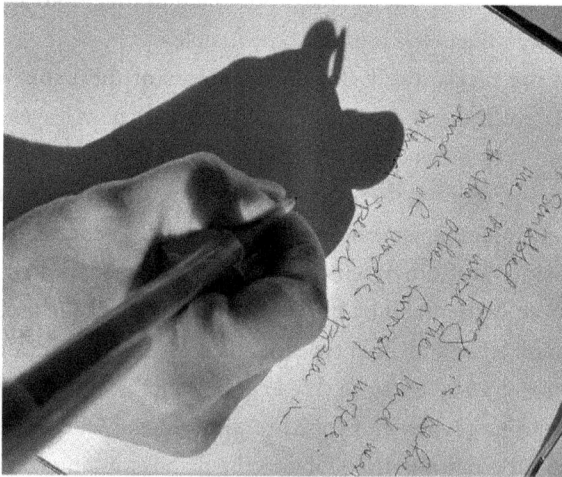

Figure 0.2 An example of visual phenomenology. Photo by Paula Droege.

These various contents of consciousness gain prominence in serial—paper, speech, clock, then tea—yet they are more or less present in my experience throughout. I have the sense that visual, auditory, tactile, and gustatory sensations[16] appear together in consciousness, even as the focus on one or another shifts over time. In other words, my visual field does not appear blank outside the page on which my foveal attention rests, nor does my auditory experience of the clock disappear when my attention shifts to the taste of tea.

Deliberately missing from my description are self-conscious thoughts such as what I will write next, regret for having said a harsh word this morning, memories of Willoughby's in New Haven where I discovered this brand of tea. A large quantity of the self-conscious ruminations that occupy the monkey mind is made up of thoughts about the past and future. One estimate is that we spend 50 percent of our time thinking about something other than what we are currently doing (Killingsworth 2013). Meditators try to still the monkey mind by attending to the contents of current sensory experience as invasive thoughts come and go. A common form of practice involves concentrating on simple elements of experience, such as breathing, to ground the mind in the present moment. The breath is a consistent and invariable marker of presence, although it is rarely represented *as* present. By deliberately attending to the normally unconscious event of breathing, you direct your mind to focus on what is present. When self-conscious thoughts of past and future appear, they can be noticed and set aside to return to the present moment.[17]

The power of this simple technique is immediately evident. I recommend that you pause in your reading and concentrate on your breath for a while. Simply pay attention to the contents of your experience, the thoughts, sensations of your body and surroundings as they come and go. Notice when the mind inevitably strays in this direction or that, and gently bring it back to your breath.[18] You are focused on what it's like to be you as you are breathing. The form of consciousness when you are attending the breath is phenomenal consciousness, the target of explanation.

Focusing on your breath is not the only way to attend to the present moment. You may experience the same form of non-self-consciousness when you are deeply engaged in a project or sport or art. Mihaly Csikszentmihaly (2008) calls this form of engagement *flow*, and it occurs when your task is appropriately suited to your abilities. If the task is too difficult, you will be frustrated, and if it is too easy, you will be bored. Flow experiences seem timeless—you look up from your project to discover an hour or more has passed. As humans, the feeling of time comes from the continual self-conscious awareness of past and future, made concrete by the passage of clock time. When consciousness remains in the present, we cease to notice time *as* time. The time is always *now*.

My description thus far highlights two essential features of consciousness: unity and flow. Each moment of experience combines various forms of content—

thoughts, emotions, sensations—into a unified experience of the world, and that experience changes over time, as attention to different objects shifts.

If you are not yet convinced that these two features are central to conscious experience, or you think that my description leaves out some essential feature or features, I encourage you to try to articulate what feature has been left out, or why you would leave out one (or both) of the features I take to be essential. Then (and this is critical), keep paying attention to your conscious experience to see if these essential features appear in different contexts. When you are playing sports or an instrument, what is that experience like? Some people interpret flow states as unconsciousness. Certainly they are not self-conscious. The question at issue is whether there is something it is like to experience a flow state. Consider also whether there is something it is like to experience driving or shopping. If so, what features of consciousness appear? Are you aware of your self as the subject of experience, or are you conscious exclusively of your body and the world without self-consciousness?[19]

Because any description of consciousness involves self-conscious reflection, your observations will necessarily be after the fact. You've been absorbed in an activity for an hour and then wonder: what was my experience like? Was I consciously appreciating the music or intensity of the game or the traffic signals on the drive home? It is surprisingly difficult to be sure. Some amount of practice and a kind of covert attention are needed.

Directly introspecting your current conscious experience in the way I recommended earlier yields useful data, although even in this case caution is in order. The nature of consciousness is not immediately and infallibly revealed just by looking. Introspection is an essential but unreliable tool for investigating consciousness. Most people, for example, would say that a good bit of their conscious experience is in detailed focus while the edges are fuzzily colored to span about 180 degrees. To see how mistaken this judgment is, try another phenomenological experiment using our thematic playing cards. Keep your eyes facing forward while you draw a card and hold it at arm's length on the very edge of your visual field. Can you tell what number the card is? The suit? The color? If you slowly move the card from the periphery toward the center, when do these features become identifiable? If you do this, you will probably be surprised at how little of your conscious experience is in focus at any given moment (Schwitzgebel 2008).

The general lesson is that the nature of consciousness is not obvious. Though we have been conscious all our lives, we use our consciousness to investigate the world; we rarely take time to investigate consciousness itself. If we are to have any hope of solving the problem of consciousness, the first step must be to try to get a better sense of our own conscious experience.

At this point in our investigations, we will concentrate on everyday experiences of work and leisure, sport and thought. We won't worry about unusual states of consciousness like dreams, drug-induced experiences, or advanced meditative states. Though I recommend meditation as a way to focus on the present moment of consciousness, the training required to achieve a deep and sustained meditative state makes it unusual. Some might argue that meditative states should be the paradigmatic object of study due to the purity of this form of consciousness. On this view, the goal of meditation is to experience a kind of consciousness that lacks any contents, empty of any thought or sensation at all, even of your own body. From a biological perspective, however, purity is not an indicator of the nature of things. Unusual sorts of experiences will need to be explained in due course (see Chapter 7), but first we need to grasp everyday conscious experience, the sort of experience we might share with other animals and that may have evolved to serve an adaptive function. Basic meditation practices such as focus on the breath help reveal how the mind tends to worry about things that might happen and fret about past mistakes. The breath grounds experience in an activity we share with other animals, reminding us of what consciousness is like without language and self-reflective thought.

As you go about your conscious life, then, pay attention. Notice the way the contents of your experience shift over time. Different types of activity bring different qualities of experience. Even in the course of quiet reflection, as you sit there reading this book, various sensations will appear in consciousness and then recede. As with the breath, you can observe unconscious sensations enter consciousness by deliberately shifting your attention to them. Normally, your posture and limb positions are unconscious; you don't consciously feel the pressure of your back against the chair, for example. By directing attention to that pressure, the sensation becomes part of your current conscious experience. Perhaps this shift of attention already happened due to the simple act of reading and thinking about that part of your body, and now you do consciously feel the pressure of your back against the chair.

One question to ask yourself as you experience sensations and thoughts entering and leaving consciousness is what differences need to be explained between unconscious and conscious states. For example, is the sensation of your back against the chair essentially the same sensation when it is unconscious and conscious, or is there some fundamental quality that is added to the sensation when it becomes conscious? Some people think there are extra properties, called *qualia*, that appear only in consciousness. If so, there is something, some property or object, that appears and disappears when that sensation is conscious.

Others would say that the same sensation was there all along, and consciousness does something like illuminate it. The metaphor is problematic, because there is no light in the brain and no inner eyes to see the now-bright object. Nonetheless, there is a reason that light and illumination metaphors are so compelling. Things that were previously unnoticed suddenly seem to pop out, as if in a beam of light surrounded by darkness. The limits of the light metaphor are obvious when the example is changed to a sound like the clock chiming. The bells may be unobtrusively ringing four, five, six times when somehow—the details are interesting—you consciously hear the sixth bell and realize you are late to a dinner party. While the earlier bells were unconscious, they were heard and even counted. Then the final bell is *illuminated,* or whatever the auditory equivalent might be.

As you may have guessed, I favor the view that sensations are essentially the same when unconscious and conscious. The difference consciousness makes has to do with the way those sensations appear, or what those sensations *do*—as I will argue, appearance and function come to the same thing when properly understood (see Chapter 1). On the face of it, this claim seems like a category error—an appearance is the way something *looks* and a function is what something *does*. For many things, though, appearance is determined by function. A bench looks like it can be sat on, because that is its function for me. An apple looks tasty, because its function for me is nourishment. The apple has evolved to look tasty to me in order to fulfill its own function of spreading its seeds. Something might be a broken bench or a rotten apple; it may fail to fulfill its function. Nonetheless, function determines appearance.[20]

This brings us to the third and fourth cards in our house of explanation. The third Definition Card will elaborate on the essential features of unity and flow to identify how conscious states appear and how they differ from unconscious states. That is, this card will offer a definition of what consciousness is. The fourth Function Card will connect the appearance of conscious states with their function; this card will show how the function of consciousness determines what it's like to have experience.

## The Hard Problem

The contrast between conscious sensations and unconscious sensations described in the previous section is very difficult to consider, if you are inclined to think all mental states are conscious. Chapter 2 will provide experiential and scientific evidence in support of the claim that many sorts of mental states operate unconsciously as well as consciously. To warm up for those arguments, think of the integration of information from visual, auditory, and kinesthetic sensory systems that is needed simply to walk down the street. Your motor system must be finely tuned to modulate your gait to match changing elevations, avoid obstacles, keep pace with a walking partner, recover from a stumble. The bulk of these processes occur unconsciously. Your consciousness can be nearly completely occupied with conversation and still manage to walk smoothly along.

However, consciousness cannot be *completely* occupied with conversation. While you need not be conscious of walking, you remain generally aware of the world as you focus on your conversation or phone or daydreams. If something unexpected happens—a bicycle crash or someone calls your name—your conscious representation immediately incorporates that new information which is fed into the decision-making system to facilitate response. The most important responses are the unconscious ones—in both cases you will probably stop immediately. But the ongoing response system needs to consciously assess the new situation in order to determine the next appropriate action.

The central thesis of this book is that consciousness is a representation of the present moment (the Definition Card) that is necessary for responding flexibly to changes in the current situation (the Function Card). These two cards together form the Temporal Representation Theory that claims consciousness represents what is happening now in order to serve the function of responding effectively to opportunities and dangers. How things appear consciously—as unified, flowing serially, and occurring *now*—is determined by function, that is, flexible response.

This claim—that consciousness represents the present moment in order to serve the function of facilitating flexible action—is essential to solving what is known as *the Hard Problem of Consciousness*. David Chalmers famously described the "easy" problems of consciousness as those that can be explained in terms of function. Among the easy problems are: perception, introspection, the focus of attention, and the deliberate control of behavior. According to Chalmers:

> The easy problems are easy precisely because they concern the explanation of cognitive *abilities and functions*. To explain a cognitive function, we need only specify a mechanism that can perform the function. The methods of cognitive science are well-suited for this sort of explanation, and so are well-suited to the easy problems of consciousness. By contrast, the hard problem is hard precisely because it is not a problem about the performance of functions.
>
> (Chalmers 1995: 202)

The intuitive appeal of the Hard Problem lies in this apparent disjunct between conscious experience and function. How could the colors and sounds and tastes of consciousness be simply a matter of stimulus and response relations? The "raw feels" of sensations seem to be qualities that go beyond the ability to discriminate red things from green ones, or coffee from tea. The functional aspect of sensations seems to be distinct from their qualitative aspect. Chalmers pushes this intuition by asking us to imagine a world where the functional and qualitative aspects of consciousness do come apart. In this world, you have a zombie twin, a being with a mind that performs all of the same functions that your mind does, except without consciousness. Your zombie twin would not be the movie version of a stumbling murderous robot; a *philosophical zombie* would act like you, think like you, speak like you, even perceive the world in the way that you do. Your zombie would be self-reflective, consider the beauty of a sun-lit meadow, and wonder about the function of consciousness. The only difference is that none of these mental processes would actually be conscious; there would be nothing it is like for your zombie twin to act, see, or reflect.

There are a number of ways to respond to the possibility of zombies (Gozzano and Hill 2012; Kirk 2017; Levin 2012). As well argued as many of these responses are, I suspect the only ultimately satisfying response is to show that consciousness serves a function after all. A description of the nature of consciousness in terms of its function means that a mind could not do *all* of the functions of my mind without consciousness. Consequently, zombie twins are not even logically possible.

It seems we can imagine zombies, because we do not have an adequate conception of the nature of consciousness or the function it performs. Similarly, my thin grasp of chemistry makes it seem possible to imagine water is not $H_2O$. A closer observation of water reveals liquidity and translucence as essential (albeit insufficient) properties, and the study of chemistry shows how these properties are constituted by their chemical substrate. The explanation of any observable property requires this sort of dynamic process whereby property and substrate are illuminated in relation to one another.

In this chapter, and throughout the book, I will direct you to investigate your own consciousness in order to develop a clearer conception of it in relation to the brain, body, and world that constitute it. To the extent that we reflect at all on the nature of consciousness, our expectations are conditioned by cultural traditions that take consciousness to be unusual, an exception to the patterns of everyday physical causation. Even Buddhist traditions that posit a continuity of consciousness with all things maintain that consciousness alone produces the illusion of discontinuity. As a result, the intuitions of the dualist run deep and make it difficult to see how consciousness could be explained by anything like neurons and their interactions.

The first step toward dispelling these intuitions is to reflect more carefully on exactly what consciousness is, to identify the properties to be explained. A good place to begin is with the phenomenologists, whose central philosophical program was to examine consciousness in order to determine its essential features.[21] Edmund Husserl (1905), the founder of *Phenomenology*, took temporal representation to define the structure of consciousness, underlying the two features that came up in my description earlier: unity and flow. Consciousness binds sights, sounds, thoughts, and bodily feelings together to form the experienced world, yet that world is constantly in flux as attention and its objects shift in space and time. The famous metaphor of time as a river fits perfectly with the metaphor of consciousness as a stream. Time and consciousness flow in synch, manifest in the present, moving toward the future, having come from the past.

Following this insight from Husserl, I suggest that consciousness is a representation of the world at the present moment. This is the Definition Card in the house of explanation. A vital but difficult distinction is between *representing* time and simply happening in time. A representation *of* the world now is not simply what is *occurring* now. Some of what is occurring now will not be represented at all, and some representations that are occurring now will not be incorporated into my representation of now. Consciousness is selective in processing only some of the available sensory and cognitive representations. Because consciousness serves a biological function, on my view, this selective process is designed to meet my needs as a human being. The next section (the Function Card) will discuss what that function might be.

Even without the specifics, illusions demonstrate this selective function by making it malfunction. Let your eyes rest on the motion illusion in Figure 0.3.

Developed by Akiyoshi Kitaoka, this image demonstrates the way visual motion detectors are triggered by asymmetric luminance steps. The illusion depends on eye movement, so if you don't experience illusory motion, try scanning across the image. The technical explanation for this illusion is that fast luminance changes as the eye moves across the pattern activate global motion detectors that are designed to adjust to the slow changes in luminance patterns of static objects (Backus and Oruç 2005).[22] The static image fools the visual system into representing motion. What is *occurring now* is a static image. What is *represented as now* is a moving image.

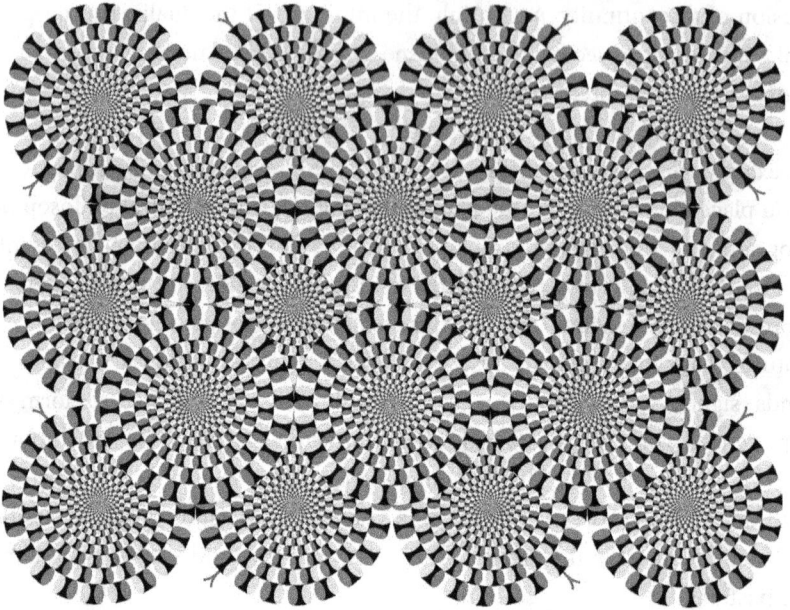

**Figure 0.3** Rotating Snakes Illusion. Akiyoshi Kitaoka, by permission.

What we see as now—stationary or moving object—is not necessarily what is occurring now; it is the best approximation of what is occurring now based on how the representational system has been designed. Chapter 2 further explains this difficult distinction between what is represented as now and what is occurring now.

## The Function of Consciousness

The fourth Function Card in the house of explanation is to say why our representational system has been designed to represent the present moment. The challenge for any proposed function of consciousness is: why think consciousness does *that* (you can fill in any function you think can only be done consciously: perceiving colors, creating music, making decisions)? Couldn't a zombie do *that* without conscious experience? Here is where the definition of consciousness in terms of the representation of presence can help connect phenomenology to function.

Given that unconscious mental states can serve the function of representation, what *additional* function could be served by consciousness? What is gained by selecting some of these unconscious mental states and combining them into a representation of the present moment? The answer is flexibility. A representational system needs to represent what is happening now in order to respond in different ways depending on how things are going. Maybe everything is operating smoothly, but maybe there should be a change in plan. A system that has the capacity to adjust its actions according to its plans needs to keep track of what is happening now in order to make those adjustments.

An automated system doesn't need a representation of what is happening now, because the action is coded to automatically follow from the sensory input, as when the heat of the stove causes you to withdraw your hand. An immediate, inflexible response is designed to ensure quick action when the delay needed to allow for conscious processing would be deadly.

On the other hand, a *conscious* response is required when different actions are possible. Say you are waiting for a pot to boil. Though this is a fairly simple task, it requires you to be conscious of its progress. You might turn your attention to other tasks, but if you fail to monitor the pot, you will not be able to respond when the water boils. At that point, a variety of things could happen. You might have been planning on spaghetti but discover you have none and so put in linguini instead; the water might start boiling over and require that you reduce the heat; you might decide you are too tired to cook and call for take-out instead. Your conscious representations are needed to monitor progress toward your goals, and more importantly, consciousness provides the ability to shift actions or goals in response to new situations.

My claim is not that conscious representations are needed to *initiate* action or to *decide* on the appropriate action. In Chapter 6, I will review the neuroscientific evidence that suggests processing leading to action or resulting in a decision occurs unconsciously. The function of a representation of the present moment is *descriptive* not directive. It says what is happening *now* so that the system can determine what to do *next*. In other words, your representation of now can't do you any good now, because it takes time to produce a conscious representation and more time to causally influence the stochastic decision-making procedures of the brain. Nonetheless, I will argue that a representation of the present moment distinguishes past from future, and that distinction is necessary to evaluate how things are progressing toward goals. Chapter 3 provides the reasons in favor of the fourth card: the function of consciousness is to facilitate flexible action.

If my argument is correct, the phenomenological structure of consciousness involves a representation of the present moment, and flexible behavior also requires a representation of the world as it is now in order to assess progress toward goals. This is the Bridge Card: the description of the nature of consciousness determines its function. The hard problem becomes one of the easy problems.

## Operationalizing Flexibility

Of course, none of the so-called easy problems is so very easy. Chapter 4 considers the problem of operationalizing the proposed function of consciousness: the capacity to select action and shift goals in response to new environmental conditions. I had the great fortune and honor of working with the renowned animal cognition researcher, Victoria Braithwaite, before her recent death from cancer. Combining my theory of consciousness with her expertise in fish sensation and behavior, we developed four categories for assessing the capacity for temporal representation through flexible action:

1. differential response to the environment,
2. adaptation to novel situations,
3. manipulation of the environment to accomplish goals, and
4. explicit representation of absent objects.

In the chapter, I show how the actions described by each category demonstrate flexibility, explain why temporal representation is necessary to perform those actions, and give an example of the capacity in a fish species. My claim is that the ability to represent a goal as *not present* requires the ability to represent the *present* environment as distinct from the past and the future. Consciousness is a representation of presence; its job is to tell us what is happening now so that the rest of the system can determine the best course of action.

An important consequence follows from the claim that consciousness is necessary for flexible behavior: demonstration of the capacity for flexibility is sufficient to demonstrate consciousness. If we could devise adequate tests for flexibility—again, not easy—we could determine which animals have conscious experiences. We would no longer need to rely on analogy and intuition to research animal consciousness; we could gather evidence. The examples of fish demonstrating each of the categories of flexibility are compelling, but inconclusive. Tests would need to be applicable across the animal kingdom, yet adaptable to the ecosystem of the species. The potential to operationalize flexibility in order to demonstrate animal consciousness is perhaps the most significant consequence of a solution to the explanatory gap.

Before we even consider this possibility in depth, let me address an objection to the very idea of a scientific research program on animal consciousness: anthropocentrism. Some people are inclined to say that any claim about an animal's consciousness is necessarily anthropocentric. On this objection, I am taking a theory about human consciousness and testing animals to see if they measure up to humans. Animals have their own talents and abilities, so it seems a mistake to judge them by human standards. One advantage of a functional theory of consciousness, however, is that the capacity for which we are testing is defined by its *function* not by the fact that humans have the capacity to perform that function. Looking for a human ability in animals is not anthropocentric when there are good general, functional descriptions of the capacity and evolutionary reasons for its convergent evolution in other animal species and taxonomic groups.

For example, it is anthropocentric to define tool use in terms of a power or precision grip that requires opposable thumbs, possessed only by humans and other primates. It is not anthropocentric to consider how the behavior of different animal groups might perform the function of using an object instrumentally to achieve a goal.[23] A theory can also be anthropocentric by assuming that the ability at issue must be identical to the human ability in every way. Chimps use tools differently than humans, and octopus tool use would differ even more significantly due to its radically different physiological and ecological structures. As long as we are attentive to differences, using the same term to recognize similarities can be instructive.

The opposite objection to designing a test for animal consciousness is anthropomorphism, an unwarranted assumption that animals are similar to humans. Even if flexibility indicates consciousness in humans, animal behavior can be explained in terms of more simple forms of associative learning.[24] Just because animals demonstrate similar behavior to humans, we cannot assume that their consciousness is similar. Here again, the claim is that consciousness serves the function of facilitating flexible action. If consciousness is a necessary condition for the evolution of flexibility, the similarity with humans follows from this shared function, and it is not an anthropomorphic assumption.

There is a well-known tendency when theorizing about something unfamiliar to either assimilate or exoticize it. Animals are just like us; animals are entirely alien. Neither position considers evidence about similarities or differences. One good check on this tendency is to adopt the perspective of the other being to whatever extent possible. For animals, including fellow humans, the best way to do this is by learning how they represent their world: what they need and want, and how they act to satisfy these goals. If we can understand how animals use unconscious representations differently from conscious ones, then we can explain how consciousness evolved based on function.

## The House of Cards

Once more, let me review the cards that will form the house of explanation. Beginning with the top card that connects the other cards into a structure, the Bridge Card is a solution to the explanatory gap. To understand how a physical system becomes conscious requires a description of consciousness in terms of its function. A fully satisfying explanation of consciousness will require more: details about the mechanisms that perform the designated function and further consideration of the nature of consciousness to determine whether anything essential has been omitted. Chapter 7 discusses some of the areas for further research. This book certainly does not aim to be the last word on consciousness. It does aim to offer the conceptual connection between consciousness and the function that grounds it in the physical world.

The first foundational card in the house of explanation is the Mind Card, the claim that minds are things that represent the world. To have a sensation or a thought is to have a state that stands for some feature or object. For a materialist, these mental states are constituted by states of the nervous system. The second foundational card, the Representation Card, explains that physical states become mental when they acquire the function of representing something. Various neurons in my visual cortex (and elsewhere, I leave the details to the professionals) represent the color and shape of my pen, because they have the function of varying in accord with those features. An important explanatory advantage to thinking of representation in terms of function is the ability to articulate a continuum of functions from simple to complex forms of representation. Different sorts of physical structures can serve different sorts of representational function.[25] The mind of a snail can be radically unlike the mind of a giraffe and yet both can be compared with respect to the functions their representations perform in negotiating their respective environments.

The definition of consciousness as a representation of the present moment is the third and most important Definition Card. Its strength depends on its ability to capture essential features of conscious experience. My proposal is that otherwise unconscious sensory and cognitive representations become conscious when they are selected and coordinated into a representation of *now*.

This Temporal Representation Theory highlights the way conscious experience presents its contents as unified and flowing serially through time.

Adjoining this definition of consciousness is the fourth Function Card that claims the representation of presence serves the function of facilitating flexible action. In order to evaluate a situation in relation to multiple actions and multiple goals, an animal must be able to represent the way things are *now* as distinct from how they have been or might be.

The description of consciousness in terms of its function now allows us to place the top Bridge Card gingerly on the house. A solution to the explanatory gap rests, somewhat precariously, on four mutually supporting cards. If a case can be made that physical systems are conscious when they have the capacity for flexible action, the conceptual gap between mind and body has been bridged.

## Getting On with It

With this rather lofty goal ahead of us, let me sketch the plan for achieving it. Chapter 1 gives reasons to believe that the mind is a thing that represents and function determines its representational content, the Mind and Representation Cards, respectively. I will consider several different theories and argue that Ruth Garrett Millikan's *Consumer Theory* (Millikan 1989a, 2004) offers the best explanation of the individuation of content. The peculiar representational issues raised by sensory qualities—paradigmatically color—will be addressed as well.

Chapter 2 argues that most mental states, which is to say most forms of representation, can occur unconsciously. Though it is tempting from the subjective perspective to identify the mind with consciousness, there are good empirical and conceptual reasons to include unconscious states and processes as part of the mind. One of the strongest conceptual reasons has been mentioned already: the explanatory advantage of a representational continuum from simple to complex forms. Drawing on the Consumer Theory of representation, I will describe the transition from an unarticulated representational form, where action is fixed in relation to the current environment, to a more articulated form, where action can be flexibly adjusted according to the goal best achieved in the current environment. This chapter introduces the Definition Card—consciousness is a representation of the present moment—and the Function Card—the function of consciousness is to facilitate flexible action.

Chapter 3 further develops the case for both cards, beginning with reasons for defining consciousness as a representation of *now*. We will engage in some more phenomenology and then consider what possible function phenomenal consciousness serves. The representational differences underlying fixed and flexible action show why a representation of presence is necessary for flexibility. Some technical issues are discussed, such as how long "now" might be, and how successive representations might relate to one another. Because the theory proposes that unconscious mental states become conscious when they are integrated toward the pursuit of goals, useful comparisons can be made with similar proposals such as the Information Integration Theory, the Global Workspace Model, and the Attended Intermediate Representation Theory. The chapter ends with a review of a current debate among consciousness theorists, the Iconic Memory Debate, and suggests how the Temporal Representation Theory provides a solution.

By this point, all the cards in the house of explanation will be in position. The remaining chapters consider cards that stand on *top* of the theory, such as a demonstration of animal consciousness. Chapter 4 looks at the scientific literature in Comparative Ethology to refine the operational definition of flexibility. I will propose an array of tests to begin the collection of data that exemplifies conscious, flexible action, and I will apply those tests to fish with surprising results.

Chapter 5 addresses the issue of conscious memory and planning for the future. Humans consciously represent times other than the present, so the theory needs to account for these sorts of mental states. Because they are self-conscious states, their higher-order representational structure allows for each level to reference a different time without contradiction. Conscious memories are representations of past experiences that are represented as part of my experience now.

In Chapter 6 I tackle the perennially puzzling question of free will. My topic will be the role of consciousness in causing action, rather than the philosophical opposition of free will and determinism. Whatever the outcome of that debate, I am interested in whether my conscious deliberations can causally affect my future decisions and actions. Evidence suggests that they can. More fundamentally, the sense in which my future is caused by *me* is deepened by the recognition that my unconscious states—beliefs, emotions, memories, values—are an essential part of my self.

The final chapter looks toward the future. Several areas of research have the potential to support or undermine the strength of the Temporal Representation Theory of consciousness proposed here. Neurobiological mechanisms responsible for producing consciousness need to be identified in human and nonhuman animals. The theory should be able to offer new insight into related mental phenomena such as social and emotional capacities as well as psychopathological forms of consciousness. The possibility of an artificial consciousness should be connected to the possibility of genuine representation: what would it be for a robot to have functions of its own rather than functions derived from its designer?

This glance ahead further underscores the message that we are not alone in our consciousness. Although each of us has a mind and body of our own, the mind is part of the body and as such is part of a shared world. A careful examination of the way a life comes to have a mind and a mind comes to have consciousness reveals the essential role that the physical and social environment plays in forming a person.

An appendix is included for those who are especially interested in how time is experienced. There is a long-standing philosophical debate about how consciousness presents temporal phenomena such as movement, change, and succession. I consider this debate in an appendix rather than throughout the book because the Temporal Representation Theory is an explanation of how consciousness evolved, not how temporal contents appear in consciousness. Nonetheless, it is worthwhile to show how the theory addresses issues raised by temporal phenomena and how it relates to the central theories of temporal consciousness.

# In Defense of Function

*Intelligence is based on how efficient a species*
*became at doing the things they need to survive.*

Charles Darwin

## Thinking about a Banana

The title of this chapter is an homage to Ruth Garrett Millikan's article "In Defense of Proper Function" (Millikan 1989b) where she explains the importance of a historical, teleological description of mental representation. What it is to have a thought about a banana as opposed to an apple is for the banana thought to have served some function in relation to bananas. You need a banana thought to get bananas. Quite simple, really, although as we will see, the details get complicated quickly.

In the Introduction I suggested that a convincing solution to the explanatory gap will depend on a description of consciousness in terms of its function, specifically its function as a particular sort of mental representation. A critical card in the house of explanation is a theory of how representations might be constituted by physical states and processes. This chapter will show how several contemporary theories fail to adequately specify mental content; that is, they fail to explain why a thought is about a *banana* as opposed to an apple or a yellow fruit. The key feature, as the chapter title suggests, is identification of the function of representation as articulated in Millikan's Consumer Theory. A number of objections to the theory will be addressed, as will the particularly difficult problem of qualitative character—the reds and stinks and clangs of conscious experience. The goal of this chapter is to show how physical vehicles like brains could come to have content like "banana" by serving the function of representing things in the world. Before we can understand the particular function of consciousness, we need a broader sense of the function of representation in helping an animal navigate its environment.

Note for nonspecialists: The two interludes and the objections in this chapter are fairly technical and aimed toward those with some background in the philosophical debates about these issues. These sections can be skipped if you are satisfied with the general explanation of how representation works. Try not to skip the whole chapter, though. The theories and arguments are not simple, but they are worth the effort to understand them.

Note for specialists: The arguments in this chapter sketch the reasons in favor of the views I advocate, but they are not comprehensive, conclusive, or particularly original. The point is not to convince opponents, it is to demonstrate how the Consumer Theory of representation forms the foundation of a solution to the explanatory gap. The original move is to show how the Consumer Theory supports a description of consciousness in terms of function, and that move requires at least some defense of function. For a fuller defense, see the authors and texts referenced.

## A Potted History of the Mind-Body Problem

The word "representation" is used in many ways. Within philosophy of mind alone, there are numerous different theories of representation, and each defines the term in line with the theory. So take a moment to put aside your preconceived ideas of representation in order to see the particular problem about the nature of mind that a philosophical theory of mental representation aims to solve.

Prior to René Descartes, the standard way for Western philosophers to think about the mind and body was as two aspects or parts of a person. Plato conceived of a tripartite soul composed of spirited, appetitive, and rational parts, all of which operated to regulate the body. Aristotle took the soul to be the form of living matter; it is the capacity of the body to develop into the sort of thing it is. Even the medieval philosopher St. Thomas Aquinas took great pains to show how the soul is substantially unified with the body. Though the rational soul can continue to exist in heaven after the destruction of the body, Aquinas maintained that its nature depends on its capacity for action as a living animal.[1]

Thinking of the mind as essentially separate from the body emerged with Descartes and Dualism, partly in response to Isaac Newton's application of mathematical principles to the motion of bodies. If the body is regulated by physical law, the mind must be distinct from the body in order to be regulated by rational law. In the *Meditations*, Descartes reflected on the properties that seem to be essential to his mind and found that a mind is a thinking thing, entirely different from a body, which is located in space and has spatial dimensions (Descartes 1641). Even Descartes realized this stark division between mind and body failed to adequately address phenomena such as emotions that cannot be clearly split into a mental and a physical component (Brown 2006). Contemporaries of Descartes recognized that a deeper problem with mind-brain duality was causal interaction. If mind and body are separate, how does the body cause the mind to have ideas, and how does the mind cause the body to act?

And so the mind-body problem was born: how is the mind (essentially rational) related to the body (essentially physical)? One way to answer this question is to focus on the way ideas seem to be about things in the world. My ideas might be mistaken about the world, but there is undoubtedly the *appearance* of a world. There appears to be a banana, roughly two feet in front of me, resting on the table in a green kitchen with windows looking out on a grey winter day. Though the reality of these things may differ from the way they appear, their appearance is undeniable.

Fast forward 400 years and the mind-body problem has been transformed from a question of the relation between mind and body to a question of the relation between appearance and the world, or in representationalist terms, between representation and the object represented. When a banana appears to be on the table to my left, I represent the banana as on the table to my left. The task for the contemporary materialist is to explain how a brain (or whatever aspect of the nervous system is the appropriate vehicle) represents objects like bananas and tables, and how it comes to be accurate or inaccurate in its representations.

## On What a Representation Is *Not*

To better understand how the problem of representation can be solved, we can begin by reviewing three popular theories that do *not* solve it: the Picture Theory, the Computational Theory, and the Causal Theory. Each theory offers a tempting but inadequate way of thinking about representation. We can avoid these tempting options by seeing where they go wrong.

### The Picture Theory

First, the *Picture Theory* was the original and remains the most intuitively satisfying theory of representation. John Locke famously considered the mind a blank slate, a *tabula rasa*, and took ideas to be impressions stamped on the mind by objects.

> These simple ideas, when offered to the mind, the understanding can no more refuse to have, nor alter, when they are imprinted, nor blot them out, and make new ones itself, than a mirror can refuse, alter, or obliterate the images or ideas which the objects set before it do therein produce. As the bodies that surround us do diversely affect our organs, the mind is forced to receive the impressions, and cannot avoid the perception of those ideas that are annexed to them.
>
> (Locke 1689 Book II, Ch 1, §25)

The force of sensation gives the mind a picture that mirrors the objects that produced it. The Picture Theory seems right because it reconciles the recognition that the mind is separate from the world with the experience of full IMAX immersion in the world. On one hand, everyone knows that perception involves a relation to the world that may be mistaken. Illusions and hallucinations present the world in a way that it is not. On the other hand, the world appears to be immediately available; details of the branches and leaves outside my window are present in a way that feels direct. If my representations are pictures of the world inside my head, providing a kind of mirror image of my environment, then both the immediacy and distance of the world make sense.

Also worth noting is the way Locke describes perception as passive. The mind, in its blankness, awaits the impression of colors, sounds, and tastes. On the basis of this input, then, more complex ideas are formed, such as the idea of a tree composed of branches and leaves, which are in turn composed of simple color and shape ideas. Without the input of the senses, there would be no ideas at all, on this view. This commitment to sensation as a passive source of knowledge is the hallmark of Empiricism, which has been a significant influence in theories about the mind.[2]

Despite its intuitive appeal, however, the passive view of sensation is false, and the Picture Theory of representation fails. Research on implicit bias, priming, and other forms of cognitive influence on perception demonstrate that sensation is active.[3] What we see is determined in large part by what we expect to see and what we need to see. This is a point about the operation of attention as well as the nature of perception. A wonderful illustration of the power of expectation was given by Dan Simons and Chris Chabris (1999). If you haven't seen it already, google "selective attention test," and follow the instructions on the video.[4] Now for the spoiler: your expectation directs your attention to the people bouncing a ball, so you fail to notice the gorilla. When pursuing a goal, we are likely to see things that relate to that goal and miss unrelated things, even enormous and surprising things, like the gorilla. Our sensory system actively seeks out some things and ignores others.

Likewise, the Picture Theory fails both factually and logically. As a matter of fact, there is no place in the brain where a picture of the world is displayed.[5] While it is true that patterns on your retina preserve the spatial relations of the visual scene (albeit upside-down), this is just the beginning of visual processing, and vision is just one sense. My representation of the world includes both sight and sound, and it is not clear what a picture of a sound (or a smell for that matter) would involve. Moreover, even the retinal pattern hardly satisfies the intuitions that support the Picture Theory. None of my neurons are yellow or banana-shaped, yet I see a yellow banana before me. The brain simply doesn't picture the world in the way required by the theory.

As a matter of logic, the idea that representations are pictures before the mind implies that the mind is somehow looking at the pictures. If so, the mind must have inner eyes by which to view the picture and an inner mind to represent it. The inner mind must have yet another inner mind and so forth. This infinite regress shows that the Picture Theory cannot explain the mind, because it assumes there is a mind (with inner eyes) to see the picture.[6]

Picture theorists can avoid these problems by accepting the vehicle/content distinction discussed in the Introduction. They can then argue that sensations are brain vehicles (in other words, neurons) that represent yellow bananas, and do so simply by being the sensations they are. What it is for some neurons to represent yellow bananas and others to represent red cups is for there to be a covariation relation between the neurons and the things they represent. Neurons "picture" bananas when the neuron pattern changes in relation to the banana's movement, shape, color, etc. No inner mind is required to see the sensations, so long as the neurons match the object in the appropriate ways. The picture is a mirroring relation rather than a mirror image. At this point, though, it is unclear that the neural "picture" bears much resemblance to the photographs and paintings that inspired the Picture Theory.

Moreover, there is a deeper problem. Picture Theories are committed to *Indirect Realism*, the view that the mind represents the world by means of representing sensations. When I see a banana, I am actually seeing my mind's picture (or representation) of the banana. I then infer that there is actually a banana in the world causing this picture. My sensations appear immediately before my mind, but the object causing these sensations is only known indirectly. What if I am wrong? Worse yet, what if I am massively wrong?

One of the most fun and familiar philosophical mind games is to wonder whether *everything* we sense could be caused by something other than the real world. A current version of the game involves being snatched by clever neuroscientists who put your brain in a vat wired to simulate the world. Instead of a banana causing my banana sensations, the vat produces electrical signals that are indistinguishable from a banana.

Here is one of the first tests of an adequate theory of representation: the Vat Test. Remember the challenge is to figure out how a brain represents objects like a banana. On a Picture Theory, neurons picture or match the banana. If my brain were in a vat—or a matrix or a dream—the neurons might be in the same pattern as they would be when there is an actual banana. For the Picture theorist, all there is to representing the banana is to be in the "banana" brain state, whether or not there are or ever have been real bananas. This means that my brain might right now be in a vat and so I cannot know if there is *anything* that my brain state truly represents. More troubling, this radical skepticism renders the existence of bananas irrelevant from the internal perspective of the picture. The banana would look the same no matter what the situation outside of my brain.

In my view, this result fails the Vat Test. While the possibility of hallucination and illusion must be explained, a theory of representation should first and foremost connect banana representations to bananas. The object should determine representational content in such a way that absence of the object makes a difference to the representation in some way. Either the representation is false or has no content at all. If representational content would be exactly the same in a vat, then the theory is not an adequate theory of representation. My point here is not that it is impossible for me to be a brain in a vat; I address skepticism later in the chapter. The Vat Test indicates whether there is a meaningful relation between the representation and the object it represents. Because my banana representation would have the same meaning, even if there were no bananas, the Picture Theory fails the test.

## Metaphysical Interlude: Representation and an Alternative to Reduction

Intuitions differ on this point, which is why materialists sometimes favor the Picture Theory. In the Introduction I mentioned that materialists take mental states to be constituted by physical states. As Lynne Rudder Baker puts it, "every concrete particular is made up entirely of microphysical items" (2009: 110). *Reductive Materialism* makes the further claim that higher-order properties and relations, like mental states and their causal powers, can be entirely explained in terms of microphysical properties and their relations. That is, given a set of physical properties, the mental properties that are instantiated follow as a law of nature.

So, on Reductive Materialism, any brain that is microphysically identical to your brain right now would necessarily have the thoughts and sensations you are currently having, even if that brain is in a vat. Bananas can have no essential role in determining the content of your banana experiences, because you could have exactly the same experiences even if no bananas exist. The best you can hope for is that your internal picture of a banana somehow matches something in the world that relates to yellow-colored, banana-shaped things.[7]

It may seem that *Non-reductive Materialism* is an oxymoron. A commitment to Materialism may seem to entail that *only* physical properties have any metaphysical status; anything other than properties described by physics has at best a nominal status, a kind of shorthand for referring to collections of microphysical particles. Without canvassing the array of positions and arguments, let me motivate the possibility of Non-reductive Materialism with a sketch of Baker's Constitution View.

The task is to provide a connection between mental and physical properties that avoids two problems posed by *Dualism,* the view that the mind is a different sort of stuff or property from physical properties. The first problem is the possibility of zombies, physically identical beings that are not conscious. Because we can imagine zombies, Chalmers (2010) argues, the nature of consciousness must be distinct from, albeit systematically connected to physical structures. To avoid zombies, a materialist theory needs to describe how mental properties depend on physical properties in a sufficiently determinate way.[8]

The possibility that mental properties are caused by physical properties but do not themselves have any causal power is the second problem, posed by *Epiphenomenalism.* Your experience of the red of the stop sign is caused by the neural activity in your visual system, according to the epiphenomenalist, but the redness plays no role in your response. The neural activity alone causes your foot to move to the brake, not your conscious experience of the sign. This view has the virtue of preserving dualist intuitions about the differences between consciousness and the brain that produces it while avoiding any conflict with physical law (Robinson 2018).

The cost is the denial that your experiences play any role in your life. We will see in Chapter 6 that consciousness cannot be the direct source of our decisions and actions due to the time constraints required to produce a conscious state and execute a motor command. Nonetheless, it would be better to preserve some causal power for consciousness. First, evolution can only select on the basis of causal consequences. If consciousness has no effects, it cannot have been selected for itself. Natural selection can only have operated on whatever neural system causes both consciousness and the advantageous traits. Second, a theory that bridges the explanatory gap is preferable to one that leaves it in place. It is more satisfying to understand how consciousness is part of the physical word, if possible. So to avoid Epiphenomenalism, a materialist theory needs to explain how mental properties have causal power that is independent of yet consistent with physical causal processes.

According to Baker, every instance of a mental property is constituted by some set of physical properties and relations, but the physical items alone are insufficient to entail the instantiation of the mental property as a law of nature. The physical conditions alone are insufficient, because mental properties have independent causal power, considered counterfactually. That is, mental properties *could have had* the same effect given a different physical substrate, and the physical substrate alone *would not have had* the same effect in the absence of the circumstances required to specify the mental property (Baker 2009: 17–20).

An example from Baker about the causal power of voting helps make this rather abstract explanation more concrete. Consider the property of Jones voting against Smith, which is constituted by the property of Jones's hand going up. This causes Smith to be angry, which is constituted by his neural state. Voting is constituted by the hand movement, though there are other ways that voting could have been constituted: paper ballots, voice vote, standing up. Still, nothing supernatural is going on. Furthermore, the hand movement in itself could not have caused Smith to be angry. The circumstances required for the hand movement to constitute the property of voting are part of a system of properties and relations that together explain why the vote caused Smith to be angry. All of the circumstances involved in Jones's vote are physically constituted, but the constitution base is too broad and varied to be useful in causal explanation (Baker 2009: 19).

Later in the chapter (Objection 1) I will return to the Constitution View to explain how thoughts do and do not depend on physical properties for their causal power. For now, I will take as a condition for an adequate theory of representation that a banana thought depends on its relation to bananas in order to ground representations in the physical world. The theory must past the Vat Test. This means that representation cannot be determined by a brain state alone.

## The Computational Theory

A second plausible theory explains how a brain state represents an object by looking at the causal-functional role of the representation. A representation, on this view, is a node in the network of causal relations; its content is defined entirely by the functional role it plays within that network, the inputs and outputs of that node. In the *Computational Theory* a thought is about bananas when it plays a particular role in relation to other mental and physical states. Thoughts about bananas are *caused by* bananas, they can *cause* a desire for bananas, which in turn can *cause* me to walk to the kitchen and eat a banana. On the Computational Theory, if we could map all functional relations such as these, we would have a complete explanation of the mind.

The affinity with computers is obvious in the very name of the theory and gives rise to the familiar idea that the mind is like the software running on the hardware of the brain. One form of artificial intelligence research is to design computational models of the functional relations involved in various kinds of mental processing, such as playing chess, using language, and making decisions. Given the right inputs (bananas) and the right functional relations (the causal network), you get the right outputs (eating a banana).

These models can be very useful in the development of technology that performs these tasks far more efficiently than humans can. More controversial is the claim that computational systems are actually performing mental—that is, representational—processes. The claim rests on the assumption that any system capable of manipulating symbols according to input-output rules is doing what minds do, and so it is also a mind. In other words, what is required for a system to have representations about bananas is for that system to reproduce the functional role that "banana" plays in a human mind.

If we apply the Vat Test, we find that that the Computational Theory is more successful than the Picture Theory in connecting the representation to the object it represents. The functional role of the representation is determined by both input relations (bananas) and output relations (eating bananas). So computational representation is causally tied to the world more firmly than Picture Theory representation. If you were in a vat, you would be mistaken about the *source* of your representations. You would think bananas were the source when actually the computer-simulation of bananas was the source of your sensations. Nonetheless, you are not mistaken about representing a world outside your mind. There is *something* your mind is representing, even though it is not quite the world you think it is. I'll say more about how this solution to the

Vat Test works in the Epistemological Interlude. But first it is important to see why the Computational Theory cannot simply adopt this solution.

A famous thought experiment by John Searle (1980) lays out the objection vividly. Imagine you are in a room with no access to the outside world except a slot where papers with Chinese writing occasionally appear. Your job is to look up the character sequences in a set of rule books which specify the algorithm for determining the character sequences you are supposed to write down. You then deposit the results back through the slot. Unbeknownst to you, the incoming and outgoing sequences form a coherent conversation about bananas in Chinese. But you do not understand Chinese,[9] so the character sequences are meaningless to you.

Though the Chinese character sequences are about bananas to Chinese interpreters *outside the system*, for you, the person who is manipulating the symbols according to the rules, the characters are not about bananas or anything else. For a representation to be meaningful, its content must be meaningful *for the system*, for you. The trouble is that functional role is defined entirely abstractly in terms of computational rules, but the rules only generate meaningful action if the content is already meaningful. Think about how your computer uses representations in word processing. You type in letters and it manipulates that input according to a program in order to produce letters on a screen, which can be saved in the form of bits in a file. Whenever you type "banana," there is a sequence of bits that represent bananas. As should be obvious, your computer doesn't know this. The input-output relations are insufficient to *determine* meaning because their success *depends on* already being meaningful to the user.

Computational representations seem meaningful, because we can build systems to do things that are meaningful to us: word processing, tax forms, Google searches. As Searle argues, this meaning is derived from its meaning for us, the users of these systems. In Chapter 7 we will revisit the question of artificial intelligence to consider what would be needed for a system to determine its own meaning, independent of the designer's uses. Until this question is answered, the computational mind remains stuck in the vat. Even if representations are actually about the world, a computational system has no more understanding of their meaning than Searle has of Chinese.

## Epistemological Interlude: Externalism versus Internalism

In different ways the Picture Theory and the Computational Theory fail to appropriately connect the content of the representation to the object it represents.

The view that representational contents are defined by their relation to objects is called *Externalism*. The Picture Theory fails because the same representations could be "pictured" in the absence of the objects they are supposed to be about, as in the case of the brain-in-a-vat. The Computational Theory fails because processing rules alone are insufficient to make representations meaningful for the system. That is why you could process Chinese writing without understanding the meaning.

One way to respond to these failures is to invert the criterion for success. *Internalism* is the view that contents are defined entirely in terms of internal properties and relations. The mind is not shaped by the world; the world is shaped by the mind. The basic claim is expressed in a slogan from Gottlob Frege: sense determines reference (1948). Frege wanted the term "sense" (*Sinn* in German, also translated as "meaning") to do a lot of work, very little of which will be discussed here. Nonetheless, it is worth keeping Frege in mind as one of the most influential figures in the development of Internalism. For Frege, the meaning of my thought that "bananas are yellow" is determined by the mind's grasp of the concepts "banana" and "yellow" as well as the logical relation "is" and a quantifier like "some" or "all."[10] Whether this thought is true or false depends on what these concepts refer to in the world. Imagine that the concept "banana" puts all of the bananas in a basket. The predicate "is yellow" then takes all the bananas in the basket and sorts out just the yellow ones. If none of the bananas are yellow, then the thought "bananas are yellow" is false. If some but not all of the bananas are yellow, then the thought is true if it means "some bananas are yellow" but false if it means "all bananas are yellow."

One appeal of Internalism is that it preserves the intuition that the meaning of experience is determined by the way things look to *me*. If a banana looks the same whether I am in the world or in a vat, then what it *means* to experience a banana must be the same in both cases. The difference, according to the internalist, is in the world, not the mind. In the world there are bananas, so my thought that "I am seeing a banana" is true. In the vat there is only the appearance of a banana, so my thought is false. In both cases, though, my experience presents the appearance of a banana. All this is very reasonable until you start to wonder what sort of thing a "banana appearance" is. An appearance can't be an object because the failure of banana appearances to be proper objects is what prompted the move toward Internalism in the first place. Things only get worse when you realize that the "banana appearance" is what you are seeing in the vat *and* in the world. Suddenly, you realize that you are never actually seeing bananas, only banana appearances. This is the Picture Theory again, except with the epistemic direction reversed. Rather than figuring out whether the picture matches the world, you try to figure out whether the world matches the picture. When the world fails to picture the mind, as when I am in a vat, my thoughts are false. Nonetheless, internalists maintain that banana appearances are *about bananas* even if I had never encountered a banana in my whole, sorry, envatted life.

For some people, this *Internalist Intuition* is a fundamental truth: meaning is determined by the mind. If this is your view, everything I say in this book will probably seem incomplete to you. You will feel something—you can't say what—is left out of the explanation, something about how your experience is meaningful in a way that transcends its relations to the world. The intuition runs very deep and may be the place where, as Wittgenstein would say, my spade is turned (1953: §217). There is always a point in a philosophical argument where a basic disagreement prevents further argument.

Even if I can't talk you out of Internalism, let me give you some reasons in support of the *Externalist Intuition*: Meaning is determined by the world. The first, somewhat counterintuitive advantage of Externalism is that it is the best defense against skepticism. A central objection to theories of representation has been that the gap between a representation and its object opens the possibility that representations are radically false. We might be living in a vat and have no way of knowing this. But on an externalist theory, the meaning of representations is determined by the objects they represent. Consequently, if you have been living in a vat your whole life, your representation of a banana is *about* a particular set of stimuli produced by the vat.[11] It may be cold comfort that your banana thoughts are true but about a very different kind of thing than you might have expected. But then physics is continually revealing unexpected details about the nature of things like bananas. Meaning and truth are inextricably connected to the world; there can be no meaning without successful reference to the objects represented. My thoughts in the vat are not radically false, they are about different objects than the objects in the physical world.

What disturbs me about being in a vat is not that my thoughts are radically false. What is really disturbing is the possibility that all my thoughts and experiences are disconnected from a world outside them. In other words, solipsism is the real worry, not skepticism. And this worry is also addressed more effectively by Externalism. While the radical scenario of the vat is logically possible, the probability of actually being in a vat is infinitesimal. All evidence stands in favor of banana thoughts referring to things composed of chemicals, which are composed of atoms, and so forth, according to the best current science. While it could be that all of these things (including the scientists) are in fact sets of stimuli produced by a vat, there is no more evidence for this possibility than that there are angels dancing on your nose right now. Lots of things are logically possible that we have no good reason to believe. In contrast, the assumption that my thoughts are determined by the world—that is, the Externalist Intuition—gives me good reason to believe that there is indeed a world they are determined by.[12]

A second advantage of Externalism is its better explanation of the way thoughts are *individuated*. That is, the theory says what it is for a thought to be about a banana *as opposed to* an apple or something else. So far I have only discussed the difficulties that internalists have in getting a thought to be about the world at all. An additional difficulty is to say why the thought is about one aspect of the world rather than another.

Internalists assume you know what you mean when you are thinking about bananas. If you have a thought about a banana today and another tomorrow, how could you be wrong in taking these thoughts to be about the same thing? This intuition is even stronger if you have a perception or image of a banana.[13] Two banana images must both look to me to be about bananas, right? Not necessarily. While we often know what we are thinking, we can sometimes be mistaken. Moreover, our successes are dependent on the physical and social environment in essential but unnoticed ways.

Consider the Pepsi Challenge. In blind taste tests, Coke drinkers discover they prefer Pepsi. Why do they choose Coke if Pepsi really does taste better? One answer is that Pepsi is sweeter, and sweetness is preferable in a single sip. In a full glass, though, a good thing can be too much. Another answer is branding. Neuroscientists Read Montague and colleagues (McClure et al. 2004) had subjects take the taste test both blind and non-blind, and they recorded the brain activations. It turns out that in the non-blind test Coke drinkers prefer Coke even after a single sip. In the blind test, when they picked Pepsi, the brain areas associated with distinguishing tastes were more active. In the non-blind test, when they picked Coke, the brain areas associated with semantic memory and decision-making were more active. The point is that the same sensation is not always identified as the same. If it were, people would consistently choose the same beverage as preferable.

Even for something like a banana, there is a problem ensuring that representational content is consistent across time. Say you are familiar with bananas and come across a plantain for the first time. Is this new experience a "banana" experience or a "plantain" experience? What would determine the difference? For an externalist, the difference in fruits makes a difference.

Theories differ on whether that first encounter with a plantain will be sufficient for you to experience it as different (see discussion below). But all externalists agree that the influence of the object on your perception is what makes the difference. Even to be able to identify the very same banana twice involves the ability to interact with the object. You look at it from several angles, smell it, peel it, taste it. Perceptions aren't static images in your mind, they are interactions with objects in the world, or so an externalist maintains.[14]

## The Causal Theory

If the meaning of representations is determined by objects in the world, how might this occur? An obvious suggestion is that objects *cause* representations. The *Causal Theory* is the inverse of the Picture Theory.[15] Where the Picture Theory starts with the banana representation in the mind and infers that the real-world banana matches it, a causal theorist starts with the real-world banana and argues that it alone can cause banana representations. Bananas cause banana representations, apples cause apple representations, and so on.

On the Causal Theory, there is no requirement that a representation match or picture its cause. Though we represent bananas as yellow and solid, we know that physical properties of objects are not similar to the way we represent these properties. Solid objects are composed of tiny spinning atoms in empty space, for example. Nonetheless, there must be a relationship between the physical property and its representation that ties them together. Differences in physical features are correlated with differences in representations. This external correlation, rather than internal software, determines the content of the representation. The result is that the representational system provides a guide or map for navigating the world.

The view that representations serve a purpose or function like a map is another important advantage over indirect realist theories like the Picture Theory. Not only is the representation caused by the object, but the representation causes action that is object-oriented. My banana representation causes me to do things like pick up and eat bananas. The map is a tool you use to *directly* engage the world. A representation is simply the way the mind registers and responds to the object it is using. As I am using the term,[16] Direct Realism is the view that representations put the mind directly in touch with the world. We do not represent our sensations, we use our sensations to represent the world. This direct connection with the world is another reason to favor the Causal Theory over the Picture or Computational Theory.

Despite its straightforward explanatory appeal, two problems call for a more refined account. First is the *problem of multiple causes*. The banana is certainly one of the causes of my banana representation, but there are multiple intermediary causes as well: the light waves traveling from the banana to my retina, the neural activation from my retina through my visual system. There are also background conditions such as the medium of air, and prior conditions such as the light source reflecting on the banana. In the midst of this causal swirl, why single out the banana as *the* cause that determines the content of my representation?

There are various ways that causal theorists solve this problem. One of the most well-developed accounts by Fred Dretske (1981) borrows the technical notion of *information* from Communication Theory. According to this theory, the amount of information transmitted from source to receiver can be calculated in terms of the reduction of uncertainty among possible states to specify a single state. Dretske argues that the content of a representation can be determined when the information received specifies the source with a probability of 1. Continuing with our banana example, when the sensory signal carries information about a banana with a probability of 1, that signal is 100 percent likely to represent the banana.

Even if this solves the problem of multiple causes, the Causal Theory of representation faces the more difficult *problem of error*. So far we have considered how a representation might come to be about a banana, but the reality is that sometimes we are mistaken. Sometimes things look like bananas but are actually plantains or hallucinations or made of plastic. Though indirect realists are overly impressed by the possibility of error, direct realists certainly must explain how error is possible. The paradox for a Causal Theory is that success in securing a causal relation between an object and a representation entails that the representation is accurate. There can be no error. A solution to the first problem means that there is no possible solution to the second problem.

Dretske's theory exemplifies this dilemma. Because there is a probability of 1 that a banana representation is about bananas, there is no possibility of error. In recognition of this problem, Dretske tries to separate the process by which the representation acquires meaning, the training process, from the process in which that representation is used. When you are learning what bananas are, your representation absolutely must be caused by bananas. If you are not 100 percent accurate in picking out bananas from non-bananas, you do not yet know what they are. After the training period, however, you might get sloppy and represent something as a banana when it is not one.

This solution is unsatisfying. The division between training period and post-training use is arbitrary. Perhaps your later errors mean you never learned the meaning of "banana" in the first place. More fundamentally, learning and error are intertwined throughout the life of a mind. You may know perfectly well what a banana is prior to having any idea that things like plantains exist. Then you taste a plantain and take it to be a banana. Must this be a mistake? Say you go on to use your "banana" representation to include both bananas and plantains for the rest of your life. Does it follow that you will forever be mistaken about what you mean when you use your banana representation to think about plantains? Or is there some point when your "banana" representation comes to have the function of carrying information about both types of fruit? At what point does that happen and, crucially, what accounts for the shift in meaning?

## Determining Content by Consumer Function

### The Consumer Theory

To answer these questions we need to think of the way representations are *used* by the mind. The meaning of your "banana" representation is determined primarily by the way you use that representation to do things, like eat bananas. This is the part of the story that the Computational Theory gets right. As you may recall, the problem for the computationalist was to connect the content of the representation to its *object*. The causal theorist successfully connects content to object but has the problem of connecting the content of the representation to its *use*. Putting these two functions (to connect to the object and to be used by the mind) together, then, can explain the way representations come to be about *objects* as well as the role that *use* plays in securing that critical content-object connection.

On Millikan's Consumer Theory, a representation stands for something, such as a banana, if (1) it varies isomorphically with that thing, (2) because this covariation relation has been beneficial in the past. The first condition ensures a particular sort of causal connection with the object. An *isomorphic variation* means that changes in the object—its position, color, size—correlate by a mathematical rule with changes in the representation (Millikan 1993: 90, 2004: 48–50). If the banana shifts position, the representation changes accordingly. If the banana turns brown, the representation must change too. Of course, the representation vehicle doesn't shift position or turn brown. Changes in the neural patterns correlate with object changes rather than picture them.

That is, neuronal patterns change to represent the banana as brown, they don't themselves turn brown.

The astute reader might ask: how does the representation determine what the *right* correlations are? The second condition answers this question. The correct covariation relations are determined by the uses that specify which object needs to be tracked. Say you want a banana. Why? Because its potassium and vitamin B6 and other healthy contents satisfy essential nutritional needs. Satisfaction of these needs is one of the reasons your representational system has for getting you to bananas. Keep in mind that the ways a representation covaries with the object it represents are not identical with the uses of the representation. I identify bananas by color, shape, and smell, not by potassium and vitamin levels. These latter attributes serve the nutritional functions that give the identifying features their representational function.

There may be several uses you have for bananas, each of which involves some use or *consumer*. Personally, the taste and texture of bananas does not appeal to me. Rather than satisfying my nutritional functions, my banana representation satisfies my very different sort of need for a philosophical example. Consumers are not restricted to serving basic biological functions, because humans have evolved to live in complex social environments. Consequently, there are all kinds of uses that humans now have for representations, well beyond survival and reproduction. Whatever representational use, successfully fulfilling its function depends on the covariation relation between the representation and the object, between my banana thought and bananas.

It is worth pointing out that there is no way a consumer mechanism can guarantee (with a probability of 1, for example) that the covariation relation holds. Global commerce introduces that pesky plantain and—bam—I have a banana representation in the absence of a banana. Here, in addressing the problem of error, we can see the most important contribution of the Consumer Theory. At first, the conflation of plantain and banana is simply an error, since my representation is supposed to be about bananas, not fruits that look like bananas. The reason my banana representation was successful in the past was that it satisfied my banana consumers. All the needs I have had for bananas (potassium, vitamin B6, etc.) were previously satisfied by getting me to bananas, not plantains or plastic bananas or anything else.

But then I eat the plantain and it provides even more potassium, although a bit less Vitamin B6. Overall, though, it satisfies my nutritional needs, so I go on indiscriminately purchasing bananas and plantains, thinking of them both as "bananas." In this case, my representation comes to mean "banana or plantain" because both types of fruit have been successful in satisfying my banana representation consumers.

Now wait. How can "banana" mean "banana or plantain"? Isn't this just an error? Keep in mind that there are different ways to be wrong (and right). My banana representation is wrong relative to the way the English language categorizes these two fruits, yet it is right relative to my own representational system. Each mind has different needs and different interactions with the world that satisfy or do not satisfy those needs. That is why no two minds are exactly alike. Even so, we all live in the same world and face similar challenges in navigating it. Humans have designed languages to codify a representational system that everyone can use to share information and so to interact more effectively with the world. On the Consumer Theory of representation, the English word "banana" is only one way of meaningfully representing bananas. My way of blurring together bananas and plantains may be perfectly adequate to my needs, and so my representation is perfectly meaningful for me.

Which is not to say that representations are correct always or even most of the time. As a matter of biological function, a representation only needs to be successful enough of the time to be worth the cost of reproduction.[17] I may occasionally see a plastic banana and mistake it for the edible kind. This is a full-on error because the plastic banana has never and could never fulfill my nutritional needs. Since I rarely eat bananas, I may not notice the mistake. In cases where costs are low, false or poor representations might flourish; where costs are high, a more accurate representational system is needed. If I actually tried to eat that plastic banana, for example, you can bet my banana representation system would get corrected very quickly.

To review, my banana thought comes to represent bananas by covarying in accord with bananas, because this covariation relation has been beneficial to me. When my banana representation occurs in the absence of a banana—caused by a plastic banana or a hallucination—the representation fails to fulfill its function.[18] There is no banana for the representation to covary with, so it cannot do its job. So long as the representation is successful enough of the time to warrant reproduction, it will continue to mean "banana" despite these mistakes. However, its meaning may become equivocal ("banana or plantain") or hopelessly confused in the face of repeated failure.

## Objection 1: Swamp You

One of the most counterintuitive consequences of a Consumer Theory is that two identical physical systems might differ with respect to their mental states.

This point can be made by the usual bizarre philosophical thought experiment[19]: Imagine a freak electrical storm that miraculously produces a molecule-for-molecule duplicate of you out of the dreck and debris in a nearby swamp. Though this SwampYou has exactly the same sensations and brain processes as real you, none of these states are meaningful until they have proven themselves useful. (That's why it's called a "consumer" theory—use is essential to meaning.) Since all the same causal relations hold, bananas will cause all the same responses in SwampYou as they would in you. The difference is that these relations and responses will not be *meaningful* to SwampYou until they are used. Presumably the usefulness of bananas would be proven fairly quickly if SwampYou is hungry and eats the banana on the table. When SwampYou uses its sensorimotor systems to peel and eat a banana, they acquire a functional history that secures their value in SwampYou's strange representational system.[20]

*Mini-metaphysical interlude.* SwampYou provides an example of the Non-reductive Materialism I discussed in the metaphysical interlude earlier. In that section, I considered Baker's case of voting, where the physical act of raising a hand is insufficient to constitute voting in the absence of a political system within which that act occurs. In the SwampYou case, causal relations to bananas are insufficient to constitute a meaningful banana representation in the absence of a functional system that interprets the relations in order to make use of bananas. There are no mental states that are not constituted by physical states—that's the Materialism part—yet physical states alone are insufficient to constitute mental states without the appropriate historical, functional relations—that's the non-reductive part. *End interlude.*

SwampYou also shows why your laptop does not have mental states. Though computers are paradigmatic representational devices, a computer's representations serve no functions for the computer. Your laptop functions to satisfy your needs rather than its own, because it has no needs, no representation consumers of its own. It may be possible to program needs into a computer or robot that can serve the function of representation consumers and thereby ground representational content. This is the crucial question to determine whether true artificial intelligence is possible or whether the best we can do is to build sophisticated forms of computation.

A representation consumer is something that needs representations in order to fulfill its function. Still, it is insufficient to program a robot to plug itself in when its battery is low, as some Roomba vacuum cleaners now do. In such a case, the need for more power (the consumer) does not make plugs meaningful to the Roomba, because the plug representation was also programmed. The designer simply added a low battery indicator to cause the activation of the plug representation. Both representations are meaningful to the designer, not the Roomba, because the Roomba does not have needs of its own, distinct from its designer.

Saying exactly what will count as "needs of its own" is a project for another time (see Chapter 7 for a start). Let me just say that the question of whether any sort of artificially designed needs can serve the function of representation consumers must be solved before there can be any discussion of artificial consciousness. As I will argue in Chapter 3, consciousness fulfills a particular representational function. Unless robots are capable of mental representation, they cannot be capable of consciousness.

## Objection 2: Direct Perception

A second line of attack on Consumer Theory comes from proponents of a more direct relation with the world. Most of the arguments against representational theories are aimed at the idea that representations form an internal model or picture that we see (Noë 2012: 30ff), and that representational theories take perception to be passive and detached from the world (Noë 2010: 82ff). As I argued earlier, the Consumer Theory does not involve models or pictures, and representations are formed through active, engaged processes.

Nonetheless, there remains the argument that representations are unnecessary. You just don't need something in your head to stand for bananas, the argument goes. All you need are the skills to be able to get to bananas in the world. Perception is an ability to utilize *sensorimotor contingencies*, rules about how your exploration of the world provides access to different aspects of it.

On the *Enactive View*,[21] perception involves an appreciation of the regularities in your interaction with the world. Seeing a banana is not a matter of having an internal picture of the banana in your head, or a matter of bananas causing a particular sensory signal. When you see the banana, you see it as a whole object, you see the back side, despite the fact that no sensations are available from the back side. Your perception of the banana is rooted in your ability to explore the banana, your expectations of how it will change as you move your eyes and your head and your body around it. Ongoing dynamic relations between you and the world provide you with the skills to explore things in the world, and this capacity for exploration is all there is to your experience (Noë 2012).

In many ways this description of perception is perfectly in line with the account of sensory representation I have given. According to the Consumer Theory, there are no pictures in the head; the meaning of a representation is determined by your interaction with it, your use of it. Physical, neural processes are not sufficient to constitute your representation of a banana or any other feature of the world in the absence of the ways you have used those neural processes to get to bananas. The only disagreement I have with the Enactive View is their claim that representations can be dispensed with in favor of something like sensorimotor contingencies.

Two reasons suggest representations are still needed in a theory of mind. First, the *problem of error* cannot be solved by sensorimotor contingencies. The dynamic relation between you and the world is always successful. The world is available to you by virtue of your skills in accessing it. So here comes that plantain. Presumably you would apply the perceptual skills acquired in your interactions with bananas to explore the plantain. There is no possibility of a mistake here, since your perceptual skills will function perfectly adequately with regard to this new fruit. Discovery of a different smell or taste may well lead you to treat these fruits differently in the future, say by only using bananas in smoothies. But if you then put a plantain in a smoothie and don't notice, is this a mistake? What constrains the exercise of your skills such that your use of them is successful rather than unsuccessful?[22]

There is a corollary problem about objects that are beyond your sensorimotor skills to access. According to enactive theorist Alva Noë, you don't actually see stars, because they are just too far away (2012: 70). All you can access are points of light, so that is all you see. Yet it seems like our perception of stars is far more complex. We know that the source of the light is or was a star. Moreover, information about stars is necessary to make sense of the patterns of light over time. For astronomers in particular, use of telescopes and computer simulations informs their perception of the night sky in a way analogous to perception of a banana. Perceiving points of light as stars is not an error due to lack of sensorimotor access; it is a successful use of a theoretically grounded star representation.

Second, the Enactive View fails to adequately address the capacity to represent an object when it is absent. Right now I can think about bananas even though there are no bananas within sensorimotor range. A partial account can be given in terms of potential access (Noë 2012: 26). Just as you see the banana as whole, as having a back side, because you can move your head and body around the whole banana, you can think of a banana in the kitchen because you can go into the kitchen to get it.

Here again, however, the account depends on the possibility of access. There must actually exist an object in order for you to be able to access it. So, what happens when there is not actually a banana in the kitchen? You think you'd like one and then discover the last one has been eaten. This failure is a puzzle for the Enactive View. As Noë says, "Where there is no really existing thing there can be no access or genuine availability; at most there can be the illusion of such" (2012: 27). The puzzle is, without some sense of a failed representation, it is unclear what exactly constitutes the illusion. Noë admits that illusory cases involve "apparent content" (64) but fails to say what the appearance of content involves, if not representations.

An enactive theorist might want to say that the sensorimotor skill that is *supposed* to get you to a banana has failed. In this case the apparent banana content is the ability to get to bananas in the next room, if they were there. A consumer theorist would of course endorse this move and note that this sensorimotor skill seems to be serving the function of representing bananas. That is, sensorimotor skills function to keep track of bananas, because those skills have been useful to get to bananas in the past. In other words, sensorimotor skills just are representations, according to Consumer Theory. It seems that we cannot do without representations after all.[23]

## How Can *That* Be a Representation?

### Yellow

Throughout this chapter I have been arguing that understanding the representational relation between your mind and the banana is fundamental to solving the mind-body problem. These are the first two cards in the house of explanation. The first card claims that what it is to be a mind is to represent the world. The second card claims that physical states are mental when they have the function of representation. If these cards fall, the house collapses. There may be a way to support the remaining two cards with another theory of representation or another solution to the mind-body problem. I leave that project to others. My goal in this book is to show how all the pieces in the puzzle, all the cards in the house of explanation, fit together to demonstrate the possibility that consciousness is the product of a physical, functional, evolutionary process.

My externalist, Consumer Theory of representation is an essential component to that explanation. Whether or not you accept it, there remains a question that no theory provides a fully satisfactory answer to: what about yellow? You might agree that the banana is in front of me and not in my head, and the representation that is in my head comes to be about the banana by helping me get to bananas.

The yellow color is certainly one of the features by which I recognize bananas, but we know that color is not a straightforward property of the banana in the way that, say, size is. An 8-inch banana is 8 inches (or whatever unit) no matter where it is or who is looking at it. The color, however, depends on available light and the visual system of the viewer. Bananas don't look yellow in a dark closet or if you have infrared vision.

Scientists refer to the light reflectance properties of objects when speaking about the physical properties of color. When a light source hits an object, the wavelengths that reflect off the surface depend on factors such as whether the object absorbs or transmits frequencies, and whether the reflectance is mirrored (nail polish) or scattered (cotton fabric). The wavelength and frequency ranges that are used to categorize colors in the visible spectrum are rough divisions in a continuous spectrum. The borders of colors, for example, between yellow and orange, vary somewhat across individuals and cultures ("Color" 2016).

Nonetheless, people from very different cultures perceive roughly the same colors due to the structure of the human visual system. The activation of rods and cones in response to the physical properties of light determines a *color space*. A quality space of relative similarities and differences can be determined for the structure of auditory (pitch, volume), tactile (texture, temperature), and even olfactory experience. Dimensions of these experiences can be graphed geometrically by asking subjects to discriminate among fine-grained presentations of stimuli in standardized conditions.

Specifying uniform laboratory procedures is necessary for establishing any sort of standard color perception, because context is another complicating factor. For example, perception of a color in shadow will result in the same objective light reflectance properties as a color that appears to be a brighter shade.[24] Angle of illumination and other sorts of perceptual cues can also affect the perceived color.

In other words, color perception highlights the role of the visual system in determining the position in color space that the yellow of the banana occupies. The earlier distinction between the vehicle of representation (the neural system) and the content of representation (the object) explains why brain states needn't be 8 inches long and crescent-shaped to represent bananas. The explanation of colors, however, does require an examination of the way the vehicle represents content. We need to know something about the visual system to understand how it represents yellow. On the account developed by Austen Clark (2000), "yellow" is ambiguous between the property the banana is represented as having, call it *yellowP*, and the property of the visual system, call it *yellowQ*.

Q stands for the *qualitative character*, the way an object looks, and *P* stands for the color attributed to the object. A banana looks *yellowQ* to you because its light reflectance properties activate the neural vehicles in virtue of which you represent the banana to have the property of *yellowP*. The yellowness (Q) of the banana is a feature of your visual system that you use to identify yellow (P) things. Bananas are not actually yellow (Q), you represent them to be because they activate the yellow (Q) position in your visual system's color space.

The beauty of this account is the way it deals with both subjective and objective aspects of color. On one hand, qualitative character (yellow) is entirely subjective in the sense that the idiosyncrasies of an individual's sensory system— its peculiar genetic and developmental structure—determine how things look, sound, and smell. While the banana looks yellowQ to you, it does not look yellowQ to a fly. Since houseflies have only two kinds of color receptors, they have trouble distinguishing yellow and white. Yet they can tell the difference between polarized and unpolarized light, whereas humans cannot (Masters 2018). The structural properties of the fly visual system mean that it sees the color of the banana differently than you do. The same banana with the same light reflectance properties causes different color experiences in different visual systems.

The structural differences between fly vision and human vision also mean that flies and humans sort objects differently according to the colors they perceive. This doesn't mean that bananas aren't actually, objectively yellowP. The color reflectance properties in virtue of which bananas look yellowQ to you are out there in the banana, along with its size and shape. That's why bananas are yellow, not the visual system. The experience of yellowQ represents bananas as yellowP.

The objective content is essential to understanding color, because otherwise there is no place for the yellow to go. The yellow is not an absolute physical property of the banana (the color appears differently to different observers and under different conditions), and it is not a physical property of neurons (no neurons are yellow), nor is the yellow represented to be a property of the mind itself. There can be hallucinated colors and dream colors, but even these are represented to be properties of hallucinated and dream objects.[25]

Colors and shapes and textures are the ways the mind has of representing external physical patterns (even when they don't exist!). There need be no similarity between the thing (light reflectance properties) and the way it is represented (yellowQ), or between the way it is represented (yellowQ) and the neural vehicle that carries its content. YellowQ varies in accord with yellowP and thereby satisfies the appropriate consumers, even though it betrays no hint of the mechanisms by which it operates.

Addressing the colors of things is important because debates about consciousness often invoke the specter of *qualia*, which are taken to be properties of experience such as yellowness that can't be explained in physical terms. The representational account of color explains two features qualia are supposed to have: (1) the qualitative similarities and differences between, say, yellow and orange or the visual and tactile sensation of roundness, and (2) the appearance of qualitative character in consciousness.

First, questions about qualitative similarities and differences can be answered in terms of the way sensory systems represent physical properties. As mentioned above, quality space relations can be specified for every modality, and cross-species comparisons can be drawn by examining how different animals discriminate stimuli of various kinds. Though humans and flies have different systems, they can be compared in various ways.[26] Likewise cross-modal comparisons can identify the structures that allow round shapes to be distinguished from square ones in both vision and touch while noting the different way each modality represents round and square.

Second, qualitative character is not exclusive to consciousness; unconscious states may be yellow or even painful. The very idea of unconscious sensations is counter-intuitive to many people, so I'll provide reasons to accept this idea in the next chapter. Even if you are prepared to accept some kind of unconscious sensory process, you may well think there must be something distinctive about the conscious experience of yellow or pain. While there is indeed something distinctive about consciousness, the qualitative character that distinguishes yellow from orange, stabbing pain from burning pain, is the same whether conscious or unconscious, or so I will argue.

In his description of the explanatory gap that a theory of consciousness needs to bridge, Joseph Levine helpfully separates these issues:

> There are two questions a Materialist theory has to answer: (1) what distinguishes conscious experiences from mental states (or any states, for that matter) that aren't experiences? and (2) what distinguishes conscious experiences from each other; or, what makes reddish different from greenish, what determines qualitative content?
>
> (Levine 1997: 338)

Essentially, I am arguing that the answer to the second question can be answered independently from a theory of consciousness. The qualitative character of *yellowQ* is determined by the structure of the visual system in its capacity to represent things as *yellowP*. This book offers an answer to the first question about consciousness in terms of the representation of features like *yellowP* as *present*, a feature of the banana before me *now*. When conscious, representations gain significance as selected and integrated into my representation of the present moment. The peculiar qualitative character, the distinctive *yellowQ-ness*, is the way I represent the color of the banana before me now. Nonetheless, this character is determined by sensory processes prior to consciousness.[27]

## Joy

Emotions, like joy, can also occur unconsciously and can be explained in terms of representation. Some might object that emotional states are often too diffuse to be representational. Doesn't there need to be an object, like a banana, for the mind to represent?[28] Certainly there is a class of emotions that involve objects, as when I am joyful about finding a long-lost earring. In this case the earring is the object of my emotion. Yet even here, one could wonder what the *joy* represents.

In his *Embodiment Theory*, Jesse Prinz (2004, 2012a) argues that joy and other emotions represent bodily states. The light and animated feeling of joy represents high dopamine and endorphin levels. In contrast, the heavy feeling of sadness represents low dopamine and serotonin levels. Joy is also represented in other bodily states such as a smile and spring in your step when joyful, and an ache in your chest and tears when sad. While this simplistic sketch cannot capture the full experience of emotion, it demonstrates the direction that a representational theory can go in providing a more complete picture.

On this view, emotions are representational, because they inform action or other response to events. My being joyful, for example, combined with my previous anxiety about the lost earring, motivates better safe-keeping procedures.[29] My emotions have been useful to *me*, and relate to *my* bodily states, yet they need not be conscious or self-conscious in the sense of being recognized *as* states I am now undergoing. I may be oblivious to my sadness until someone asks me why I look so down. Self-conscious emotion can be useful to better address the issues causing sadness, even though I might be sad without this reflective awareness.

What is essential to emotion, on this view, is to represent the appropriate bodily state in a way that can be used to respond more effectively in the world. Joy reinforces the actions that led to it; anger motivates aggression; fear induces fight, flight, or freeze responses. As with color sensation, the characteristic conscious feeling of joy may seem essential to its nature. Even so, all of us are familiar with cases where a person's behavior indicates emotions—anger, resentment, love—that the person herself does not realize she has.[30]

# Conclusion

In the course of this chapter, I have described a way of thinking about the mind in terms of its capacity for *representation*. Some aspects of this view are intuitive: thoughts are *about* things; mental states are constituted by brain states yet are somehow more than just the brain (Non-reductive Materialism). On some aspects intuitions go both ways: whether you experience your sensations and only indirectly perceive the world or whether your experience is about the world itself (indirect vs. direct perception); and relatedly, whether things determine the content of thought or whether the thought determines what it is about (Externalism vs. Internalism). For other aspects, intuitions run entirely against the view I have described: a physical duplicate of you may not have identical thought contents; sensations and emotions can occur unconsciously. These intuitions may be hard to dispatch, but I encourage you to hold them at bay in order to see the whole house of explanation. Only then can you see what might be gained from revising some otherwise appealing ideas.

In the next chapter I will provide some empirical evidence and additional arguments for thinking that the qualitative character of sensations and emotions can be unconscious, and in Chapter 3 I will describe what consciousness contributes to unconscious representations, which is the sense that they are present. Consciousness represents what is happening *now*.

But we can't skip ahead to consciousness without understanding the parts of the theory on which it rests. If we begin with Descartes by introspecting the conscious mind, we will never escape the mind-body problem. Conscious experience from the inside feels categorically different from brains and bodies. The only possible way to explain this difference is to begin where evolution begins, with the representational capacities of simple organisms trying to survive in the world. We need to begin to see how environmental challenges demand the development of increasingly articulate forms of representation in order to better tailor behavior to conditions and needs.

William Paley (1802) famously argued that an eye must have been designed intelligently because its operation is too intricately structured to have appeared as a random mutation. Now of course we know that the fabulous precision of human vision, or the more fabulous vision of birds of prey, is the result of gradual steps, each of which provided just a tiny bit of advantage for its possessor over previous versions. Presuming the mind evolved to be conscious, we should expect the same gradual process from dull to spectacular. This chapter and the next are devoted to taking you through these relatively dull but important steps toward explaining why and how consciousness evolved.

2

# Ants Go Marching

## Reclaiming Your Unconscious Self

Descartes' motto is compelling. I am my thought. Whenever I reflect on what I am, I find myself thinking, consciously thinking and perceiving. Everything else— my body, my belongings, my relationships—is an aspect of me only in relation to my consciousness of them. If I lose my consciousness, I cease to exist. Except, as Locke reminds us, consciousness disappears when we sleep without dreaming. Few people worry that going to sleep really means that a person ceases to exist. After all, we can watch others sleep and confirm that they remain essentially the same before and afterward. Sigmund Freud took the power of the unconscious to the extreme and claimed that your *real* nature is your unconscious thought. Your consciousness (Ego) is simply struggling to balance your unconscious desires (Id) against the unconscious rules imposed by social order (Superego). As we will see, consciousness is more than the pawn of Freudian unconscious forces, although less than the Cartesian ruler of its own destiny.

Consideration of the role of unconscious sensations and thoughts will prepare us for the next chapter where we will consider the role of consciousness.

Unconscious processes are the evolutionary precursors to consciousness, and they do most of the work of the mind. However, consciousness is important to unconscious processes as well. The critical question is: why? If so many processes occur unconsciously, why be conscious at all? A hint of an answer will appear at the end of the chapter, and a full-fledged account will be developed in Chapter 3.

## The Phenomenology of the Unconscious

Unconscious phenomenology is an oxymoron. Phenomenology is the study of appearances, where "appearance" refers to how things appear in consciousness. One would seriously underestimate the resources of Phenomenology, however, to conclude that the theory had nothing to say about processes outside of consciousness. By careful observation of the regular patterns of change within consciousness, a great deal can be learned about processes outside consciousness.

Consider the feeling of losing and regaining consciousness as you fall asleep and then wake up again in the morning or after a nap. (Feel free to take a nap now in the interest of phenomenological investigation.) Sometimes the transitions are quick, and it seems as if no time has passed between lying down and getting up again. Even in this case, you can tell that you have slept. The clock has moved forward, for one thing. Dawn has come. You feel bodily changes as well, at first sluggishness, and then after coffee, a renewed alertness. Something was happening during that time, both to your body and to your mind. While no one yet knows exactly what value sleep brings in exchange for roughly one-third of our lives, there are some reasonable hypotheses. Evidence suggests that sleep functions to consolidate memories by strengthening neural connections recently formed ("Sleep, Learning, and Memory" 2007). A nap of 20 minutes to an hour improves mood and the ability to learn new information (Anwar 2010; Cellini, Torre, Stegagno, and Sarlo 2016). These are changes you can consciously observe, if you pay attention.

Other phenomenological evidence of unconscious processing is the discovery of a solution to a problem after a period of inattention. There you are, struggling with your taxes or a difficult book of philosophy or even a crossword puzzle. You take a break, go for a walk and suddenly, out of nowhere you understand how to calculate depreciation or what transcendental deduction involves or the seven-letter word for dream.[1] Either a miracle has occurred, or your mind has been churning through the information unconsciously while you were consciously admiring the day.

Creativity research suggests that unconscious thought can generate relevant connections among ideas, but conscious thought is needed to determine which of these connections is actually useful (Markman 2012). When awake, the novel connection can be immediately vetted, generating that "aha" moment. When asleep, on the other hand, things don't usually go so well. I regularly suffer from insomnia at three in the morning, my mind churning through ideas about the self, robots, free will. My speculation is that unconscious processes have generated an overload of possible solutions and demands from the day, and consciousness needs to sort through them. These unconsciously produced solutions would be great and worth the disturbance if they were actually useful. But left to its own devices, the unconscious mind makes too many connections, resulting in a flood that quickly swamps a groggy consciousness. So it is better to sleep well at night and take walks (and naps) during the day to most effectively utilize these unconscious resources.

Here is another exercise in phenomenology of the unconscious: pay attention to your conscious experience when talking to a friend. Notice how your words just appear without consciously thinking about them in advance. Your consciousness is occupied with thoughts about the content of the conversation—perhaps you are trying to decide what movie to see. You might have a mental picture of a particular actor, or a memory of a review. You will probably not have any conscious representation of the words you intend to say before actually saying them. Somehow the right words appear in mostly grammatical sentences without any conscious planning.

This is not to say language production is never conscious. In some situations, such as in a heated debate or testifying in court, precise wording is crucial to avoid misunderstanding. Prior to saying anything out loud, you might consciously rehearse your response in your mind. Even in this case, however, the process of producing a word and arranging it syntactically is unconscious. The words simply appear in a particular order. You can consciously assess the result, but you can't peer into the process of language production itself. Has this ever happened to you? You are in the middle of a sentence and realize you are saying something you shouldn't—it is rude or a secret or just a mistake. You can't stop yourself. The best you can do is to try to apologize or correct yourself afterward. Consciousness seems to function more as an overall guide rather than the causal source of language.

Various sorts of phenomenological evidence for unconscious processing are described by David Rosenthal, one of which occurs when another person knows our emotional state before we know it ourselves:

we will occasionally recognize that we ourselves are sad or angry only after somebody else points it out to us. Subliminal perception and peripheral vision remind us that perceptual sensations can occur without our being aware of them. It is arguable that even bodily sensations such as pains can at times go wholly unnoticed, and so can exist without being conscious. When one is intermittently distracted from a relatively minor pain or headache, it is natural to speak of having had a single, persistent pain or ache during the entire period. It would be odd to say that one had had a sequence of brief, distinct, but qualitatively identical pains or aches.

(Rosenthal 1997: 731)

In all these everyday instances, we readily acknowledge the role of unconscious states in accounting for our behavior. By its very absence, consciousness recognizes unconsciousness.

The last form of unconscious experience to be considered is, counterintuitively, subjective experience. Subjectivity is often taken to be synonymous with consciousness; there is something an experience is like *for the subject* (Nagel 1974). To see why subjectivity is necessary yet not sufficient for consciousness, notice your body position right now. Feel the weight of your legs, the press of your back against the chair. Consider where your arms are located and how you can feel their location even with your eyes closed. The world is arrayed spatially around you, coordinated so that the sights and sounds of things like the clock across the room appear to be a definite distance from here.

The egocentric geometry of your sensory representations (everything is centered on *you*) is the structural basis of subjectivity. Thomas Metzinger calls this the *weak first-person perspective* (weak 1PP), because it is simply a spatial frame of reference, prior to the formation of a conscious sense of self. Subjectivity is constituted by the weak 1PP, the sense of your body in space, and the sense of ownership you have of your body.[2] These three conditions necessarily inform every conscious experience, but they arguably structure unconscious processes as well. In dreamless sleep, the body coordinates its movement to avoid falling out of bed, and may even hit the snooze button without requiring conscious direction. Before directing attention to your body position, you were able to remain upright and periodically shift in your seat to relieve pressure on one or another limb. The unconscious sense of your body in space, your subjectivity, can thus be revealed by being brought into consciousness. Nonetheless, subjective experience in this weak sense is usually unconscious.

## The Science of Yellow and Joy

The possibility of unconscious qualitative character and emotion is also counterintuitive. In Chapter 1 I promised empirical evidence that the experience of yellow and joy could occur unconsciously.[3] A large and growing literature on the differences between conscious and unconscious processing speaks to the variety of psychophysical and neuroimaging methods that have been developed in recent years. I will consider only a few examples from this literature as illustrations, and encourage the skeptical reader to explore the many books available on the neuroscience of conscious and unconscious processes (Dehaene 2014; Eagleman 2012; Koch 2012; Seth 2014).

Let's start with color and a curious phenomenon called *binocular rivalry* that you can try at home. Go to Eric Thomson's Neurochannels blog (2009) and follow the instructions for experiencing rivalry between an image of a face and a house:[4]

> Most people do not see a simple fusion of the house and face, but rather the patterns alternate. For instance, you might see the house for a few seconds, and then the face will dominate for a while, and so on. That is binocular rivalry. During transitions, the new percept will spread across the old in a kind of traveling wave, in which case you might see a dynamic quilt-like pattern.

Binocular rivalry is useful for studying unconscious perception, because the stimuli are the same throughout the experiment. The pictures remain; only your conscious perception changes from green face to red house. Evidence from psychophysical and neuroimaging studies shows that simple features like color and grating type continue to be processed even when the image is unconscious. However, participants are only able to identify more complex perceptions like face or house when the image is conscious (Blake, Brascamp, and Heeger 2014; Lin and He 2009; Tong, Meng, and Blake 2006). Using the binocular rivalry paradigm to study the neural dynamics of consciousness is a useful method for investigating how representations become conscious and why (Kang and Blake 2011; Maier, Panagiotaropoulos, Tsuchiya, and Keliris 2012).

Another source of neuroscientific evidence for unconscious color perception comes from people with a strange capability called *blindsight*. In these cases, a lesion in the visual cortex causes a region of the visual field to be blind; when a stimulus is shown in that region, blindsight subjects say they see nothing.[5] Yet when prompted to guess between two choices (red or green, vertical or horizontal), subjects are usually right, guessing correctly as much as 90 percent of the time (Cowey and Stoerig 2004; Stoerig 2006).

Take a minute to try to put yourself in the position of someone with blindsight. The researcher asks you what you see, and you see nothing. The world looks exactly the same to you as it did before the stimulus was there. Then the researcher asks you to guess whether the stimulus is red or green. Ridiculous, how can you guess the color of something you can't see? But you agreed to participate, so you ought to try to cooperate—red, you say. Right! 90 percent of your guesses are right, even though you are not consciously seeing the stimulus. The results must seem like magic. The reason they aren't magic involves unconscious sensory processes that can inform action, like guessing, even without becoming conscious.

More surprising results come from research on unconscious emotion. It can be hard to think about emotions like joy or fear in the absence of their characteristic conscious feelings. Chapter 1 suggested that emotions are representations of bodily states. Joy is the representation of physiological changes—such as high dopamine and endorphin levels—that serve to reinforce whatever action or situation brought about these changes. The best evidence that emotional representations occur unconsciously comes from *masked priming studies*. If a stimulus is presented briefly (under 100ms) and then immediately followed (masked) by another stimulus, such as a random pattern of dots, subjects do not report having seen the first stimulus even though it influences their responses. This unconscious influence is called *priming*. Using this paradigm, researchers have found that when the prime shows an emotion such as joy, subjects will interpret the neutral probe image as positive. If the prime is negative, like a face showing fear, the probe face is interpreted as negative (Axelrod, Bar, and Rees 2015).[6]

Going back to the research on blindsight provides further evidence. When blindsight subjects view emotional faces presented in their blind field, they spontaneously mimic the emotion of the stimulus. Known as *emotional contagion*, this sort of unconscious imitation of emotion may serve as an evolutionarily early means of sharing emotions (Tamietto et al. 2009).

## The Cognitive Unconscious

Perhaps you are convinced that sensory and emotional processes can occur unconsciously. After all, it makes good evolutionary sense to be able to process these sorts of stimuli quickly in order to respond to life-threatening dangers. Moreover, very simple-minded animals like bees can distinguish colors, and it is unlikely that they are capable of consciousness (see Chapter 4). Yet you may share the tendency of philosophers such as Descartes in believing that the higher cognitive functions of language and reason are the true indicators of consciousness. You may accept that simple sensory and emotional processes can be unconscious, while consciousness is required to think and make decisions.

On one hand, you do need to be conscious to make decisions. On the other hand, growing evidence indicates that even our most sophisticated forms of thought and decision-making depend essentially on unconscious processes. The priming paradigm used above to illustrate unconscious emotion was originally developed to investigate *word priming*, the unconscious semantic influence of words. Researchers found that the presentation of a masked word (salt) inclines subjects to choose a semantically related word (pepper) from a list rather than an unrelated word (lotus).[7]

A more familiar and troubling context of unconscious influence in decision-making occurs when racial and gender stereotypes affect the evaluation of job applicants. *Implicit bias* refers to the way a person tends to make judgments based on familiar categories, and the most entrenched cultural categories are gender and race. Several studies have shown that white, male job candidates are favored over Black and female candidates with similar resumés.[8] Though this sort of bias is sometimes conscious and intentional, more often it is the result of unconscious processes. Whenever we make choices—simple ones like what to wear or complex ones such as which career to pursue—past experience weights factors as more or less salient to the decision. A positive response to that red dress or a successful chemistry class appropriately sways future choices. Past training is problematic when packaged in cultural norms that result in discrimination against disadvantaged groups. Even computer programs exhibit bias when trained using internet language and images (Caliskan, Bryson, and Narayanan 2017; Lohr 2018).

Unlike computer programs, humans can self-consciously work to correct our implicit bias. By understanding how unconscious processes influence our perception and action, we can deliberately seek out experiences that will challenge our stereotypes. As I will argue in the next chapter, consciousness is necessary to prevent a habitual response. If we consciously attend to the specific features of the person in front of us, it is possible to overrule the weight of cultural norms in evaluating the situation.

The upshot of research on the power of unconscious processing is that many of our perceptions, thoughts, and responses are influenced or entirely determined without conscious oversight. Despite this evidence, you may remain unconvinced. The methodology regarding unconscious processes is fraught with difficulties (Newell and Shanks 2014). Subjective report is the primary method of gaining access to conscious experience, but this procedure conflates evidence of consciousness with evidence of reportability.[9] In the absence of report, however, it is more difficult to satisfy skeptics who believe there can be no objective evidence for a subjective state. This sort of skepticism is the motivation behind the Hard Problem—all the neural and behavioral evidence could be the same without any consciousness.

As I said in the Introduction, the solution to the Hard Problem involves a description of consciousness in functional terms. If we can determine a *function* of consciousness, then we can look to see when that function is performed and when it is not. The evidence presented up to this point, both phenomenological and empirical, supports the claim that similar sorts of sensory and cognitive processing occur both unconsciously and consciously. If we knew what function consciousness performs, we would better understand these similarities and, crucially, why these processes differ. One clue is the earlier observation that consciousness is required for using language and making decisions even though most of the machinery for these cognitive processes occurs unconsciously. The trick is to figure out why.

## Evolution of Mind Time

In taking this functional view, we shift our perspective from humans to look at the evolution of the mind from very simple organisms to non-human animals capable of conscious experience. I began with the human case because humans are reading this book. Ultimately, arguments about consciousness are more compelling when they are suited to our own consciousness. Yet the best reason to think the mind functions unconsciously is the fact that many animals perform similar functions without the aid of consciousness, or so I will argue. At this point, then, we leave behind the phenomenology of our own experience and its associated neuroscientific evidence. We turn now to the possible evolutionary sources of consciousness.

Let me begin with a sweeping history of the universe to give you a broad sense of the possible origin of mind from matter. Physical processes after the Big Bang gradually led to the primordial soup out of which life formed. With the dawn of life came the need to distinguish good and evil, nutritious and noxious. Natural selection favored organisms that responded appropriately to their environment based on their particular needs. Beings that succeeded in acquiring nutrients and avoiding toxins survived and reproduced. Successive generations inherited these capacities to distinguish good from bad,[10] that is, they inherited the capacity for *representation*. Given the diversity of environments and the randomness of mutations, different organisms acquired different forms of representation. More challenging environments demand more sophisticated representational systems. An examination of these demands reveals the general structure of development from simple stimulus-response association to more flexible forms of representation, from unconscious to conscious representation.[11]

## Tracking Change

Taking a biological view of representation shows how different sorts of representation serve different functions, and how those functions are adapted to particular environments by the organisms that inhabit them. Consider the lowly nematode worm *Caenorhabditis Elegans (C. Elegans)*. Although a very simple organism, it has a nervous system capable of basic forms of learning. With just 302 neurons, *C. Elegans* is able to sense the chemical gradient in its environment and move toward nutrients and away from toxins by flexing and relaxing bands of dorsal and ventral muscle cells (Edgley 2015).

The sensory system of *C. Elegans* satisfies the two conditions on representation mentioned in Chapter 1: (1) sensory cells have the function of varying in relation to features of the environment (chemicals), (2) because that covariation relation has been helpful in the past. Sensory representations have been effectively used by the muscle system to move toward nutrients and away from toxins.

As I argued in Chapter 1, using the word "representation" for stimulus-response association emphasizes the continuity among the sorts of physical states that are mental. Even if it initially seems odd to say that a worm (or a plant, see Chapter 4) has a mind, the capacity for representation is a conceptually useful defining feature. Representation is the thread that binds perception, thought, memory, higher-order capacities like mathematics and language, and even artifacts like computation and art. Everything that involves mental capacities involves representation.

My suspicion is that the reluctance to ascribe a mind to *C. Elegans* stems from two sources: (1) identification of mind and consciousness, (2) worries about panpsychism. The goal of this chapter is to undermine the first objection. *C. Elegans* has a mind yet is not conscious. The second objection takes the form of a slippery slope; if *C. Elegans* has a mind, why not a rock or a table? *Panpsychism* is the view that the rock and table and absolutely everything else also has a mind. While this view has adherents, it obscures the radical transformation of physical processes that took place when life and mind originated. There is a reason the mind is mysterious in ways that geology is not (although rocks have their own secrets, of course). If we are to understand the source of these mysteries, we need to have a sense of how the mind is distinct from other physical things.

Taking Panpsychism off the table, the question for this chapter is what distinguishes the simple mind of *C. Elegans* from us, or more narrowly, what distinguishes unconscious representations from conscious ones. My proposal is that conscious states represent the present moment in order to facilitate flexible action.[12] Consciousness represents what is happening *now* in order to determine what to do *next*.

But wait. Don't all representations have to represent the present environment in order to be effective? No, some representations *track change* without representing time.[13] All representations make use of timing relations in order to coordinate actions with the feature of the environment that is represented. The appropriate response must occur at a specific time after the stimulus to be effective. It is no good for the frog to zap its tongue out after the fly has gone. Furthermore, actions often follow precisely timed sequences in response to environmental cues. These are ways representations use temporal relations to *track change*, and these forms of representation can occur unconsciously. The remainder of this chapter will explain how this works. Chapter 3 will explain how consciousness *represents time*. Only conscious states include the present moment as part of the content of the representation. From among the various changes an animal is tracking, some selection is represented *as now*.

Before we can see why an animal would need to represent time, it is important to understand how animals track change. Sequences such as *before and after* are, in a certain way, timeless. If X regularly comes before Y, this relation holds whether the sequence is past, present or future relative to me. If a tree always blooms before it bears fruit, the relation *bloom-then-fruit* is not tied to a particular time. Whenever the bloom happens, the fruit appears afterward. Consequently, no representation of time is needed. To track the change from bloom to fruit in order to get something delicious to eat, an animal only needs to represent the two events in relation to each other. Likewise, when the frog tracks the fly from right to left, it represents the fly at one location *and then* at the next. In order for the frog to capture the fly, its representations of the fly's location must change as the fly moves, and the frog's actions must be in synch with those changes.

## Pushmi-pullyu Representations

This all seems very simple, and it is. The frog can track the fly in the world and respond effectively by means of representations that connect the way the world is with the right way to respond. In behaviorist terms, these are the most simple stimulus-response associations. In terms of representational function, this stimulus-response association combines two jobs that could be done separately: it both describes the world and directs behavior.

To borrow Millikan's terminology, a *descriptive representation* is object-oriented; it is designed to vary according to what it represents in order to alert the animal to useful things in the world, such as location and distance from a fly. A *directive representation* is goal-oriented; it is designed to vary its activity so as to create the state of affairs represented. The frog's goal is to create the state of affairs where it is eating the fly. The directive representation aims behavior in such a way that its goal is achieved. Descriptive representations get the frog to align with the world; directive representations get the world to align with the frog.[14]

According to Millikan, the ability to acquire purely descriptive or directive representations is an evolutionary achievement that requires prying apart two elements of a more primitive representational form, whimsically called *pushmi-pullyu representations*. A pushmi-pullyu representation is one that ties a descriptive (pushmi) function to a specific directive (pullyu) function. Animals like the frog develop pushmi-pullyu representations in response to particular environmental challenges, such as the ability to spot flies in order to eat them (Millikan 2004: 77–81). The two aspects work in tandem to engineer appropriate behavior.[15]

Pushmi-pullyu representations do not need to represent time, because the timing of action to environment is built into the representation relation itself. The animal is able to exploit cause-effect relations in the world by tuning its responses to particular cues. In some cases the timing from detection to action is absolutely fixed. As Millikan explains,

The P-P [pushmi-pullyu] neural impulse produced in the frog's optic nerve by a passing fly reports when and at what angle the fly passes and provokes a corresponding response from the frog's tongue. This impulse forms part of a simple reflex arc that cannot be inhibited, even if the frog is completely sated. It reports a fact and issues an unconditional command.

(2004: 164)

As we will see, pushmi-pullyu representations need not be so rigid. Indeed, behavior can become quite complex and still be regulated by pushmi-pullyu representations. So long as the way things are determines what to do in a 1–1 relation, the time at which things happen will specify the time to respond. In this way, the use of timing relations is built into the representation. An important advance occurs when *different* things might be done in response to a given situation. Only then can the animal choose which action is best in relation to its current goals. Only then does the animal need to move beyond tracking the timing relation to *representing* time.

*C. Elegans* does not represent time; it makes use of timing relations in its tracking of nutrients and toxins. In order to move toward nutrients and away from toxins, the nematode worm compares chemical concentrations at one point and then again at a later point. We might translate the pushmi-pullyu representation as "more food, go this direction" or "icky acid, go back." To form these representations, one chemical concentration must be taken *before* the other, and action must follow immediately *after.* The worm uses the timing relation between sampling points to determine whether its direction is a good one or a bad one, and to respond accordingly. Nonetheless, the relations are timeless in the sense that they are fixed to the structure of the worm's environment. Given that the environment and the worm are configured in the way they are, the worm's action is fully specified by the environment. The timing relation of *before and after* is used to calculate the relations, but it does not need to be represented *as time.* Another mechanism might do the calculations in relation to distance, for example.

Psychologist J. J. Gibson (1986) referred to such perception-action sequences as *affordances* and argued that perception is essentially the ability to appreciate the ways one's environment allows or "affords" action. A chair affords sitting (to humans); flies afford eating (to frogs). We don't first see the chair and then consider what to do with it. We see the chair *as* a sitting affordance.[16] Pushmi-pullyu perception includes a representation of appropriate action, not merely as a hypothetical possibility, but as a trigger that initiates response. So the representation of flies triggers consumption, which has the function of sating hunger. Temporal representation at this level is limited to the ability to register environmental markers in relation to an appropriate response. In other words, pushmi-pullyu representation is the ability to exploit cause-effect relations, to appreciate the difference between before and after. Because causes come before effects, the sensitivity to their temporal order facilitates appropriate action.

## Implicit and Explicit Representation

Another way to make the point is to say that *C. Elegans* represents time *implicitly*. There are a number of ways that a distinction between implicit and explicit representation can be drawn.[17] As I will use the term, an *explicit representation* accounts for the success of an animal in using whatever is represented; the success of explicit representation is the reason that the representation is reproduced. In the case of the nematode worm, nutrients and toxins are explicitly represented. When movement toward nutrients and away from toxins is successful, the worm thrives. An *implicit representation* is a necessary condition for explicit representations to function properly but is not itself the reason that representation is reproduced. Timing relations are the means by which the worm accomplishes its representation of nutrients and toxins. While correct timing is essential, its role is instrumental to the success of the explicit representation.[18] For *C. Elegans* the method of sampling the environment at two points is useless unless it is used to represent the direction of nutrients and toxins.

Biological organisms have developed a remarkable variety of timing mechanisms that function in this implicit way. The marine Palolo worm *Eunice viridis* times its reproductive cycle to a two-hour period in late Fall. How thousands of these organisms manage to synchronize their timing with such astounding precision is attributable to a combination of biological mechanisms. Diurnal, lunar, tidal, and annual cycles provide external signals for tracking change (Gallistel 1990: 236). Circadian rhythms and hormonal cycles provide internal signals for tracking change (Dunlap, Loros, and Decoursey 2003).

These timing mechanisms are amazing feats of engineering in their ability to coordinate response precisely to environmental conditions. Even so, time remains implicit in these systems because success does not depend on any particular time, only the timing of action relative to perception. To represent a situation *as now* would require distinguishing it from the past and future in some way and would include the possible *mis*representation of time.[19] Pushmi-pullyu representations do not do either of these things. The time is specified entirely in terms of the behavioral sequence, so the failure of timing is not a representation of the wrong time, it is a failure in the behavior. The Palolo worm with a fast-running oscillator will arrive early to the meeting location, and so its behavior will fail to satisfy its need to reproduce. Yet the time component of this repertoire cannot be adjusted independently of the entire perception-action sequence. The worm has no means of recognizing that it is early, or even what it means to be early, and so it can't decide to wait a while. Because the timing mechanism is built into the perception-action relation, there can be no reevaluation of action when the mechanism fails.

To use a more familiar example, compare two-timing mechanisms in your dishwasher. The first is the washing mechanism that is designed to pump water through the system according to the kinds of dishes to be cleaned. It runs longer on the "pots and pans" setting than on the "normal wash" setting, yet it does not need to represent the time it takes to wash pots as opposed to other dishes. When functioning properly, the mechanism simply varies its operation according to the wash setting, not according to the passage of time. In contrast, the delay mechanism does vary its operation according to the passage of time. When functioning properly, the "one hour delay" setting will delay the wash for one hour from the time you push the button. For the wash settings, the timing is implicit in the function of proper washing; whereas for the delay settings, the timing is explicit in the function. Both of these timing relations depend on humans, of course, since their representational abilities were designed by the manufacturer, not by evolutionary success. And the dishwasher is no better than the Palolo worm at compensating for a failed mechanism. Still, the two settings illustrate the difference between a mechanism that *implicitly* varies according to time and one which *explicitly* represents the period of time as its function. There is a parallel difference between the implicit way an organism such as *C. Elegans* utilizes timing relations to track changes and the explicit way a conscious animal represents time.

## The Joys and Sorrows of a Pushmi-pullyu Animal

Canvassing the ground covered thus far, we have seen various forms of evidence for unconscious representation in humans and pushmi-pullyu representations in various organisms that use timing relations without representing time. In my view, unconscious representation and pushmi-pullyu representation are connected: any task performed by pushmi-pullyu representations can be done by unconscious processes. When there is no need for an explicit representation of the present moment (because time is implicit in pushmi-pullyu representations), there is no need for consciousness. It is worth carefully examining exactly what capacities can be performed unconsciously by pushmi-pullyu representations in order to better understand exactly *why* an animal ever needs consciousness.

Pushmi-pullyu representations use timing relations but don't represent time explicitly. If, as I suggest, pushmi-pullyu representations are unconscious, another way to ask why we need consciousness is: why couldn't all behavior be regulated by pushmi-pullyu representations? For some animals, call them *pushmi-pullyu animals* (Millikan 2004: 165), this is exactly the case.[20] Such an animal is in the happy situation where behavior is tailored to environmental cues, so that appropriate responses are either innate or finely tuned by past learning episodes. Quite sensitive and intricate sequences of behavior can be formed when pushmi-pullyu representations become linked. As Millikan observes, "The activities of insects may be largely or entirely governed in this way, by hierarchies of perception-action chains, or as ethologists call them, chains of 'behavior releasers'" (2004: 166).

The foraging patterns of an ant demonstrate how remarkable yet inflexible pushmi-pullyu representations can be. Leaving the nest, an ant will loop back and forth in search of food. When a morsel is found, the ant does not retrace its steps. Instead, it takes a direct path back to its nest. The ant accomplishes this efficient navigational maneuver by computing the geometric relation between the starting position and the ending position. By keeping track of its turns left and right, the ant can head in the correct direction and go the right distance to return home (Gallistel 1990: 58–65).

Before you get too impressed with ant super-intelligence, consider what happens when entomologists move the ant over a few meters after it has found food. The ant automatically returns to the place where the nest was *supposed* to be based on the calculation of the original starting and ending positions. If moved again, the ant will take the new location as where the nest should be and restrict its search pattern to that spot. Despite the very elaborate chain of pushmi-pullyu representations that an ant uses in its navigation, its behavior is conditioned to respond exclusively to a given set of cues.

The drawback of a pushmi-pullyu animal is that it lacks "the ability to recombine various segments of behaviors in its repertoire in new ways so as to achieve new goals. It could achieve new linkages of behavior chains only by reinforcement of accidental connections after the fact, never by inventively looking ahead" (Millikan 2004: 168). Because pullyu goals are linked to specific pushmi facts, the pushmi-pullyu animal is guided entirely by the affordances in the chain as they present themselves rather than by a general representation of the ultimate goal. The ant is guided by its representations of starting and ending positions in order to get food to its nest. The nest is its goal, but the ant does not represent this *as* its goal. Once the ant has found food, it simply walks in the direction specified by its navigational calculus. Natural selection has shaped the ant's representational system to respond to its environment in particular perception-action sequences.

Consequently, pushmi-pullyu goals are oddly backward-looking. As humans, we expect goals to be in the future, hoped-for yet unrealized events. For pushmi-pullyu animals, goals are linked to past successful behavior. The lost ant cannot dream of a new path home. Its search pattern is dictated by the navigational tools that have been successful in the past.

The sad story of the digger wasp is another example of the failure to separate pullyu goals from the pushmi facts that trigger them.[21] These wasps dig tunnels in loose dirt to serve as nests for larvae, hence the name digger wasp. After paralyzing its prey with a sting, the wasp will drag it to the edge of the tunnel, set the prey down outside, check to be sure the tunnel is intact, then emerge to retrieve the prey. When researchers moved the prey a few inches away from the edge of the tunnel each time the wasp went inside, the wasp got sent back to step one: drag, check, emerge, drag, check, emerge, and so on indefinitely. The wasp failed to realize that its goals in checking the tunnel had been successfully fulfilled. Its behavior is tied to a chain of affordances that is probably quite useful in the absence of pesky entomologists but nonetheless strikingly inflexible.

## Consciousness and the Need for "Now"

The story of the digger wasp is poignant, because we immediately appreciate the futility of its behavior. *We* can see that the tunnel doesn't need to be checked again, but the wasp cannot. Tunnel-checking is just what happens after prey-moving. What we have that the wasp lacks is a representation of the goal as distinct from the situation absent the goal. For us, most situations offer possibilities for action in relation to a goal rather than preset connections between means and ends. Animals like us are capable of what Millikan calls a *goal state representation* (2004: 198); we can consider a variety of different means toward a goal and can determine when that goal has been realized. Unlike a pushmi-pullyu animal, a *practical animal* represents situations independently of actions in order to evaluate which action has the best chance of success.[22]

In contrast, a pushmi-pullyu animal like a bee cannot evaluate its actions in relation to its goals. It may either fly to the right or fly to the left in its search for nectar, since either direction might be fruitful. Nonetheless, the factors that determine which direction it will fly are specified by the bee's history and that of its species. This history ties direction to nectar as a function of past successful behavior. If "fly-to-the-right" is reinforced by nectar, the bee cannot decide one day to see if there might be some nectar on the left. Because the bee does not represent the nectar independently as the reason for flying right, it cannot consider other options for reaching this goal.

A practical animal such as a bear can represent its goal separately from a specific path. So the bear is able to decide among several paths or even to construct a *new* path toward its goal.[23] The practical animal can assess how things are now in relation to how it would like things to be. This moment of possibility is the moment when consciousness appears. Consciousness is a representation of the present moment that serves the function of facilitating flexible action.

An animal that no longer simply acts on available cues is an animal that needs to determine how past learning episodes apply to the current situation. Conscious states are a selection of sensations and thoughts[24] that together form a representation of what is happening now. Unlike unconscious states that *use* timing relations to track change, conscious states *represent* time.

Pause a moment again to observe your conscious experience. Notice that your conscious experience is *always* current. Anything you are conscious of at all, is a thing you are conscious of now. Chapter 5 will discuss conscious experiences that include past and future times, but already it should be obvious that even memory and imagination are experienced as occurring in the present. I am *now* remembering my conversation with Monique in Berlin and imagining how I would like to go back to that great city again. Both my memory of the past and wish for the future are represented as part of my conscious experience *now*.

On the Temporal Representation Theory, a conscious state is a complex representation of colors, shapes, sounds, and textures that represent what is happening now. In addition to the physical environment, consciousness represents bodily states like pains and emotions, as well as thoughts, beliefs, and desires. Something is experienced consciously when it is part of my experience of the present. A continually updated, complex representation allows for the ongoing evaluation of opportunities and dangers as well as feedback on the effects of actions in the environment. This ongoing evaluation is necessary for flexible action.

The practical animal keeps track of the present moment in order to ensure its behavior is successful in moving toward its goals. If not, or if a new goal arises, a change in behavior may be required. While the pushmi-pullyu animal can also respond to opportunities and dangers, its response is based entirely on associations formed in the past. It cannot consider actions and goals in light of the current situation.

Keep in mind that the capacity to represent the present moment as distinct from past and future does not mean that the practical animal conceives of time abstracted from its lived experience. A bear does not think of the present moment as a point along a single timeline from the remote past to the remote future. An ability to collect information about places and times completely separately from practical use requires an additional developmental step that may well depend on the conceptual resources of a language.[25] We *theoretical animals* can conceive of time in a way that goes beyond both tracking change and representing the present moment. We can theorize about the origin of the universe, as I did earlier in the chapter, and hypothesize about the climate crises in the rapidly approaching future.

Even though bears cannot represent time in this abstract way, there is good reason to think they can represent future goals as distinct from the present moment. Chapter 4 will look at the reasons to believe animals like bears are capable of flexible behavior and how this capacity can be used to investigate animal consciousness. If an animal can assess alternatives in relation to a goal, that goal must be represented separately from the way things are now. If consciousness is a representation of the present moment—the central claim to be argued in the next chapter—an animal capable of flexible behavior demonstrates consciousness. A practical animal like the bear needs to compare its alternative actions in relation to its goals in order to respond in a variety of ways to a given situation. For example, the bear needs to represent the location of the honey separately from its representation of its own current location in order to determine the best path.

Before we get to animals, though, more argument is needed for the third card in the house of explanation: consciousness is a representation of the present moment. This chapter has argued for a distinction between unconscious and conscious representations based on phenomenology, psychological research, and cognitive evolution. The capacity to represent features in the environment and respond rapidly by means of fixed perception-action sequences is the grounding layer of the mind. These pushmi-pullyu representations operate unconsciously because they do not require temporal representation; action is temporally fixed to follow perception. In the next chapter we return to phenomenology to connect the experience of consciousness as a representation of the present moment with the function of consciousness in facilitating flexible action. Consciousness allows the practical animal to assess alternatives in relation to how things are *now*.

# The Power of Now

*What then is time? If no one asks me, I know;*
*if I want to explain it to a questioner, I do not know.*

Augustine *Confessions* XIV

Enough foundational cards are in place that it is time to take on the puzzle of time. At the end of Chapter 2 I proposed an explanation of consciousness in terms of the representation of the present moment. But what *is* the present moment? The quote above from Augustine invariably accompanies any treatise on time, because the phenomenon of time continues to mystify anyone who theorizes about it. One reason that time is particularly puzzling is the question of whether time depends on the mind or the mind depends on time. According to Augustine, all of reality is limited to the present. Events that occurred in the past are gone, and events in the future have not yet occurred. Time is created by the mind through its capacity for memory and imagination. Alternatively, Newton claimed that relations between events are eternal, and so time is absolute. In his view, our experience of time unfolds as we move through the pre-existing structure of time and space.[1]

Happily, we don't need to answer the metaphysical question about the nature of time.[2] On a representational theory, mental time is the representation of change, such as before and after, past/present/future, next week. Either the mind *creates* time by means of this representation (as Augustine thought), or the representation of time *depends on* positions in absolute time (as Newton argued). In either case, the mind represents the relations between events in order to exploit consistent causal connections, regardless of whether these causal relations are fleeting or eternal.

Putting aside the fundamental metaphysical question about time, there remains the question of *how* the mind represents change. Chapter 2 argued that animals can track change by forming *pushmi-pullyu* representations that both describe the world and direct appropriate action. This sort of representation needs to be coordinated with time so that action is effective, but it need not include time as part of its content. What, then, is the difference when an animal comes to represent events *as present*?

The answer is the single most important card in the house of explanation, the Definition Card: an animal that represents events as present is conscious. What it is to be conscious is to represent the present moment.[3] According to the Temporal Representation Theory, consciousness evolved when an animal developed the capacity to respond to the current situation in multiple ways. Recall that pushmi-pullyu representations connect the description of the situation directly with the appropriate response in a 1–1 relation. While these representations can be tuned by past experience, there is no possibility for planning or decision-making. The environment specifies action. When an animal is able to represent goals independently of situational features that cue them, a representation of the present moment is needed to keep track of whether action is progressing toward the goal or whether a shift of goals might be worthwhile. This description of the function of consciousness is the fourth Function Card in the house of explanation: a representation of the present moment serves the function of facilitating flexible response. These two cards that form the theory can be stated succinctly:

> *Temporal Representation Theory (TRT):* Consciousness is a representation of the present moment, which evolved to facilitate flexible response.

This chapter defends TRT in three ways. First is phenomenological description: conscious experience appears as present. Second is neurophysiological explanation: the brain coordinates the contents of consciousness to represent the present. Third is functional analysis: temporal integration is important for flexible response.

## Phenomenological Description: Experiencing Now

After such a long examination of representation and the ways a mind can function perfectly well *without* consciousness, it is worthwhile returning to our experience of consciousness to remember why we thought consciousness was so interesting after all. Theorists who forget this critical step are often inclined to argue that consciousness is somehow extra, an evolutionary accident that just happened to accompany some other useful ability (Carruthers 2000; Rosenthal 2008). Or they argue that there really is no phenomenon of consciousness at all, that an explanation of attention, memory, perception and other representational capacities of the mind is sufficient to account for all the phenomena that exist (Dennett 1991, 2006; Frankish 2017). On one version of this view, "consciousness" doesn't pick out any particular target for explanation. It functions as a hodge-podge word to refer to such a diverse array of phenomena that we would be better off just getting rid of it in favor of more specific terms (Wilkes 1988).

Certainly there are a number of ways that people use the word "consciousness," and a number of quite distinct phenomena that the word picks out. The Introduction was designed to isolate the sort of consciousness this book claims to explain. So let's return to consciousness description with our new resources for thinking of the mind in terms of its ability to represent. Here is another description of my phenomenology, this time from a hike in the Rothrock State Forest on a warm, spring day.

> Cool wisps of breeze waft down from the slope. Rocks and roots draw my attention as I look for stable footing. When I notice my phenomenology, I realize my breathing has become labored and my body is warm. The path becomes smooth and even on the ridge, and my mind is released from the trail. Robin-egg sky contrasts with new-leaf green. My dog Goldie leaps like a deer through the underbrush. I think that I should buy new sandals and then reflect on the privilege of my life that this phenomenological exercise reveals.

The first feature of consciousness this description suggests is its flow. One experience follows another that follows another. Even during the apparent break as I negotiated the stream, there is no reason to think that I lost consciousness. The experience is entirely unlike what happens when I fall asleep or go under anesthesia. In fact, it is very much like my everyday experience when I am not self-consciously observing my phenomenology. Consciousness flows continuously from the time I wake until I go to sleep, even as the contents of consciousness shift from world to body to thought.[4]

A second feature of consciousness is not captured by my description, however. Even as the focus of consciousness tends to shift from one object to another, many of the contents remain in experience from one shift to the next. While I am thinking about new sandals, for example, I continue to consciously see the trees and path and hear Goldie rustling leaves in the distance. Consciousness is characterized by its unity at a time as well as its flow over time.

Some argue that the apparent unity of consciousness is a Grand Illusion (Noë 2002). Daniel Dennett has provided the most sustained and developed argument for this view (Dennett 1991, 2006; Dennett and Kinsbourne 1992).

Because the sensory and cognitive processes of the brain are ongoing and run in parallel, Dennett maintains, there is no place or time where all the contents of consciousness "come together." So while it may seem that the world is presented to you in a continuous and unified display, that experience is illusory, the last vestige of Dualism.[5] If we reject the Cartesian theater, as Dennett calls this tempting illusion, we will realize that consciousness is nothing more than what we report it to be. Brain processes continually produce several simultaneous representations of how the world is, and these representations are combined and revised as they are fed into decisions and actions. On his Multiple Drafts Theory, consciousness is whatever draft is produced when we ask ourselves about our experience. Consequently, consciousness is not unified except with respect to self-report, and anything that is not included in this narrative does not count as conscious.

In addition to parallel and distributed brain processes, worries about the Picture Theory of representation motivate Dennett's rejection of conscious unity. If we think of consciousness as producing a show to be displayed inside a Cartesian theater, we are immediately faced with problems of *who* is watching the show and *where* in the brain it might be displayed. As argued in Chapter 1, these are insurmountable problems.

Yet we needn't think of consciousness as a show inside a Cartesian theater to preserve its phenomenological unity. On the Temporal Representation Theory of consciousness, these features describe the way consciousness represents the world as *now*. The world is represented as unified in the present moment, and the transitions from one moment to the next are connected by the things in the world that I represent.[6] The show is just the world as represented by neural patterns.

To appreciate the difficulty of convincing the skeptic to accept conscious unity, consider your own phenomenology. You may agree with me that the world is represented as present to you, or you might agree with Dennett that your conscious experience is limited to what you can report about it. Note that anything you could say is a report and so is consistent with Dennett's position. At this point in our understanding of consciousness, it is not clear what evidence could prove that it is not a Grand Illusion. So for now, you need to be the judge. Pay attention to your conscious experience. Think about which view seems to make the best sense of the way consciousness seems to you. Ultimately, any theory will need to satisfy both the data of experience, even if that involves an explanation about why it is illusory, and the data of science. To me, the data of experience presents consciousness as unified, and the goal of this book is to show how it is consistent with the data of science.

What appears to me *now* is what I am conscious of, and what I am conscious of, appears to me as *now*. The laptop screen reflects my words back to me as I type, the sound of the keys as I type punctuates the low hum of the fan. Periodically I stop to rehearse a phrase in inner speech before recording it on the page. In contrast, my unconscious sensations and thoughts are *not* part of the world as it appears now. My sense of body position must be constant to keep me upright, but that sense is not conscious unless I direct my attention to observe it or something goes wrong, as when I lose my balance.[7]

Moreover, the features that appear as *now* are unified with one another. Sights and sounds are experienced together with pains and thoughts. These features are not disjointed but are all included in a representation of the world at the present moment.[8] The flow of consciousness comes from the change in contents of what appears as now. How contents are integrated into a moment and how moments might be related to one another to constitute the flow of consciousness are topics to be considered later on. For now I only want to point out that the contents of consciousness at least phenomenologically *appear* to be unified into a representation of the world at the present moment, and those moments *appear* to flow from one to the next.

## Neuropsychological Explanation: Coordinating Conscious Contents

If unity and flow are two central features of conscious experience, how might they be produced by brains? This is known as the *consciousness binding problem*. Neuroscience faces a number of binding problems in dealing with the brain, because different structures are dedicated to different functions. Visual stimuli are primarily processed in the occipital lobe toward the back of the brain; auditory stimuli are processed in the temporal lobes on the side; olfactory and gustatory stimuli each have their own tiny pieces of dedicated cortex. If these brain areas are destroyed, the ability to see, hear, smell, and taste is diminished or disappears entirely.

Given this cortical division of labor, it is surprising that your experience has any unity at all (as Grand Illusion proponents argue). Massive quantities of sensory stimuli are impacting you all the time in the form of light waves, sound frequencies, nociceptive and proprioceptive input, chemical and thermal changes. Your sensory receptors respond to this onslaught immediately and efficiently through reflex and also by sending the signal forward for further processing in the cortex. Each part of the cortex is therefore continually buzzing with sensory information from its designated source. Given this cacophony of stimulation, how on earth does visual information get connected with auditory information? How does visual information about one object (red square) get distinguished from the visual information about another object (green triangle)?

Somehow it does. A book in your hand both looks and feels to be a single object. It doesn't seem to you that there is one book that you see and another book that you feel. By means of *object binding*, your brain takes both sorts of stimuli as representing a single book and easily distinguishes the book from every other book on your desk. No one disputes that object binding takes place. At issue is *consciousness binding*, where your brain represents the book as part of a unified representation of book, hands, room, chair that together compose your experience of the present moment.[9]

It is important to keep these two different binding problems separate, because the brain can accomplish object binding in the absence of consciousness binding (Lyyra, Mäkelä, Hietanen, and Astikainen 2014; Treisman 1998). Chapter 2 argued that most routine tasks can be accomplished by means of unconscious representations, and this is one reason that some theorists assume consciousness has no function at all. What could be the evolutionary value to *experiencing* things if most actions can be done without conscious direction?

According to the Temporal Representation Theory (TRT) the answer is that consciousness represents the present moment in order to keep track of progress toward goals. While binding of sensory information into objects happens unconsciously, that only tells you *what* things are in the world. Object binding does not tell you *when* things are relative to you and your goals. Are things *now* more or less satisfactory, or is a change in plan needed? Consciousness provides a continued update of the world as it is now, so the brain can assess its current situation in relation to the desired situation. On TRT, consciousness is a representation of the present moment that evolved to facilitate flexible action. What is happening *now* helps determine what to do *next*.

Take the example of my hike, described in the previous section. Unconsciously, my brain was busy processing all forms of sensory input in separate brain regions; it coordinated these widely distributed representations into distinct objects (trees, rocks, stream), and it initiated appropriate motor responses to the objects sensed (place foot here, shift weight). *In addition*, another process coordinated some of these representations into consciousness, into a representation of the present moment. During the more relaxed phase of the hike, my consciousness was occupied by the beauty of the day and reflections on justice. Meanwhile, my unconscious sensory systems continued to adjust to any obstacles on the trail and its change in incline. The consciousness binding problem is the difference between the binding that was necessary for effective integration of my motor processes in order to walk (unconscious object binding) and the binding that produces the unity and flow of my sensory and conceptual experience (consciousness binding). The TRT solution to the consciousness binding problem explains how the brain coordinates contents into a representation of the present moment.

A number of theorists agree that the consciousness binding problem is the central issue in explaining consciousness and have proposed various forms of neural integration as a solution.[10] Three theories are worth considering for their prominence, plausibility, and points of connection and contrast with TRT: Information Integration Theory (IIT), Global Workspace Theory (GWT), and the Attended, Intermediate-level Representation (AIR) theory. I will review each theory and then turn to the TRT explanation of conscious binding.

## Information Integration Theory (IIT)

Originally proposed by Guilio Tononi (2004, 2008, 2012), Information Integration Theory (IIT) claims that consciousness corresponds to the number and type of information relations among neurons. Unlike many neuroscientists, Tononi usefully begins by considering the phenomenological features of consciousness to be explained. He identifies two key features: (1) the *quantity* of consciousness, whether you are awake, asleep, or in a coma, and (2) the *quality* of consciousness, what colors, sounds, and feels you experience. IIT accounts for these features in terms of a measurement of the causal relations among neurons within and between brain regions.

*Information* is a technical term derived from Signal Detection Theory that is defined as "the reduction of uncertainty among a number of alternative outcomes" (Tononi 2004: 3). In the simplest case, a photodiode that is either light or dark generates just one bit of information, because the uncertainty between two possible states is reduced by one. The more complex a system is, the more information is generated by its state changes. Individual neurons can be viewed as similar to switches that are turned on when they reach a threshold. This state change thereby generates one bit of information. Neurons never fire singly, however; they are always connected with other neurons by synapses into patterns of activity.

Let me digress a moment with a brief description of basic neural processing to give you a sense of how the brain manages to produce such a wide range of perceptions, thoughts, and actions. When one neuron fires, it sends a pulse through its axon and on to the next neuron. If a sufficient number of other spiking neurons are connected to it, the next neuron fires, and the next and the next. Different patterns of neurons fire in response to different forms of stimulation. These patterns are the representations that form the contents of our minds: one pattern for blue, another for red, another for a house or a face. Neuroscience has not progressed far enough to determine exactly which patterns constitute which representations. The fine-grained structure would be different for each person in any case. Just as the specific pattern of genes and muscles and bones that form my body is unique due to my genetic sequence and epigenetic development, each brain has a unique structure and history. Nonetheless, there are commonalities in bodies and brains that allow for comparison. Biology and neuroscience offer theories about how these common features are formed, even though the details differ in each case.

Going back to IIT, the brain's approximately 100 billion neurons, each with multiple synaptic connections, generate a mind-boggling number of potential informational states. Current neural and computational technology cannot measure or model such an enormous amount of information. Evidence for the theory comes from generalizations about functional connectivity by means of an analysis of data from the brain's electrical activity (measured by an electroencephalograph, or EEG), and computer simulations of more simple networks (Tononi 2008). Since our interest is theoretical, we can ignore the criticism that the resulting predictions are highly abstract. Intuitively, the theory is quite compelling.

The *quantity of consciousness* refers to the level of arousal from sluggish exhaustion to energized exhilaration. IIT calculates the quantity of consciousness by measuring the amount of information generated by the whole system in relation to the information generated by each of its parts. When exhausted, the information generated by the whole system is low; when energized, the quantity of information is high. The *quality of consciousness* refers to the contents of experience and is determined by identifying what type of information is integrated into the whole. In my hiking example, visual and conceptual systems are integrated into the complex of information that constitutes my admiration of the weather and concern about inequality.[11]

One problem for the theory is accounting for the *unconscious* integration of information. IIT proposes that only those processes integrated into the *largest* complex are conscious. Smaller integrated complexes remain unconscious. For example, the cerebellum is not essential to consciousness, despite its very large number of neural connections, due to the lack of integration in its synaptic structure. The cortex, by contrast, often exhibits a high degree of integration and so is critical to consciousness (Tononi 2008: 221). However, it is unclear why highly integrated complexes, such as sensorimotor systems responsible for walking, remain unconscious. In my hiking example, most of the information necessary to my activity is unconscious while I contemplated the beauty of the day. Yet it seems that walking requires significant sensorimotor integration.[12]

This problem leads to the next problem: the theory gives no reasons *why* some signals and not others are integrated into the largest informational complex. Yet it is a manifest phenomenological fact that contents flow into and out of consciousness over the course of time. A functional story could be told about the importance of integrating information relative to current goals. (Later I will tell a version of this story in defense of TRT.) Yet Chalmers' question from the Introduction can still be asked: why should this sort of integration be *conscious*? Unless a theory can connect the *description* of consciousness with the *function* of consciousness, the best a theory offers is correlation, not explanation.

A final objection comes from the identification of information integration with consciousness. If the largest complex of information integration in a system is the consciousness of the system, then a very simple system would nonetheless have a small degree of consciousness. Remember that photodiode? It's a teeny tiny bit conscious, according to IIT. The only thing preventing you from possessing 100 billion-plus consciousnesses (one for each neural state change) is that some of your neurons are integrated into larger systems and only the largest complex is conscious. Why, then, don't my subsystems become conscious when the larger complex goes to sleep? Maybe they do, and I am not aware of them. But then, what happens to *them* when I wake up? The intuitive plausibility of IIT derives from its description of the phenomenological quantity and quality of consciousness in terms of information. But the inability of the theory to offer a principled distinction between conscious and unconscious information integration undermines this plausibility.

## Global Workspace Theory (GWT)

The Global Workspace Theory (GWT) does not suffer from this problem, because it arose out of a comprehensive list of contrasts between unconscious

**Table 3.1  Capabilities of Conscious and Unconscious Processes**

| Conscious Processes | Unconscious Processes |
|---|---|
| 1. computationally inefficient: e.g. mental arithmetic<br>- many errors, relatively low speed, and mutual interference between conscious processes | 1. very efficient in routine tasks: e.g. syntax<br>- few errors, high speed, and little mutual interference |
| 2. great range of contents<br>- great ability to relate different contents<br>- great ability to relate conscious events to their unconscious contexts | 2. each routine process:<br>- a limited range of contents<br>- relatively isolated and autonomous<br>- relatively context-free |
| 3. high internal consistency at any single moment, seriality over time, and limited processing capacity | 3. diverse processes, can sometimes operate in parallel, and together have great processing capacities |
| 4. The clearest conscious contents are perceptual or quasi-perceptual, e.g. imagery, skill learning, problem-solving, action control, etc. | 4. Unconscious processes are involved in *all* mental tasks, from perception and imagery, inner speech, and internally into memory, knowledge representation and access, generated bodily feelings, etc. |

*Source: Adapted from Baars 1997, 182.*

and conscious processes (see Table 3.1). Bernard Baars (1988, 1997, 2003), who originated the theory, took the contrastive method to be an essential starting point in isolating the phenomena of consciousness. Based on the operational difference that consciousness makes to mental functioning, Baars suggests that consciousness serves as a broadcast mechanism to inform the system about decisions and goals. *Global workspace* is an information technology term referring to the computational structure that integrates information from several processing modules.

Notice in Table 3.1 that conscious processes are relatively slow, serial processes. They are highly internally consistent and can relate multiple forms of information to a context. Baars compares this serial, interconnected process to a theater where sights, sounds, thoughts, and feelings take the stage to present a coherent show of experience. The theater metaphor for consciousness should not be taken too literally, Baars cautions, since there is no audience (1997). The Global Workspace is simply the architecture that integrates the output from several sources (sensory systems, attentional modulation, memory, etc.) and broadcasts the result to motor systems as well as back to the input systems for continued coordinated action.

According to GWT, the need to make a single decision for action is the reason parallel processes are integrated into consciousness. So long as action is habitual and consistent, there is no reason to slow down processing to integrate information into consciousness. Think again about the unconscious integration of sensory and motor processes during the hike while my consciousness was occupied with aesthetic and moral contemplation. As long as those unconscious processes function effectively on the basis of routine training, they can bypass the Global Workspace entirely.

Recent work by Stanislas Dehaene has added empirical support to the GWT by using a computational workspace to model conscious processes. Dehaene and his colleague, the late Jean-Pierre Changeux (2005), developed a computer simulation of neural activation processes to show how signals are propagated, amplified, and dampened across brain areas. Instead of focusing on the *amount* of information processed, Dehaene and Changeux were interested in the *distribution* of information. Their model showed that brief, weak signals failed to initiate the global activation of multiple brain areas characteristic of conscious processes. Moreover, stronger signals could be inhibited when followed by a second strong signal, as in the case of masking (see Chapter 2).

Evidence from this model fits with images taken of the brain showing high levels of activity across the brain when subjects are conscious of a stimulus, whereas only visual areas are activated when a stimulus is unconsciously processed (Dehaene and Changeux 2011). According to the Global Workspace Theory (or the Global Neuronal Workspace, as Dehaene calls it), parallel processing by sensory systems, memory systems, and executive systems needs to be integrated in order to make a single decision. These different systems compete for access to consciousness, and the result is made available globally in order to coordinate movement.

A virtue of GWT is its clear description of conscious processes. The empirical investigation begins with the subjective experience of the contrast between conscious and unconscious processes. When a subject reports a stimulus as seen, it is conscious; when a subject reports seeing nothing, the stimulus is unconscious. Dehaene defends this reliance on subjective report as "the perfect, indeed the only, platform on which to build a science of consciousness" (2014: 43).

Yet subjective report conflates at least two aspects of consciousness: the experience and the capacity to monitor the experience. These two aspects are obviously closely linked, so evidence about conscious monitoring of experience will provide evidence that the experience is occurring. Even so, conscious experience extends beyond the ability to report it. To test this claim, look up and let your eyes wander around the room a moment. Then close your eyes and describe your consciousness for that brief time. Your report will fail to capture the complete contents of your experience, partly due to the limits of language, partly from lack of time to describe all the detail, and also partly, I believe, because conscious contents appear and disappear so rapidly that the monitoring system cannot capture them.

The claim that there can be conscious experience without conscious access is a matter of considerable debate. Ned Block (1995) introduced the distinction between *phenomenal consciousness* and *access consciousness* to argue that the phenomenal aspect of conscious experience cannot be explained in terms of subjective report. According to Block (2011a), a representation is access-conscious when it is available for cognitive processing, such as to make a report or a decision. Phenomenal consciousness is "what it is like" to have an experience (567). The debate concerns whether phenomenal consciousness does indeed occur without cognitive access, or whether the sense that we experience more than we can report is a Grand Illusion.[13] Block insists that there are cases of phenomenal consciousness without access consciousness.

Theorists like Dehaene would say that the gap between phenomenal and access consciousness is more apparent than real. Counterintuitively, Dehaene claims that conscious access is limited to as little as one item at a time, and any sense that there is more content to conscious experience is due to the fact that attention can shift to bring different items serially into consciousness (2014: Ch 1). Just as it seems that the refrigerator light is always on, because it is on every time you open the door, you seem to be conscious of everything around you at the present moment, because anything can be brought to consciousness by attending to it.

To see which side of this debate you favor, consider results from a set of experimental procedures called the *partial report paradigm*. Originally developed by Gene Sperling (1960), the idea is to gain information about the critical period *after* the early stages of sensory processing and *before* the full-fledged cognitive processing needed for subjective report. Subjects are shown a visual stimulus, typically an array of letters or shapes. After the stimulus disappears, subjects are cued to report on just one part of the array, either by naming the letters or by saying whether a shape changed position. Sperling found that subjects could name three to four items in whatever row was cued, whereas they could only name three to four items from the whole matrix when asked for a full report. The critical question is how to interpret this remarkable difference in reportability.

On one side of the debate, the Rich View (Block 2011a), these results indicate that subjects possess a detailed, conscious visual image of the whole array prior to forming their report. Known as "iconic memory," it is characterized as high-capacity, short-term, and pre-categorical. These attributes are in direct contrast to "working memory," which is characterized as limited-capacity, capable of being maintained through attention, and categorical. Due to the limited amount of information that can be processed into working memory, reports about the whole array identify a smaller percentage of items than reports about part of the array. Because the visual information is available to any part of the array that is cued, adherents to the Rich View assume that information about the whole array is available. A further assumption is that any visual information available for report is conscious.

Advocates of the Spare View (Irvine 2011) object to the assumption that the availability of visual information about any part of the array indicates consciousness of the whole array. Because visual processing occurs in disjointed stages (for example, color is processed in a different brain area than location, and at a slightly different rate), there can be no detailed, conscious visual image that subjects use to form their report. The conclusion is that our impression of a rich, detailed conscious experience is an illusion. Our conscious experience is limited to the reportable contents of working memory.[14]

I see two serious problems with the Spare View. First, illusion arguments are unsatisfying. Ever since Plato's cave[15] philosophers have proposed one form of massive perceptual/cognitive error after another. Our concepts are mere images of the Truth, our perceptions are radically disconnected from the Real. These epistemological challenges are worthy puzzles to sharpen logical incision and cut down triumphal claims of certainty. In the actual world, however, it is a safe bet that our brains are not in vats, and our thoughts about things track stable and useful structures in the world. While conscious experience does present illusions of all kinds, these are mistakes about how the world is, not errors about the nature of consciousness itself. It is telling that advocates of the Spare View trust subjective report completely—Dehaene takes it to be the definitive data—yet distrust the subjective report that we seem to be conscious of more information than we can report. Why would the subject be trustworthy about one aspect of her experience and entirely mistaken about another?

The second problem with the Spare View is more serious. On GWT, the function of consciousness is to construct a single item from the vast quantity of unconscious information and broadcast it to the rest of the brain. Dehaene claims that conscious access allows a person to hold an idea in thought and manipulate it, and this provides the ability to name, rate, judge, and memorize a stimulus (2014: 14, 42). But this proposed function is implausible. Consciousness is neither necessary nor sufficient for the performance of these cognitive tasks. Simple computer programs can name, rate, and memorize information *without* needing consciousness,[16] and animals that lack these abilities *do* need consciousness, or so I will argue in the next chapter.

GWT architecture was originally introduced to explain global integration of information from multiple parallel systems. If consciousness is limited to reportable contents, however, the value of global integration is correspondingly limited. If, on the other hand, the contents of the workspace integrate information so as to represent the world at the present moment as proposed by TRT, its value is clear. In this combined Global Workspace/Temporal Representation Theory, the workspace is a relatively high-capacity yet selective processing space that tracks time in order to assess progress toward goals. In other words, much of the Global Workspace Theory is consistent with the Temporal Representation Theory. The key difference is that for TRT the workspace functions as a *source for* rather than the *result of* working memory.

## Attended, Intermediate-level Representation (AIR) Theory

A theory developed by Jesse Prinz (2012b) offers a similar description of the function of consciousness as a source for working memory. According to the Attended, Intermediate-level Representation theory (AIR), attention selects from the vast quantity of unconscious information to provide a representation of the world from a particular point of view. Low-level information about edges or a high-frequency tone is insufficient to identify an object or sound, and high-level information is too abstract to capture the perspectival quality of a conscious representation (201). Intermediate-level representations hit the sweet spot of familiar medium-sized objects, so they are selected by attention for consciousness. This conscious representation is then fed into working memory where it can be used for flexible decision-making. In contrast to the GWT, the AIR Theory maintains that working memory operates unconsciously. All of the advantages of deliberation and control accrue as a *consequence* of consciousness rather than prior to consciousness. Working memory utilizes the range of objects in consciousness that attention processes select, based on current goals and actions (202).

The prospect that a mysterious phenomenon such as consciousness could be given an account in terms of the empirically tractable phenomena of attention and intermediate-level representations is compelling. In standard cases, we become conscious of whatever is the focus of attention. If you shift your attention from this text to your body position or to the room you are sitting in, the contents of your consciousness will shift as well. Attention selects, and consciousness is selective. There is a natural match.[17]

The problem with this nice match is that it does not solve the Hard Problem: why are Attended, Intermediate-level Representations *conscious*? Why not just select the appropriate inputs to feed directly into working memory? Many theories of consciousness, such as GWT, propose just this short-circuited move; unconscious sensation becomes conscious, reportable content with no intermediary stage. Prinz's AIR Theory admirably resists this move by recognizing the phenomenological sense that we consciously experience more than we can report.

Prinz also recognizes the importance of time as the element that unifies conscious content. The objects selected for consciousness are unified at three time scales, according to AIR Theory: the instant, the now, and the present. An *instant* is formed at 25–30 ms, which is the minimum threshold of visibility. When two lights flash faster than a 30-ms interval, it may be possible to tell that they are not simultaneous, but not possible to say which light flashed first. The *now* (60–100 ms) is the unit of duration; events occurring over this span seem to extend in time and are ordered one after the other. Direction and speed of a moving object can also be identified at this time scale (257–9). As Prinz defines the *present* (2–3 sec), events are taken together as a unit or episode but they are not perceived to be simultaneous. A sentence or line of music tends to fall within this span, and repetitive motion activities like rowing and hammering divide naturally into three-second units. Perception of a bistable figure, such as the Neckar cube in Figure 3.1, also tends to flip in three-second intervals (259–260). This three-level approach to temporal binding usefully clarifies differences among perceived simultaneity (instant), conscious unity (now), and the specious present (present). When I elaborate on how long "now" is, according to TRT, more will be said on the distinction between "now" and "present."

The critical advantage of TRT over AIR Theory is an explanation of *why* attention selects representations for consciousness prior to working memory operations: representations are unified into a representation of "now" in order to facilitate flexible action. Conscious contents are made available to working memory, because without them the system could not compare how things are now against how they were (memory) and should be (goal). As will be developed further in the next section, this evaluative moment is necessary to the capacity for flexible response. Without a representational divide between what is and what follows, a stimulus would lead automatically to action. Consciousness provides a separation between representations of how things are (pushmi, descriptive representations) and representations of how things should be (pullyu, directive representations).[18] Working memory utilizes the representation of what is happening now (consciousness), together with unconscious representations, to determine the best action.

Often Prinz's Attended Intermediate-level Representations will likely serve the function of representing the present moment. But unlike AIR Theory, TRT is open to the possibility that bottom-up, non-attentional processes might generate consciousness. By focusing on attention rather than temporal representation, Prinz is forced to deny research that shows attention occurs in the absence of consciousness, and consciousness appears in the absence of attention (Jennings 2015; Montemayor and Haladjian 2015; van Boxtel, Tsuchiya, and Koch 2010).

A second problem with the AIR Theory is its restriction to intermediate-level representations. Recognizing temporal representation as the function of consciousness allows more specific (shape, color) and more general (object type) forms of representation. In ambiguous figures such as the Necker cube (see Figure 3.1), you can focus on just the lines and avoid seeing any object at all.

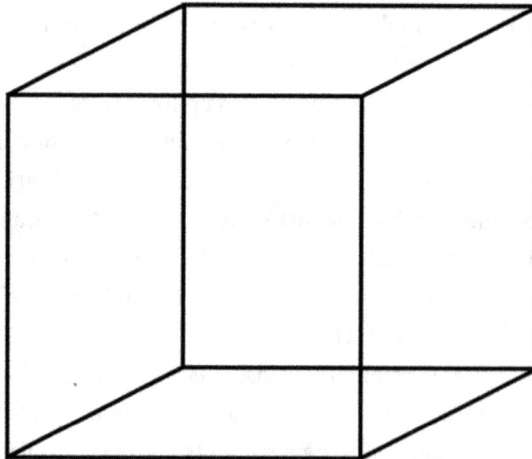

**Figure 3.1** Necker Cube (Wikimedia Commons: https://en.wikipedia.org/wiki/Necker_cube)

That process requires a significant degree of effort, however, as your perceptual system immediately attempts to interpret these elements as a familiar object. Still, it is possible to direct attention to low-level features of an image and be conscious of them, contrary to the intermediate-level hypothesis. More problematic is Prinz's claim that conscious perception just delivers the object (the intermediate level) without also classifying the object *as* a cube or a face or a vase. According to AIR Theory, *only* intermediate level representations are conscious; concepts are *never* conscious. (Prinz 2012b: Ch 5).

Play a moment with the cube, flipping it back and forth in your mind between leftward-facing cube and rightward facing cube. Are concepts involved, such as the concepts of cube, left, right, forward, backward? Prinz's claim is that there are no conceptual differences between these experiences that are not fully realized by sensory differences. While concepts can influence your visual processing, according to AIR Theory, the contents of consciousness are entirely visual (73). Similarly, your cognitive experience of reading this sentence or hearing someone speak is exhausted by the auditory qualities of inner speech together with visual imagery accompanying word meaning. To illustrate the power of imagery over conception, Prinz challenges you to interpret the word "bat" to mean a flying animal while you mentally picture a baseball bat (162). He's right—you can't do it. But failure to produce contradictory conscious concepts does not mean that no concepts are represented consciously.

One of the factors that drives Prinz to reject conscious concepts stems from his view of concepts as stored perceptions (153). For Prinz, the concept of "bat" is unconscious except to the extent that associated perceptions are activated. Consequently, any conscious bat concept is reducible to the visual or auditory phenomenology of the reanimated perception. A different way to think of concepts takes them to be abilities to track and reidentify individuals, kinds, and quantities (Millikan 2000). On this Consumer Theory (see Chapter 2), my bat concept is not reducible to my visual and auditory phenomenology nor is it an extra sort of experience that concepts add to consciousness. My concept is simply the way experience is organized. When I pick up a stick and use it as a bat, I am representing the stick *as a bat*; the *batness* of the stick accounts for the way I throw acorns in the air and swing at them.

For biological reasons, we usually interpret the world as composed of middle-sided objects by means of intermediate level representations. There is no reason to think our conscious representations are restricted to this level, however. The same sensory stimulation can generate a representation at any level of abstraction, depending on how the sensations are interpreted. A stick can be seen as a set of lines and edges, as a stick or bat, or as representing the natural kind *stick* or (occasionally) the conventional kind *bat*.[19] I agree with Prinz that the phenomenological aspects of these representations are sensory. There is no special cognitive phenomenology in addition to visual and kinesthetic sensation, imagery, and any bodily feelings associated with the sense of understanding.[20] Nonetheless, the interpretation of sensory phenomenology is part of the content of consciousness. If sensory experience is used to reidentify an object— and most experiences are used this way—concepts are included in conscious representations.

## Temporal Representation Theory (TRT)

One reason to include concepts as part of conscious representations is the role concepts play in maintaining a sense of continuity in consciousness over time. The next section discusses how the brain coordinates the contents of consciousness to represent the present, and how a representation of one moment relates to a representation of the next moment. Chapter 5 will consider how representations of the past and future come to be included in a representation of the present moment, that is, how conscious memory and future imagination develop. Before we tackle these issues, it would be useful to briefly compare the role of integration in TRT with the three other theories discussed in this section.

According to TRT, consciousness represents the present moment in order to facilitate flexible action. The temporal content is the distinguishing feature of theory. Representations are integrated in order to represent what is happening now. Integrated information that is not included in a representation of the present moment is not conscious, contrary to Information Integration Theory (IIT). Even so, it seems likely that a representation of the present moment will integrate a wide array of available contents, so IIT calculations for quality and quantity may usefully gauge levels of consciousness. What TRT contributes to IIT is an explanation of what the measurement indicates and why some integrated informational structures are not conscious.

The definition of consciousness as a representation of the present moment also distinguishes the TRT from the Global Workspace Theory (GWT). GWT takes subjective report to define conscious content, identifying consciousness with the output of working memory. Yet this view violates the phenomenological sense that our experience of the world at a moment is more rich than the few elements we can report about it. Along with the Attended, Intermediate-level Representation (AIR) theory, TRT proposes that conscious representations are a resource for rather than the output of the more restricted processes of working memory.

In contrast to AIR Theory, TRT holds that attentional processes and intermediate-level representations are not sufficient and may not be necessary for consciousness. The representation of *now* determines what representations are integrated into a conscious state. Intermediate-level representations may be the most common format, but as argued above, lower- and higher-level representations may also be included among the contents of consciousness.

According to TRT, consciousness represents the present moment in order to facilitate flexible action. I need to know what is happening now to monitor progress toward my goals. *Right now* I am thinking about the integration of conscious contents. My back pain has subsided, and I am beginning to get hungry for a snack. These contents are both fleeting and enduring. Each moment differs somewhat from the previous moment as feelings and thoughts shift, subside, resurface. Yet each moment also flows seamlessly into the next, especially when my task is clearly defined and intellectually engaging. How does this work? How are representations selected to be coordinated into a representation of the present moment? How long is a representation of the present moment? These are questions to be answered in the next two sections.

## Functional Analysis: Representing *Now*

Recall the important distinction from Chapter 2 between a representation *occurring now* and *representing "now."*[21] All representations that are part of some active mental process (sensation, thought, emotion, action) are *occurring now*. When walking down the street, several representations are occurrent, even if unconscious: kinesthetic representations of posture and leg position, visual representations of the sidewalk, curb, road and other obstacles, auditory representations of my shoes sounding on the pavement, cars passing, squirrels scrambling in the leaves, and a goal representation to guide my direction. These representations must be occurring now in order for me to be successfully walking now.

Only some of these representations are included in what I *represent as* "*now*." Perhaps I am deep in philosophical thought and consciously represent little bodily or sensory content, enough to keep me updated on my progress along the sidewalk so that I avoid cars and stop at crosswalks, but my *sotto voce* ruminations consume the bulk of my conscious content. Then suddenly I hear my name. The contents of my consciousness shift weight my visual and auditory representational system. The people and sounds around me centrally figure in what I represent as "now" so that I can find the face of my friend.

According to TRT, *representing "now"* serves the function of facilitating flexible action. An animal (like me) needs a representation of the present moment when it is capable of representing its goals independently of its representation of the current environment. Ongoing updates inform me if things are going well or if there should be a change in plan. As I walk, my conscious thoughts feed back into my thinking processes, allowing scattered ideas to be collected, reshaped, reinforced, or rejected.[22] When someone calls my name, bottom-up sensory processes cue attention to shift toward the source of the sound. The salience of my name presents a new goal, and with it a new set of conscious contents.

The distinction between representations that occur now and those that have the content "now" can be difficult to grasp, because it seems as though what we represent as "now" must be what occurs now, as a matter of logic. The function of "now" in language is to refer to the time at which a token of the sign appears. So "now" must mean now, right?

Not necessarily; the referential function of "now" is less rigid. Here are three examples that demonstrate the malleability of "now":

- On my voice message, when I say "I'm not available to take your call right now," "now" means the time of the call, not the time I recorded the message.
- When the narrator of a documentary says: "Now is the moment when the treaty is signed," she is talking about a historical event, not the time she is speaking or the time the documentary is viewed.
- "We need to go now," said by a parent, may mean some vaguely near future time, in a few minutes, or THIS VERY SECOND OR YOU'RE IN BIG TROUBLE. (from Droege 2009)

Biology seems to have provided a similar variety of ways to track events occurring now. Recall the description of the now (60–100 ms) time scale by Prinz. Within this span you get a sense of sequence even though you take events to be occurring at the same time. This apparent contradiction—how can events be sequential *and* simultaneous?—is one of the most puzzling and illuminating features of consciousness.[23]

Move your foot back and forth while you watch it. Your conscious experience represents the foot *as moving now*. That means you are representing the foot at one place *and then* at another as part of "now." To make things even more complicated, keep in mind that your experience of the moving foot occurs *after* the foot moves. It takes time for light to bounce off the foot, travel through the air, hit your eyes, and get processed (somehow) into consciousness.

The time course is very quick, less than one second, but the temporal accounting is important to understand what consciousness can and cannot do. Chapter 6 reviews neuroscientific evidence that motor areas in the brain can initiate action prior to the conscious decision to act. Whether that evidence means we have no free will depends in part on whether consciousness occurs too late in the decision-making process to have an effect. So timing is crucial.

According to TRT, consciousness represents the present moment in order to assess progress toward goals. This means that conscious contents will be shaped by the goal (or lack of goal) at hand. As we saw in the discussion of AIR Theory, attention plays a key role here. Recall my walk down the street, described at the beginning of this section. My primary task on the walk was to think about a philosophical problem, so the contents of consciousness foregrounded thoughts relevant to that problem. Nonetheless, sights and sounds do not entirely disappear from conscious experience even in the most absorbed state of concentration. As long as my eyes and ears are open, visual and auditory representations are incorporated into my conscious experience. The world does not appear to be dark or silent, although I may not remember or respond to what I see or hear when I am deep in thought.[24]

There is good reason the world is not dark or silent: I need to continue to monitor the sidewalk, the road, and passing cars while I walk. By and large, the walking process is routine and can be managed by a pushmi-pullyu system of representations to direct gait, navigate terrain, and even follow a familiar route. Think about driving a car home from work. The contents of your consciousness are happily occupied listening to the radio or having a conversation. Consequently most of what goes on regarding the manipulation of the wheel, stopping for traffic lights, and so forth escapes your attention. If something unexpected happens—a crash or an emergency vehicle—your conscious representation immediately incorporates that information which is fed into the decision-making system to facilitate response. The most important responses are likely the unconscious ones—foot on the brake, grip the wheel. But the ongoing response system needs conscious attention to assess what is happening and to determine whether your actions are moving you toward safety or danger.

Autopilot mode also explains why it is so difficult to deviate from a familiar path. Routine systems take over and before you know it, you are home and only then remember that you wanted to stop for milk. Consciousness functions to keep you updated on what is happening now, it is not responsible for planning and decision-making. Recall from Chapter 2 how a decision like what movie to see involves conscious imagery and possibly some conscious thought, while the process of weighting options toward action goes on unconsciously. Chapter 6 will say more about the role of consciousness in decision-making, given that the time required to form a conscious representation precludes the possibility of real-time control of action. Consciousness represents the present moment to provide input to decision-making systems; the final decision is determined by unconscious processes.[25]

## The Span of "Now"

To review, TRT proposes that consciousness is a representation of the present moment, which evolved to facilitate flexible action. An animal capable of pursuing different possible goals in response to the current situation needs to keep track of what is happening now. A representation *occurring now* differs from a representation *of now* in that a representation *of now* selects and coordinates the representations that best represent the world at a moment. "Best" is determined by the type of animal, the current and possible goals of the animal, and its sensory and cognitive equipment.[26] Because I am an animal that can have abstract problem-solving as a goal, thoughts relevant to that goal sometimes occupy the bulk of my consciousness. I am also a social animal who responds to the sound of my name, and a physical animal whose actions are embedded in a physical world full of obstacles and opportunities. The constant shifting of conscious contents in relation to these internal and external conditions accounts for the way consciousness *flows* from moment to moment.

How might this work? How could a brain determine which representations to select? How could representations be coordinated into a "now" moment? A good place to start is with the dynamics of action. In order to assess how well I am walking, visual information about the sidewalk and street must be combined with bodily information about movement. Rick Grush (2005) has proposed ±100 ms[27] as the appropriate range for collecting different types of sensory information into an estimate of the trajectory of your body in action.

An important aspect of Grush's model is that the trajectory estimate incorporates stimulus input from the previous 100 ms (−100 ms) and *anticipates* input from the next 100 ms (+100 ms). As noted earlier, the brain is always working with old sensory information. It takes time for sights and sounds to reach consciousness. Even sensory signals from inside the body, such as the pain in your foot when you stub your toe, must travel from the location of the injury up to the brain. If your motor system had to wait for that information to be consciously processed *before* moving, your actions would always lag behind the events in the world. The fact that you can catch a ball or move to avoid being hit by one shows that your representational system anticipates events as part of its representation of "now."

You also manage to synchronize events appropriately even when sensory signals travel at different rates. Light travels faster than sound, for example, but usually it seems that you see the glass smash at the same time as you hear it. You see a person's lips move in synch with the words you hear. Your conscious experience represents these events as simultaneous, because actions that depend on these events need to recognize them as the same. Only one glass broke and should be swept up; only one set of words is being spoken and needs interpretation.

Since a set of words that forms a sentence takes longer than ±100 ms to be spoken, the next problem is how consciousness represents the relation between now moments. It is not as if a sentence is segmented into discrete units; your experience represents the words as flowing smoothly from one to the next. Evidence suggests that 2–3 seconds form a temporal unit that connects "now" moments to give the impression of duration and structure (Pöppel 1988; Wittmann 2011).[28] William James called this type of temporal experience the *specious present*, because it connects a range of "now" moments (1890: 609). In the same way that the representation of now incorporates information about a very small span of time, the specious present incorporates a sequence of now-representations into an experienced unit, like a sentence or a musical phrase. Within the frame of the specious present, you connect distinct now moments as related.

Concurrently with James, Edmund Husserl (1905) developed a tripartite analysis of the experience of time in consciousness. In addition to the representation of an instant, or "now point," consciousness incorporates a representation of immediate past events, called *retention*, and a representation of immediately anticipated events, called *protention*. This extended temporal unit combines ordered now-representations into the experience of an event as enduring.

> Let us take the example of a melody or of a cohesive part of a melody. The matter seems very simple at first: we hear the melody, that is, we perceive it, for hearing is indeed perceiving. However, the first tone sounds, then comes the

second tone, then the third, and so on. Must we not say: When the second tone sounds, I hear *it*, but I no longer hear the first tone, etc.? In truth, then, I do not hear the melody but only the single present tone. That the elapsed part of the melody is something objective for me, I owe—or so one will be inclined to say— to memory; and that I do not presuppose, with the appearance of the currently intended tone, that this is *all*, I owe to anticipatory expectation. But we cannot be content with this explanation, for everything that we have said carries over to the individual tone. Each tone has a temporal extension itself. When it begins to sound, I hear it as now; but while it continues to sound it has an ever new now, and the now that immediately precedes it changes into a past. Therefore at any given time I hear only the actually present phase of the tone and the objectivity of the whole enduring tone is constituted in an act-continuum that is in part memory, in smallest punctual part perception, and in further part expectation.

(Husserl 1905: §7)

This famous description illustrates the power of careful phenomenological reflection to identify essential, unnoticed aspects of conscious experience. Take a moment to sing the word "lullaby" aloud, if you can do so without disturbing your neighbors. Notice that the "lul" continues to resonate while the "la" sounds. The fact that the "by" is already anticipated can be heard if you cut off the tune after "la." You will invariably fill in the last note in your head (one of the reasons to sing the tune aloud for full phenomenological effect). Try humming just the beginning of these other familiar tunes: "We will, we will, ...," the first three notes of Beethoven's Fifth Symphony *da, da, da* ..., "Oh, say can you ..."

Conscious representation includes representations of the just past and the anticipated future, giving our experience of the present a kind of breadth. As Husserl observed, by the second note, the first note is gone, past, memory. Yet the just past is unlike long ago memories recalled from last week or last year.[29] The first note is represented as a just past part of what is happening *now*, and the third note is represented as the anticipated next part of what is happening *now*. The representation of now nests into the specious present by means of these representational relations between now moments.

## Succession or Overlap?

The next question is how the brain accomplishes this curious representational nesting. Although the empirical details need to be worked out by neuroscientists, the philosophical question concerns the relation between representational content and its neural vehicle. If the content of a now moment represents events occurring in a span of ±100 ms, how is each representation related to the next representation so that moments flow together to form the specious present? A comparison of two philosophical models reveals unexpected benefits of the Temporal Representation Theory of consciousness.

On the *Succession Model*, each now-representation follows the previous one, so a given ±100 ms time frame is represented by a single brain state, as shown in Figure 3.2.

Each now-representation is depicted as the tip of a triangle in order to demonstrate that a single vehicle represents a range of temporal contents (the base of the triangle). This single point may be misleading. Given the ongoing, dynamic activity of the brain, each neural vehicle is really a brain process, with its own temporal extent. The line above the tips suggests this extent but is not intended as a definitive proposal. Exactly how representational vehicles (brain processes) do the work of selecting the appropriate content is for neuroscience to discover; however, some initial clues are already available in the distinctive firing patterns of neural processes. As Prinz points out in his discussion of the three time scales (instant, now, present), the 25 ms of an instant is the duration of one cycle of a gamma band oscillation, a frequency associated with cognitive processing; the alpha band is 100 ms long and coincides with the window of attention necessary for conscious unity (Prinz 2012b: 266–7).

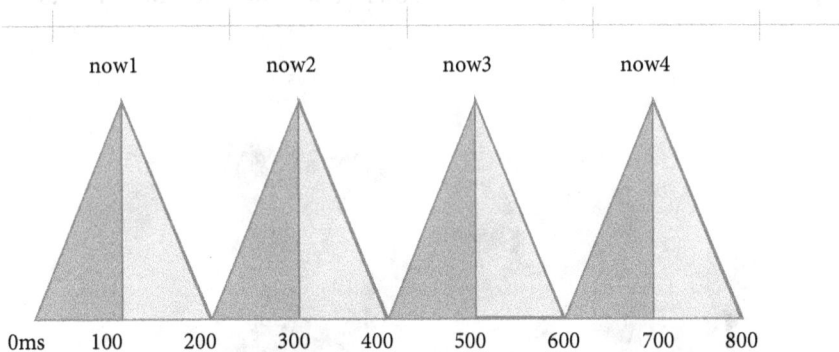

**Figure 3.2** The Succession Model. "now1," "now2," etc. indicate the vehicles representing successive ±100 ms timeframes; the line at the top indicates the potential span of the neural vehicle. The dark gray indicates the sensory input represented; the light gray represents predicted input. The timeline at the bottom is the represented time of events. (Note that the represented time of events lags behind their actual objective time of occurrence except in cases like motion where events are anticipated.)

One problem with the Succession Model is that events in between now moments might get lost. In the diagram, the light gray half of the triangle represents the estimate of future events over the next 100 ms based on the information about events from the previous 100 ms. Estimates at this time scale are fairly reliable due to the general consistency of causal relations, but the world is full of surprises. If an unexpected event happens at 110 ms, it wouldn't be consciously represented until now2. This delay would not affect unconscious pushmi-pullyu response, but events between the stimulus input phases of now moments could fail to be consciously represented.

Alternatively, the *Overlap Model* (shown in Figure 3.3) proposes that each representational vehicle only lasts for 100 ms, even though its content ranges over the same ±100 ms span as in the Succession Model. Consequently, both now1 and now2 represent events in the 100–200 ms range. On this model, the unexpected event at 110 ms is immediately incorporated into consciousness by means of sensory input into now2.

This solution potentially creates a new problem, however. If events are represented twice, why isn't experience doubled? For example, a click that occurs at 150 ms as part of a sequential series would be anticipated by both now1 and represented by now2, but only one click would be consciously experienced. This worry seems especially pressing when representations are diagrammed as in Figure 3.4[30]:

Here is another case where TRT proves resourceful. Overlapping representations would only create duplicate experiences if a person experiences the representations themselves. But now1 and now2 are the *vehicles* of

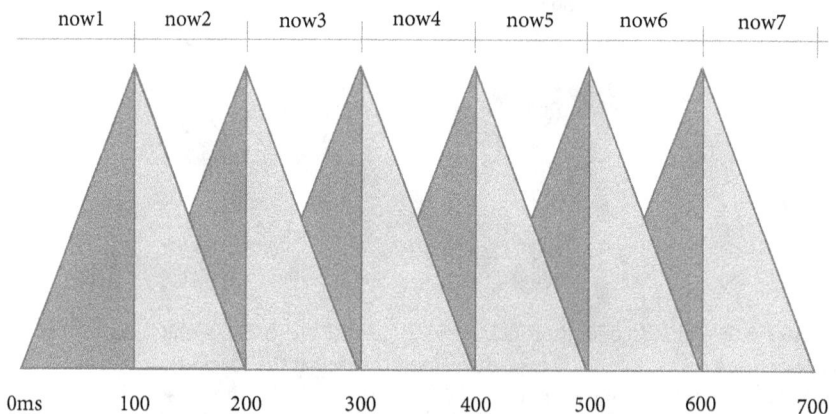

**Figure 3.3** The Overlap Model. Vehicles (now1, now2, etc.) occur every 100 ms. As in Figure 3.2, the dark gray indicates represented sensory input; the light gray represents predicted input. The timeline at the bottom is the represented time of events.

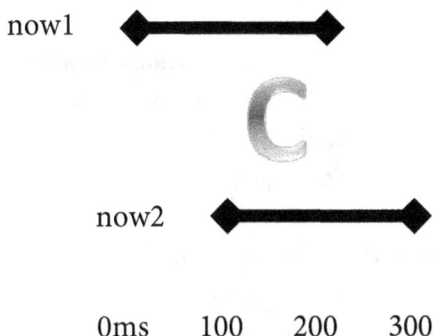

**Figure 3.4** Problem of overlapping representations. Now1 represents 0–200 ms, now2 represents 100–300 ms. Both represent event C as occurring at 150 ms, so there are two C representations.

representation, the brain processes. What you consciously experience is the *content* (the click) not the vehicle. Two vehicles representing the same click do not create two clicks any more than two newspapers reporting about the same crash create two crashes. Of course the newspapers do create two different *reports* of the crash, so the analogy is not perfect. Unlike newspapers, brain processes are designed to construct a consistent and stable representation of events. By means of dense interconnections, neural systems bind representations together to form a coherent conscious representation of the present moment. So long as the content is the same, any number of vehicles may be used to carry that content.

This means that either the Succession Model or the Overlap Model might account for the relation between now-representations. Maybe both models are used for different tasks: rapid-fire production of new representations allow adjustment to a quickly changing, high-stress environment, and relatively slow, successive representations provide a low-cost assessment of a stable, calm environment.

Another possibility is that the Overlap Model best accounts for the very short span of now-representations (±100 ms) and the Succession Model best accounts for representations of the specious present (2–3 sec). Overlapping now-representations would account for the detail in conscious experience, whereas the longer timeframe of the specious present suggests successive representations of now, just past, and anticipated future.

The distinction I have been using between a now-representation and the specious present raises the question of which type of representation is *consciousness.* Strictly speaking, now-representations constitute consciousness. What is represented as *now* is what is conscious. Nonetheless, the content of a now-representation is essentially connected to what has come before it and what is expected to happen afterward. On TRT, consciousness represents how things are going now, so that you can change your behavior if necessary. In order to fulfill this function, the content of consciousness must be responsive to a range of internal and external sources of information. This kind of responsiveness takes time, which means now-representations cannot occur without the extended representational context that shapes their content. In other words, consciousness is constituted by now-representations within the context of the specious present.

Neuroscientist Antonio Damasio underscores the importance of context in his description of the brain response to a pain signal (the names of brain regions have been omitted for simplicity):

> A wound that is mapped in the brain stem ..., and that is perceived as pain, unleashes multiple responses back to the body. ... They cause an emotional reaction and a change in the processing of subsequent pain signals, which immediately alter the body state and, in turn, alter the next map that the brain will make of the body. Moreover, the responses originating from body-sensing regions are likely to alter the operation of other perceptual systems, thus modulating not just the ongoing perception of the body but also that of the context in which body signaling is occurring. In the example of the wound, in parallel with a changed body, the ongoing cognitive processing will be altered as well. There is no way you will continue to enjoy whatever activity you were engaged in, as long as you experience the pain from the wound.
>
> (Damasio 2012: 100)

While the content of consciousness is what is represented as now, this content is shaped by its position within the sort of feedback loops Damasio describes.

## Calibrating Consciousness

Fascinating recent research dramatically demonstrates the way representations of time can be warped by context. Relative to objective time, the conscious sense of time can seem to fly or drag. Emotions such as fear have a strong effect on subjective time. David Eagleman (Stetson, Fiesta, and Eagleman 2007) famously had volunteers (graduate students) jump off a tower and free fall for thirty-one meters to test whether time really does slow down during a frightening event. Subjects wore a wrist band which displayed digits flashing at a rate too fast to be identified under normal conditions. If the rate of change in the world slowed down relative to visual perception, subjects should have been able to read the digits. They couldn't; performance was no better during free fall than on the ground. Though time doesn't *actually* slow down, it does *seem* to slow down. After watching another participant fall, subjects imagined themselves falling and timed the imagined duration. Then after falling themselves, they recalled the process of falling and timed the recollected duration. The recollected duration was 36 percent longer than the imagined duration.[31]

Even pictures that induce a slight emotional effect can influence time perception. Sylvie Droit-Volet (2014) showed pictures of angry and neutral faces to subjects and then asked them to estimate the amount of time that had passed. Participants judged the angry faces as lasting longer than the neutral faces (488). Happy faces also led to overestimation of duration, but oddly, disgusted faces did not. Droit-Volet hypothesizes that time perception is affected only when immediate action is involved. Anger and fear require immediate fight or flight response, and happiness in another person indicates social opportunities. Disgust simply warns of possible purity danger, such as contaminated food, and so does not demand a direct response (491).

Curiously, the emotional contagion discussed in Chapter 2 can also have an effect on time perception. If someone smiles at you, you smile back and time stretches a bit. In Droit-Volet's studies, the mimicry may involve very faint movements, but they are necessary to the temporal effect. When participants were shown the same smiling faces with a pen in their mouths, thereby preventing their own lips from forming a smile, the time distortion disappeared (497).

The importance of action in time perception is underscored by several studies investigating the perception of time between an action and its effects (Haggard, Clark, and Kalogeras 2002; Parsons, Novich, and Eagleman 2013; Wenke and Haggard 2009). Consistent with the idea that your conscious experience of time is designed to assess progress toward goals, when you cause an event to occur, you will experience it as occurring sooner than an event you did not cause. Your anticipation of the outcome speeds conscious processing. In fact, if you get used to the occurrence of a sound at a set time after action, say 150 ms after a button press, a sound that is presented sooner than you expect, say 50 ms after the button press, will appear *before* the button press (Stetson, Cui, Montague, and Eagleman 2006). The sound seems to magically know you were *about* to press the button.

Motion illusions are another example of the way your sensory systems fudge timing relations in order to provide a useful representation rather than an objectively accurate one. A ring moving from left to right will appear to the right of a flashed circle, even when the circle is presented within the ring.[32] To assess how things are *now*, you need to know where the ring will be by the time it is consciously processed. So the representational system advances its location relative to the stationary flashed circle. All of these studies show that what we see as now is not necessarily what is occurring now. Consciousness provides the best representation of how the world is at the present moment, based on sensory and cognitive capacities, goals, and context.

## The Power of Now

This chapter shares its title with a best-selling book by Eckhart Tolle *The Power of Now* (2004). While I do not promise the spiritual enlightenment that Tolle readers seek, TRT endorses the value of attending to the present in this bustling, future-oriented culture. One source of the power of now is that conscious feelings of happiness and satisfaction are part of your representation of the present. You cannot experience future or past joys except as they are part of what is happening *now*. Chapter 5 will consider why and how representations of the future and past are embedded in representations of the present.

As humans with the capacity to project ourselves forward in time through imagination and backward to the past through memory, concentrating on the more simple state of present consciousness is a useful reminder of the immediacy of life. Even sadness and disaffection can often be dealt with more effectively by attending to these emotions rather than trying to push them away. Most meditative practices involve attending to some aspect of the present environment, such as your breath, with the goal of heightening consciousness.[33]

According to the Temporal Representation Theory, attending to the present moment heightens consciousness, because consciousness *is* the representation of the present moment. In our busy lives we use consciousness to accomplish whatever tasks are at hand, including plans for next week and discussions of last week's mistakes. Everyday human experience obscures the fundamental nature of consciousness; meditation reminds us that consciousness is *now*.

# Beyond Analogy

*In no case may we interpret an action as the outcome*
*of the exercise of a higher psychical faculty,*
*if it can be interpreted as the exercise of one*
*which stands lower in the psychological scale.*

Lloyd Morgan's Canon

## Three Responses to the Question of Animal Consciousness

Animals do amazing things. Primates have learned sign language and demonstrate the ability to reflect on their own thoughts. Dolphins and dogs are able to follow complex commands that require discrimination of objects (ball or doll) in combination with particular actions (bring, drop, circle). Archerfish precisely target speed and distance from prey. Even bees can be trained to pull a string for a reward and then train others in the task.[1]

Do these amazing feats indicate that they are conscious? How could we know? This question is being hotly debated in several recent books (Braithwaite 2010; Dawkins 2012; Godfrey-Smith 2016; Tye 2016) and a new online journal, *Animal Sentience*. There are several possible ways to respond to the question of animal consciousness. Three will be considered in this chapter: (1) We couldn't possibly know if animals are conscious. Because consciousness is a subjective phenomenon, I can only *really* know if I am conscious. There could be no possible objective evidence for consciousness. (2) We can tell about animal consciousness by analogy. I assume other human beings are conscious due to their similarities to me, so I can apply the same reasoning to animals. Those animals similar to me are conscious. (3) We can tell about animal consciousness by looking for what consciousness does. If consciousness evolved to serve a function, then we can look for behavior that serves the function consciousness performs. Animals that can do what consciousness does are conscious.

If you've followed the argument so far in this book, you know that I adopt the third approach. Consciousness represents the present moment in order to facilitate flexible response. This chapter demonstrates one of the most significant advantages of a functional explanation of consciousness. A description of consciousness in terms of function provides an objective method for determining which animals experience conscious pain and pleasure. While it won't be a simple task to design conclusive tests for flexibility, a functional explanation tells us what our tests should show. This approach faces some significant opposition, however, so a review of the two alternative approaches is in order.

## We Couldn't Possibly Know

The first and most familiar response to the question of animal consciousness is to think it would be impossible to ever know whether or not an animal is conscious. While we might be inclined to treat animals as conscious, proponents say, this impulse is an anthropomorphic one. Humans attribute thoughts and intentions to everything we interact with, from animals to computers to the weather. (Ever notice how it rains right after you get the car washed? That must be intentional.)[2] On reflection, however, it is obvious that the weather does not have plans, so we should be wary of our temptation to ascribe a mind to computers or animals.

With regard to consciousness, the subjectivity of experience poses an additional constraint on the anthropomorphic impulse. When I reflect on my consciousness, as Descartes did those many years ago, it seems that my experience is the only thing I could know. The world and other people might be illusory, but the *experience* of those things is definitely occurring. The corollary of my certainty about my own experience is my uncertainty about anyone else's experience. If you and I disagree about the nature of the world, we might find ways to come to some agreement. But if we disagree about the nature of experience, we have no means to arbitrate the dispute. From a Cartesian perspective, no one can be wrong about the nature of her own experience, because consciousness is essentially separate from the world. So it seems we must *both* be right despite any incompatibility in our description of our experiences. This sort of reasoning is what drives convictions about an inverted spectrum: what appears green to me might appear blue to you. Even if we both call the experience "seeing green," that wouldn't make either of us wrong.

This move to epistemically isolate consciousness from objective evaluation is the source of the explanatory gap discussed in the Introduction. What is curious about the contemporary separation of consciousness with the world, in contrast with Cartesian Dualism, is that it is accompanied by a conviction that consciousness is a common and widespread phenomenon. Descartes famously advocated vivisection due to his conviction that animals lack consciousness. The howls and winces were mere mechanical responses, he surmised, not evidence of conscious pain. Contemporary dualist David Chalmers (2010) comes to the opposite conclusion; consciousness is a fundamental feature of reality. Because there is no way to account for the qualitative character of consciousness in terms of the structure and function of physical systems, Chalmers argues, consciousness should be considered a basic element of the universe, along with mass and charge, that pervades everything.

Thomas Nagel also simply assumes bats are conscious, despite his skepticism about the possibility of an explanation for this fact (1974). Nagel claims there is no way to know what it is like to be a bat, yet he is convinced there *is* something it is like to be a bat. This conviction seems entirely unwarranted given his position. If consciousness is essentially subjective and I can have no knowledge of any other consciousness, a logical conclusion is that no other consciousness exists. Without the possibility of evidence for consciousness in others, there is no reason to believe they are conscious. Notably, no one advocates this solipsistic view. Given that philosophers adopt some outrageous positions, it is instructive that no philosopher adopts this one. Even the most adamant opponents to physical explanation cling to the intuition that other beings (at least humans) are conscious.[3]

Contrary to the skeptical view, good reasons support the assumption that other people and animals are conscious. The standard argument from analogy is strong and will be considered in the next section. Further, our reasons go beyond analogy when we recognize the way consciousness is rooted in biological function.[4] Common evolutionary pressures produce similar mechanisms to solve similar problems. Our anthropomorphic impulse to ascribe conscious minds to others is not anthropomorphic at all; it is *biomorphic*. We are living beings who ascribe life to other beings. As with anthropomorphism, the impulse to ascribe life functions to other beings can be unwarranted in some cases. The challenge is to determine criteria by which the ascription of life, or consciousness, is justified.

To be perfectly clear, my argument against the very compelling position that we couldn't possibly know if animals are conscious is that we already do know that animals are conscious. We know other humans are conscious, and we know that our dogs and cats and horses are conscious. No one disputes that we know this, they just say we can't explain *how* we know this. The next two sections will discuss some ways we have of supporting our knowledge of other minds.

## We Can Tell by Analogy

By far the most common way of justifying our conviction that other humans and animals are conscious is by analogy. If others are like me, they must have similar experiences. Someone is crying, she must be feeling sad. An animal is wriggling and whimpering, it must be in pain. This simple move of inferring similar experiences based on similar behavior fits into a general capacity for identifying patterns that is basic to mental representation. On Millikan's Consumer Theory (see Chapter 1), thoughts are *about* things because they have been useful in getting me to those things. My thoughts about the feelings of others is similarly grounded in the way those thoughts have been successful. When I respond effectively to another's sadness or pain, this confirms my belief that certain kinds of behavior indicate certain experiences.

Michael Tye (2016) has developed a sustained defense of this argument. As all analogical arguments do, Tye's argument begins with himself and his own mind. Then it moves to humans, like you. Tye considers various possible hypotheses to explain your behavior and concludes that the best explanation is that you have beliefs, desires, and conscious experiences just like his own. You, dear Reader, are conscious. You are not attempting to deceive Tye about your feelings, nor are you a robot controlled by Martians, nor has your brain been replaced by a silicon chip that is designed to perfectly emulate appropriate human behavior. Though these are all logically possible explanations of your behavior, they are not reasonable explanations. "The simple fact is that the everyday causal explanation of your behavior by reference to your beliefs and desires is the best available, and as such it is rational for us to prefer it" (2016: 53).

Tye would object to my characterization of his argument as analogical (54f). A crucial difference between an inference to the best explanation, which is the sort of argument Tye is offering, and a straightforward argument by analogy is that explanation involves multiple factors that together form the most plausible account. The evidence in support of Tye's inference that conscious experiences cause your behavior comes from his own experiences, your reports about your experiences along with the reports of others about their experiences, as well as physiological evidence.

These additional forms of evidence considerably strengthen the argument, but it still depends crucially on assumptions about relevant similarities. Tye's own conscious experience of pain seems to be the cause of his own behavior, so it is reasonable for him to assume your similar behavior is caused by your conscious pain in the absence of any reason to suppose otherwise. Inferences about animal pain likewise depend on assumptions about which sorts of behavior count as relevantly similar. In cases where the similarities between human and non-human behavior and physiology are numerous and close, as with mammals, the inference to conscious experience is strong. However, in cases where similarities are few and disparate, as with bees and crabs, the inference is weak.

The main problem with Tye's inference to consciousness as the best explanation of behavior is that explanations of behavior without consciousness grow stronger the less similar an animal's behavior is to human behavior. The epigram at the beginning of this chapter is Lloyd Morgan's Canon stating that explanations should not presume a higher psychological ability if a lower ability is sufficient. Presuming consciousness is a later evolutionary development building on unconscious forms of representation, Lloyd Morgan's Canon dictates that an account of behavior should be given exclusively in terms of representation without consciousness.

So the question becomes, can animal behavior possibly be explained in terms of unconscious representation, or is consciousness necessarily involved? In the absence of a theory about the function of consciousness, the only way to answer this question is to determine which behaviors are performed consciously in humans and to look for similar behaviors in animals. In other words, an inference to the best explanation of animal behavior boils down to analogy.

Researchers often produce lists of behavior considered to exemplify consciousness. Lynne Sneddon and colleagues (Sneddon, Elwood, Adamo, and Leach 2014) propose seventeen criteria for animal pain, organized under two general principles of behavior: (1) behavior differs from simple stimulus/response, (2) stimulus processing results in long-term changes in motivation. While lists can be useful in supporting the inference that consciousness is the best explanation of animal behavior, they offer no principled reason why these behaviors require consciousness. Consequently, they are open to arguments that consciousness has not been definitively proven.

Consider the case of crab pain. After they have been given electrical shocks, crabs avoid the shells they were in when shocked (Magee and Elwood 2013). Is this behavior similar to my avoidance of a hot stove after I have been burned? We both have had a negative response to something and try to prevent that event from occurring again. Our behavior is long-term. Does it differ from stimulus/response conditioning? I continue to use the stove regularly, even though I have been repeatedly burned in one way or another. Some crabs continue to enter shells in which they have been shocked, even when another shelter is available. Our behavior is similar; is it relevantly similar?

In the absence of a theory that can connect behavior to conscious experiences, it is unclear which behaviors are relevant and which are irrelevant. Lists of behaviors are useful when the items on the list align decisively in favor of similarities between animals and humans. When dissimilarities are equal to or more numerous that similarities, there is no way to determine whether differences are due to lack of consciousness or to species differences.

The same problem applies to aspects of consciousness associated with brain physiology. Anil Seth and colleagues (Edelman, Baars, and Seth 2005; Seth, Baars, and Edelman 2005) also list seventeen criteria, some of which overlap with the Sneddon list and others diverge. In applying these criteria to non-human animals, the authors focus on neural connections that modulate level of consciousness (from sleep to waking, inattentive to attentive) and the links between perception and memory. The result is strong evidence of consciousness in mammals and birds: the complexity of neural structures and the way these structures interact is similar to the way human brains function when we are conscious.

As with the Sneddon list, however, evidence of similarity in neural structure is useful when decisively in favor of consciousness. In the face of dissimilarities, we have no way to go forward in the absence of a theory that can determine which similarities are relevant. In animals with very different neural structures, like the octopus, we have no principled way to say whether its unusual system produces consciousness or not.

Unlike the dense, functional clusters of neurons in the mammalian brain, the octopus neural system is diffuse. Two-thirds of its 500 million neurons are located in its eight arms, which house basic motor programs such as fetching. An amputated arm exhibits similar reaching movements when stimulated. By offloading much of the fine-tuned sensorimotor processing to the periphery, the central brain can adopt a more supervisory activation and coordination role. Stimulation of one of the numerous interconnected lobes that form the central brain activates a similar motion in several arms, never a single arm in isolation. This suggests the central brain generally directs and controls action while each arm individually initiates and executes the specific movements tailored to the task (Hochner 2012).

In light of the distributed nature of octopus neural structure, what conclusions can we draw about octopus consciousness? Are the neural connections among arms and brain sufficiently similar to the sorts of neural connections in humans that underlie consciousness? Might the independent motor control of octopus arms indicate that each arm is conscious on its own?[5] The authors call for further study to refine our understanding of the functions and interconnections of the lobes in the central brain to see if they operate similarly to human brains. Given that octopus and human evolution diverged about 600 million years ago and progressed in very different environments, there is no reason to assume that a similar neurophysiology emerged in both animals unless there are no other conceivable options.

This lack of alternatives seems to be the main driver of the argument from analogy. Tye claims that inference to the best explanation based on evidence of similarities is the best we can do. Theories about the nature of consciousness are controversial, he notes, and the explanatory gap raises doubt about the possibility of ever understanding the relation between consciousness and brain processes (2016: xiv). While Tye and others are right to emphasize the strong evidence for similarities between animals and humans, this approach cannot help us evaluate cases of striking dissimilarity. In these cases, we need a description of consciousness in terms of function to move beyond analogy and bridge the explanatory gap.

## We Can Tell by What Consciousness Does

My proposal in this book is that consciousness serves a function: it represents the present moment in order to track progress toward goals. Animals like you are conscious when sensory and cognitive representations are combined to form a representation of how things are to you at that moment. You need to know what is happening *now* so you can tell whether it is time to flip the eggs and when the toast is done. A good bit of your life runs on autopilot, as we saw in previous chapters. For these routine tasks, no conscious attention is needed to respond appropriately to environmental cues. You don't need to consciously direct your feet to walk over to the toaster or focus on your hand and finger movements while you fetch the toast. Your consciousness is just keeping track, maybe enjoying a daydream or worrying about an afternoon meeting. But if the toast burns or the phone rings, your consciousness quickly shifts back to the present in order to assess the situation so you can determine what the next move should be.

Is this what it is like to be a bat or an octopus? Do they represent the present moment in their respectively dark and aquatic environments? Obviously the content of bat consciousness would be different, and octopus consciousness radically different, since their sensory systems and goals are different. An often overlooked insight from Nagel's famous paper is his recognition that each mind is unique in how it represents the world. Our own personal histories shape which things in the world are relevant to us and what we do with those things. Even so, we all share a common world, and that means we can figure out how other minds work by looking at how they relate to our shared world.

Bats use sound in a way similar to the way mammals use light to identify object shape and distance. Sound waves bounce off objects, and the auditory properties of the returning signal tell the bat speed, direction, and location of its prey (Van Ryckegham 1998). Though we can't share bat experiences, we can appreciate how bats use their experience to navigate their environment. According to the Consumer Theory, the content of bat experiences is connected to the way the bats use their representations. By carefully examining the capacity of bats to avoid obstacles, hunt prey, and interact with other bats, we can determine how bats represent the world by means of echolocation and other perceptual systems. These representations tell us a good bit about what it's like to be a bat (Akins 1993).

More to the point of this book, we can determine that there is, indeed, something it is like to be a bat. If bats are capable of flexible responses, we know the bat is not unconsciously responding to its environment. *Are* bats capable of flexible responses? Here is some plausible evidence, with a full explanation of what counts as flexibility to be developed in the next section. Bats use vocalization both for spatial navigation by means of echolocation and for communication. This remarkable range of uses demands that bats be able to determine whether another bat is navigating or hunting, familiar or unfamiliar, one's own mother or pup, among other forms of information (Ross and Holderied 2013). Vampire bats are famous for sharing of blood meals within a social group, keeping track of which members share and which are stingy. Bats also engage in social grooming and a variety of other cooperative behaviors that depend on the capacity to keep track of individual relations and social interactions (Carter and Wilkinson 2013). Moreover, bats possess similar neural structures as humans for processing the emotional valence of acoustical information and social cues (Kanwal, Zhang, and Feng 2013).

The variety and complexity of these behaviors suggest flexibility. On the Temporal Representation Theory, the capacity to respond flexibly to the environment requires consciousness. A representation of the present moment is needed to distinguish past learning from future goals. Bats can select the best action to pursue by drawing on memory relevant to how things are *now*. In other words, we can tell that bats are conscious, because flexible response is what consciousness does.

## Testing for Flexibility

In the previous section I argued that the best answer to the question of animal consciousness is to determine what function consciousness performs. If the function of consciousness is to track present progress toward goals, as I proposed in Chapter 3, then we can tell whether animals are conscious by testing them for behavioral flexibility. If the animal's response is not fully determined by the stimulus, then it needs to represent the present situation in order to choose among alternative responses.

The next question is: how can we tell when a response is flexible? Finding an answer to this question is not the Hard Problem, but it is still extraordinarily difficult. As we saw in Chapter 2, unconscious, automatic responses can be quite complex. Pushmi-pullyu animals are capable of learning to associate stimuli in order to better exploit resources or avoid dangers. Their limitation is that their behavioral adaptation is entirely backward-looking. Pushmi-pullyu animals are not capable of using past learning in order to choose between different possible actions. Action for a pushmi-pullyu animal is entirely determined by its past conditioning.

The conceptual difference is clear. With consciousness, an animal assesses the current situation and chooses among its various goals and possible paths to those goals based on what its past experience suggests is the best move to make. Without consciousness, an animal responds to the current situation with whatever action has been proven best in past situations like this one. The behavioral difference is much less clear between an animal capable of conscious response and one that is not. Both learn from past environmental interactions, both will abandon a food source when threatened by a predator, both display behaviors like wriggling and twitching that look like what we do when we are in pain. So how can we tell when behavior is truly flexible?

Over the last several years I have worked on this question in collaboration with the late Victoria Braithwaite, a researcher on animal behavior and cognition. Victoria and I focused on the question of fish consciousness because this animal group resists any easy argument from analogy. Fish have a very different neural structure, and their behavior differs significantly as well. To the extent fish are at all like humans, similarities rest almost entirely on *function*. For example, certain brain areas in fish are hypothesized to be homologous to mammalian amygdala and hippocampus, because lesions to these areas disrupt the same functions (aversion to novelty and spatial memory) in both fish and mammals (Rodríguez et al. 2005). Nociceptors in fish and other animals are similar in their function of detecting aversive stimuli (Sneddon, Braithwaite, and Gentle 2003).

These common functions are suggestive, but without a theory about the function of *consciousness*, there is no reason to believe that evidence of nociception or even memory is evidence of consciousness. The Temporal Representation Theory resolves this impasse in its identification of flexible behavior as the function of consciousness. An animal must be able to represent what is happening *now* in order to distinguish the present from possible alternative futures. To determine whether fish are conscious, then, we need to determine whether fish are capable of flexible behavior. How could we test for flexibility?

Four categories of behavior connect the capacity for temporal representation and flexible action: (1) differential response to the environment, (2) appropriate action in novel situations, (3) manipulation of the environment to accomplish goals, and (4) ability to explicitly represent absent objects (Droege and Braithwaite 2014). For each of these categories I will explain how temporal representation relates to the flexible behavior demonstrated and give an example of a fish species that exhibits the appropriate sort of behavior.

## (1) Differential Response to the Environment

First, differential response to the environment is the most basic requirement for flexibility. All of the other three categories also involve this ability to respond differently to the same stimulus conditions. Simple organisms like our friend the nematode worm *C. Elegans* (the exemplary pushmi-pullyu animal in Chapter 2) can respond differently to *different environments;* flexibility means an animal can respond differently to the *same environment,* depending on its goals. The practical animal uses information learned in the past to select among different possible actions in the present situation. How things are now requires a unique assessment.

A good illustration of the way natural selection has designed different organisms to adapt to the particular demands of their environment is Daniel Dennett's *Tower of Generate-and-Test* (1995: 373–8). At the base of the tower are *Darwinian creatures*. They adapt exclusively by gene mutation and selection— good genes live, bad genes die. This group is dwindling in size as researchers discover remarkable means of learning and communication in quite simple animals and even plants. Candidates for the Darwinian category are now restricted to single-celled organisms such as the *E. coli* bacterium. The next level of *Skinnerian creatures* introduces adaptation through learning. The behavior of these animals, such as *C. Elegans,* can be modified by positive and negative conditioning. Both Darwinian and Skinnerian animals have only pushmi-pullyu representations: a specific stimulus determines a specific response.

The next level in Dennett's tower is the *Popperian creature*. Here is where an animal has the capacity to respond in different ways to the same environment. It is not driven by associative learning, because it can now anticipate which sort of action best meets its goals at the moment. Where the *Skinnerian creature* is limited to one-to-one stimulus-response learning, the *Popperian creature* is capable of response based on complex weightings of many-to-many relations. This sort of flexible response depends on learning, memory, and the integration of information. On the Temporal Representation Theory, *Popperian creatures* are conscious.

Dennett calls animals at this level "Popperian" after Sir Karl Popper who noted that flexibility "permits our hypotheses to die in our stead" (qtd in Dennett 1995: 375). My one quibble with this description is the suggestion that it involves an "inner environment." Dennett is careful to note that an inner environment does not simply reproduce the outer environment in the way suggested by Picture Theories of representation (see Chapter 1). As we saw in Chapter 3, Dennett masterfully demolishes the Cartesian theater, the assumption that consciousness involves a 360° surround-sound movie in the mind (1991). Nonetheless, the suggestion that flexible response requires imagining future outcomes is problematic. Humans can do this, as I will discuss in the next chapter, but imagination requires the next level of development in Dennett's tower.

*Gregorian creatures* are capable of developing cultural tools like language. As far as we can tell, only humans are *Gregorian creatures*.[6] We are the only animals who keep records of the distant past and think about the distant future. As I suggest at the end of Chapter 5, the ability to represent one's self in time may depend on cultural constructs like calendars. My point here is that the capacities of the *Gregorian creature* are not necessary for consciousness. There is no reason to expect that conscious animals are able to report their sensations. To be conscious requires only that an animal represents the world at the present moment. Consciousness is how things appear to an animal *now*. The capacity to report conscious experiences develops with the capacity for self-conscious expression, and this additional capacity is the special endowment of Gregorian creatures.

To return then to the bottom of the Tower, our task in this section is to examine the transition from Skinnerian to Popperian creature. What drives a well-adapted, stimulus-driven creature to become behaviorally flexible? Outside of an experimental environment, there is no time when an animal faces exactly the same situation twice. So even Skinnerian creatures will vary response to the variation in stimuli. This is why it is so difficult to design an experimental test that distinguishes flexibility from more simple forms of associative learning. Examples of the complex many-to-many relations involved in differential response involve the ability to fine-tune action to individual situations. Flexibility is essential when multiple conditions and multiple responses are available and their relations are continually changing.

The small, industrious cleaner wrasse exhibits this individual fine-tuning remarkably. A cleaner wrasse feeds on the parasites of client fish, offering its services over 2,000 times a day (Bshary and Grutter 2005). Working in pairs, these fish establish a particular location where clients return regularly for service. Often a line will form of fish waiting to be cleaned. The basic interaction between cleaner and client is mutually beneficial—the cleaner eats the parasites for nourishment, and the clients are relieved of their parasites. Things get tricky, because the cleaners would prefer to dine on the fresh and tasty flesh of the client fish rather than the parasites. Clients understandably object to being bitten and respond by shuddering, chasing the cleaner, or leaving to find a more cooperative cleaner fish. In addition, some of the client fish are predators who would in other circumstances happily eat the cleaner instead of patiently holding still for the cleaning service. One bite too many and the client might bite back, with fatal results. In addition, other fish waiting in line witness the shuddering and may decide to take their parasites elsewhere.

The challenge for the tiny cleaner fish is to judge how much cheating a particular client (and the clients in line) is willing to tolerate. For each interaction, the cleaner determines if it is best to stick to eating parasites or if it can get away with a bite or two of flesh. The cleaner can also mollify predators and offended clients by offering tactile stimulation with its fins. A little massage keeps the clients happy and prevents them from leaving or taking revenge.

The variety of possibilities for action requires the cleaner wrasse to keep track of how each interaction is proceeding in order to be able to adjust its responses. Research shows that cleaner fish are able to distinguish the identity of individual clients so as to tailor their service to the particularities of that specific client (Tebbich, Bshary, and Grutter 2002). Cleaner wrasse behavior is not only complex, it is *flexible*. At every moment a number of goals (get food, avoid predation, mollify client) and a number of actions (eat parasites, bite client, flee, massage) are in play. The wrasse needs to be able to keep track of what is happening in its environment *now* in order to adjust its goals and actions accordingly.

## (2) Appropriate Action in Novel Situations

To return for a moment to human phenomenology, novel situations are to me the most compelling sort of case for the necessity of conscious attention. See if you feel equally compelled. Imagine again that you are driving home, listening to the radio. As we discussed in the last chapter, the movements of your arms as you adjust the wheel or your feet as you move from the brake to the gas pedal, all occur unconsciously. The colors and shapes of things cycle through your conscious experience as you drive by, making little impact. And then something unexpected happens, such as a crash ahead. A novel situation immediately snaps you out of autopilot and into the present moment.[7]

The reason a novel situation requires consciousness is that appropriate action requires the ability to combine elements from various past experiences and apply them in a new way. No simple formula for weighting values of flee or feed is sufficient to evaluate the particulars of the unique event happening *now*. The animal must be able to select the relevant features of the current situation and use its knowledge of those features to choose the best action.

Of course, the world is a dynamic, ever-changing place, so all animals must be able to respond in some roughly adequate way to new environments. Consequently a test for flexibility needs to distinguish between the pre-set calculus of pushmi-pullyu response and a truly original assessment of the present situation. This distinction is quite fine and further illustrates the difficulty in designing decisive tests.

One example of appropriate response to a novel situation leverages the particular skills of cichlids, a species of fighting fish. These fish defend territories against potential invaders and learn about their opponents by watching them fight one another. In a clever experiment, cichlids watched the battles of several fish from a safe observation point behind a glass wall (Grosenick, Clement, and Fernald 2007). In contests between fish matched in size, fish A beat B, B beat C, C beat D, and D beat E. The question was what the observer fish would do when put in a tank between B and D, two fighters that the observer had not seen fight each other. The observers regularly moved to face D (in fifteen out of sixteen trials), even though it had seen both fish win one fight and lose one fight. Consequently, the observer fish needed to combine information from two different past events to utilize the information that B was the winner in a fight with C, and D was the loser in a fight with C. Only then could it know that D is the weaker fish.

A simple rule like "fight the weakest fish" is inadequate unless there is some way to assess the new combination of opponents. The observer must be able to remember which fish beat C and which fish lost to C, and it must be able to apply that information to the current situation. As in the driving case, a novel situation demands conscious attention to utilize past learning in order to respond effectively to the particular features of the current environment.

## (3) Manipulation of the Environment to Accomplish Goals

Though the previous two tests demonstrate flexibility, they both depend on applying past information in the present environment. Neither test shows the importance of explicit goal representation as a critical factor in determining which action is best.[8] The capacity to manipulate the environment in order to bring about a desired goal highlights the relation between present and future critical to the emergence of consciousness. According to the Temporal Representation Theory, consciousness is necessary when an animal is able to represent goals separately from current conditions. When the way things are now does not exactly specify what should be done, an animal needs be able to continually assess whether things are going well or whether there should be a change in plan. In order to determine how to manipulate the environment, an animal must be able to represent the difference between how things are *now* in relation to how they will be when the goal is accomplished. Only if the animal has an explicit goal in mind can it figure out what action will bring about that future situation.

When an animal uses tools to solve a problem, it is hard not to believe consciousness is involved. Just watch a wild crow solve an 8-part puzzle to get a treat and see if you can resist attributing consciousness.[9] Using something in the environment to get something else exemplifies a rudimentary form of foresight and planning. The sticks and rocks used by the crow are only valuable because they get the crow to its final goal. In order make use of the tool, the crow stops direct action toward the goal and considers how other things in its environment might help. A pushmi-pullyu animal can't use tools because it can't stop time to consider different ways to achieve its goal. All it can do is to respond to the situation in the way it has been conditioned to respond. If there is no direct route to its goal, the pushmi-pullyu animal will give up that goal and get a new one.

Paradigmatic examples of tool use are rare in natural fish behavior. Fins are not ideal for grabbing or holding things, and water slows down any effort to smash or throw things. One candidate for the capacity to use tools is the archerfish. This fish can perfectly calibrate the speed and direction of a flying insect and adjust the pressure and trajectory of its own squirt of water to hit the prey with pinpoint accuracy.

As impressive as the archerfish hunting skills are, only in the lab does the potential to use these skills as tools become clear. Cait Newport and colleagues (Newport, Wallis, Reshitnyk, and Siebeck 2016) trained archerfish to spit at one human face (A) in order to receive a treat and *not* to spit at the other face (B). Then in the testing phase, the fish were rewarded with a treat only when they continued to avoid B and spit at whatever novel face was presented. Though the number of fish in the experiment was small, just eight, they succeeded in *avoiding* B and hitting all other faces about seventy percent of the time.

Take a moment to consider the requirements of this task: distinguish one face from all other faces and *inhibit* a food-oriented response in order to get food. Having trained my dog *not* to bark at the backyard wildlife, I am familiar with how difficult it is to establish the absence of response to an ecologically compelling association. According to the Temporal Representation Theory, the capacity to act *or not act* in response to a stimulus indicates that the behavior is not stimulus-driven, that is, the behavior is flexible.

This is not to say that the stimuli don't determine the response. Every animal, including every human, decides action based on stimuli. The subtle but important difference between pushmi-pullyu response and explicitly goal-driven response is the ability to respond in different ways to stimuli in relation to goals. Since an animal only demonstrates one response in any given situation, however, it is devilishly difficult to show that it might have responded differently. My suggestion is that the capacity of the archerfish to use its spray as a tool is one indication of its flexibility in goal-directed response.

## (4) Ability to Explicitly Represent Absent Objects

The last test of flexibility sounds so sophisticated that you may wonder whether even you can pass. As noted earlier, flexibility demands the ability to represent goals as separate from the current environment. Where pushmi-pullyu animals *implicitly* represent goals as part of its stimulus-response conditioning, flexibility requires the *explicit* representation of goals. The worm represents nutrients-for-eating, while the crow can keep the treat in mind as it works to solve the puzzle.

In the crow's case, the treat is not absent; it is right there in the glass box. Yet goals are often absent, to be realized at some future time. Note that the condition here is the ability to represent the *goal*, not the *future*. To represent the future means being able to hold two different times in mind, the future time and the present time. As I will argue in Chapter 5, representing the future (and the past) in this way requires self-consciousness and probably language. To represent a goal, on the other hand, means being able to hold the absent object in mind *now*. My conscious representation of things indicates the goal object is *not present*.

If an animal is not capable of representing something as *either* present *or* absent, then the content "present" has no meaning. Such an animal could respond to things that are present, but it couldn't represent them *as present*. It is a bit like breathing air. You don't think about the fact that you breathe air because there is no alternative. Air is just what you breathe. When there *is* an alternative, such as breathing on a respirator or facing the dire prospect of drowning, you *do* think about air and appreciate it considerably. For any representation to be meaningful, there must be a contrast case to that representational content.

Absent goals demonstrate the contrast case to a representation of presence, and in so doing they demonstrate consciousness. So, how can we show that fish have absent goals in mind? Spatial navigation offers a promising possibility. To find their way from one place to another, fish sometimes follow environmental markers—left at the tall plant, right past the pile of stones, and so forth. No goal representation is needed in this sort of navigation, only a chain of pushmi-pullyu representations. Alternatively, some fish are able to map spatial relations in a region so that they can get anywhere from anywhere without following a predetermined route. The goby fish is a master of this second form of navigation. The goby lives in tidal pools, jumping from one pool to another as the tide goes out. If threatened, the goby uses its memory of adjacent pools to hop unerringly to safety (Aronson 1951, 1971).

A chain of pushmi-pullyu representations would not help the goby, because it needs to design a different pathway each time depending on the presence of predators, rate of tidal flow, and its current location. As the goby jumps, it must continue to assess the weight of its various goals to escape predators, find food, and reach deep water. In the frame of the Temporal Representation Theory, the goby needs to be conscious of how things are *now* in order to determine which way to jump.

But are goby fish conscious? These examples of flexible behavior are remarkable and may be sufficient to convince you that fish are definitely conscious. Even so, each sort of behavior is peculiar to the species, inapplicable to other fish or animal group. The next step for experimental research is to design a series of tests that could apply across a range of animal groups. Tests would need to be sufficiently general so that modifications could be made for the particular ecological niche of the species. It would be no use to try to get a goby to fight or a cleaner fish to shoot water at targets. Designing the right tests turns out to be the most challenging aspect of all the difficulties in answering the question of animal consciousness. The line between simple associative response and flexible decision-making is a fine one. Nonetheless, I believe animal researchers are up to the task.

What is most needed at this point is a convincing theoretical frame to guide research. This section aimed to provide that frame. My claim in this chapter is that the explanatory gap between the first-person experience of one's own consciousness and third-person evidence for animal consciousness can be bridged by a description of consciousness in terms of function. If consciousness is defined as a representation of the present moment, and a representation of the present moment is necessary for flexible behavior, then evidence of flexibility is evidence for consciousness. An animal needs to represent how things are now in order to choose among various alternative actions. My suggestion is that the cleaner wrasse and cichlids and archerfish and goby fish are not just operating on pushmi-pullyu representations. They are using information about the way things are *now* to determine which action best accomplishes their goals. According to the Temporal Representation Theory, these behaviors indicate consciousness. The prediction is that further research will confirm the hypothesis.

## Hard Cases: The Return of the Octopus and Ant

The word "hypothesis" should signal that ultimately the answer to the question of animal consciousness will be the result of scientific investigation. My job as a philosopher is to show the way out of the bottle, as Wittgenstein put it. The human propensity for posing puzzles to ourselves can trap us in a dead end, like a fly stuck in a bottle. The question of animal consciousness is a trap so long as we believe it is impossible to determine whether animals are conscious *and also* believe that animals are definitely conscious.

Drawing analogies between animals and humans can only take us so far in resolving this conundrum. Analogies justify the intuition that animals similar to us are indeed conscious, but they leave us with no principled way to arbitrate between relevant and irrelevant similarities. Withdrawal from something that causes injury is similar to our behavior when we experience conscious pain, so that seems a good reason to attribute consciousness. Except the withdrawal response also can occur unconsciously, so perhaps the similarity is not relevant after all. We need to distinguish the forms of behavior and types of neurophysiology that require consciousness from those that do not in order to move beyond intuition and into the lab.

By considering the hard case of invertebrates, we can get a better sense of how an explanation of consciousness in terms of function moves the question of consciousness from the armchair to the lab. Ranging from the very clever octopus to the plant-like sponge, invertebrates push analogy to the limit, because their behavior and physiology are so very different from ours.

Earlier we considered the challenge to analogy posed by the octopus. Behavioral analogy fares better than neural comparisons due to the human-like capacity of the octopus to escape from cages and look discerningly at observers (Montgomery 2016). Rather than simply list the common behaviors shared by octopus and human, however, the Temporal Representation Theory calls for a test of flexibility. In this light we can see that the ability to open cages demonstrates appropriate action in a novel situation as well as the ability to represent goals. The discerning looks and sustained attention to visitors indicates differential responses to environmental cues. Octopus behavior indicates consciousness because it is flexible, not simply because it is similar to our own. Consciousness represents the way things are *now* in order to facilitate flexible responses.

What about the ants that were featured in the chapter on unconscious, pushmi-pullyu animals? Recent research has revealed that ants and other insects (notably bees) are capable of surprising dexterity. If you missed the video at the beginning of the chapter that shows a bee pulling a string to get a reward, this would be a good time to watch this amazing feat. Another video shows how a second bee learns to pull the string by watching the trained bee. Evidence of learning such as this, as well as communication and navigation skills show that insects utilize mental abilities far beyond reflex.

Andrew Barron and Colin Klein (2016) have argued that these abilities indicate consciousness, because they demonstrate an integrated representation of the world. Insects use a centralized model of their bodies in relation to the environment to direct action tailored to context. Most admirable about the Barron and Klein approach is their commitment to "an evidence-based structural, functional, and comparative story" about the possibility of insect consciousness (4906). I am also reassured that their story about integrated action in the world is so very close to the story I am telling in this book. What is missing in their account, however, is an explanation of the function of *consciousness*. Barron and Klein provide a good explanation of the value of an integrated world model in directing action, but they fail to explain why this model is conscious. Why couldn't an animal have an integrated world model that is not conscious? This question appears in various forms from critics of the claim about insect consciousness and will continue to appear until there is a convincing theory about the function of consciousness itself.

The Temporal Representation Theory proposes that consciousness represents the world at the present moment in order to facilitate flexible behavior. Therefore, it is not enough for insects to possess an integrated world model unless that model represents *now*. While evidence suggests that insects represent the world in order to act appropriately in the present, that representation does not explicitly *represent* the present unless goals are separated from sensory input. If insects operate on pushmi-pullyu representations alone, then they are not conscious.

Does any of the evidence so far demonstrate flexibility according to the four indicators described earlier? Not yet. Insect training shows they are Skinnerian creatures, capable of learning and not just reflex. So far, however, all of the cognitive abilities of insects are based on past experience. Insects tune their responses directly to the situation. No research yet shows the ability to choose between alternative paths and/or goals. The absence of a demonstration of flexibility means that the existence of consciousness in insects has not yet been demonstrated.

What about the hive mind? People often claim that insects function as a group or *superorganism*. If a group of insects is capable of flexibility, wouldn't it be just another form of anthropocentric analogy to demand that consciousness is a feature of a single mind rather than the collective? There are two responses to this question, one based on evidence and one based on theory. First, the evidence for collective flexibility in insects is no stronger than for individual insects. The amazing architectural structures produced by termites are based on simple behavioral rules, like put the mud ball where the scent is strongest (Wilson 2015). Group efforts to carry large food items, bridges across gaps, and rafts during flooding all involve a division of labor where each individual action is a response to a specific stimulus. Collectively the result is a complex structure, yet there is no group decision or plan to produce that structure. In other words, the "hive mind" is not one mind with a representation of the present situation; it is sum of the actions of many minds making adaptively designed responses.

The second, theoretical, response is that unity and flow are essential features of consciousness. The collective action of insects is not based on unified representations that flow as they are temporally updated. So, on the Temporal Representation Theory, insect groups are not conscious. If somehow a hive mind did produce a unified representation, then the case would be different. The Borg on *Star Trek* was portrayed as interconnected in this way. Cyberspace and Wi-Fi present another possibility of this sort of collective unity. The internet as it exists now does not have any representations of its own; the web doesn't yet want or need anything that would ground mental representation. So the internet is not yet conscious. In Chapter 7 I will return to the issue of artificial forms of consciousness and why cyber consciousness is an unlikely prospect.

For now, on the basis of current research and the Temporal Representation Theory, neither insects nor the internet are conscious, although the octopus probably is conscious. More research and more developed theories of consciousness may yet prove the opposite. One of the main advantages of a functional explanation of consciousness is that we know what to look for, or in the case of artificial consciousness perhaps, what to avoid.

## Closing the Explanatory Gap

The gap between consciousness as experienced from one's own point of view and evidence from outside that point of view can seem unbridgeable. A central goal of this book is to bridge that apparent chasm with my fragile house of cards. We began with a representational theory of mind. Minds have the function of representing things in the world, because those representations have been useful to survival. Many of a mind's representations are unconscious; they operate automatically to translate environmental conditions into actions based on past learning. Conscious representations are not needed unless there is the possibility of alternative responses to the current situation. A mind capable of flexible behavior needs to represent the world at the present moment in order to determine the best action.

The keystone card is the explanation of consciousness in terms of representational function. Consciousness is a representation of the present moment, designed to track what is happening now in order to assess progress toward goals. Consider again your own conscious experience. What is it like for you now? For me, sensations and thoughts are selected and combined to form the array of books on my desk, the smell of coffee, the sound of birds chirping outside. As I observe my experience, I notice the focus of attention shifts from the external world of my office to the internal world of my thought and back again, although both worlds remain present throughout. I have not yet discussed this shifting of worlds from internal to external, and it is an important aspect of human consciousness. The next chapter will puzzle through how these worlds relate and how past and future time could be part of a representation of the present moment, as they certainly are in conscious memory and imagination. I will also say why these forms of consciousness may be uniquely experienced by humans.

The point of this chapter has been to show how the keystone card—the function of consciousness—secures the bridge to an explanation of animal consciousness. If, as I have argued, consciousness is a representation of the present moment, and flexible behavior requires this sort of representation, evidence for flexible behavior is evidence of consciousness. The subtle exchange of cleaner wrasse and client fish, cichlid fight clubs, archerfish hunger games, and goby escape rooms provide initial examples of the types of behavior that indicate consciousness. The empirical task of devising adequate cross-species tests for flexibility remains, and it is not an easy one. Yet the path forward for animal researchers is clear now that the Hard Problem of consciousness no longer stands in the way.

# Extending Consciousness in Time

*I could no longer stop anything. Not the vehicle she*
*had been driving, nor her slow, endless leave-taking as*
*we watched her body fold in on itself. We were drifting.*

William J. Doan, *Drifting*

In the remarkable play *Drifting*, William J. Doan recalls his experiences at the time of his sister Samantha's traumatic brain injury. Drawings and journal entries are interwoven with narrative and film to bring the audience into Doan's memories. They slide in time from the recent past, now several years after his sister's death, and back to his childhood, regularly revisiting the pain of injury and loss in the immediate aftermath of the accident. The disjointed, multilayered production has an oddly immersive effect. The standard dramatization of memory depicts events as a sort of theatrical re-creation as if they were present, perhaps indicating the past with a time stamp (ten years earlier) or period clothing. In *Drifting* by contrast, I truly found myself drifting along with Doan as he sifted through events. Each memory has its own temporal order, but the smooth sequence gets interrupted by other memories with their particular place in time. Doan is driving and thinking about Samantha, when he remembers their conversation about whether or not he still goes to Mass, which reminds him of when they were younger and used to go mushroom hunting.[1]

This is how memory works. The brain is not a video recorder of experience, storing the track for later playback. Familiar and important elements of experience are somehow encoded in a way that allows reconstruction. We use these elements to produce a sense of past events and our selves in time. Memories result from the capacity to leverage ourselves out of the present moment to be conscious of past experiences. But if consciousness is a representation of the present moment, as this book has been arguing, how can there be consciousness of the past? The aim of this chapter is to resolve this apparent contradiction. In conscious memory[2] a representation of past events becomes part of the representation of the present. Rather than traveling back in time, we bring the past experience into the present. Conscious memory is an experience about the past that is also experienced as happening *now*. The ability to consciously remember our past experiences and imagine possible future experiences requires a representation of oneself as the person one is in the present (quietly sitting in an armchair) and also a representation of oneself as the person one was or will be (remembering last summer at the beach and anticipating next week's return trip). Conscious memory and imagination connect our past and future selves to the present by means of *embedding* representations of past and future events into the representation of the present moment. Even when these representations are mistaken, as memories and dreams notoriously are, the production of a *temporally extended self* serves the valuable function of maintaining an identity in time. Even if I falsely remember only sunny days, when it actually rained almost every day of my beach vacation last year, the sense of my self as the same person in the past, present, and future allows me to tell the story of myself as a character within the history of my community, nation, and world. As *Drifting* brilliantly demonstrates, the function of memory is to understand one's self through narrative, rather than factual accuracy.

## Experiencing the Past

Take a moment to bring to consciousness some experience from the past. Try to find a memory that is particularly vivid, either because it is recent (your experience of eating breakfast), or because it is significant (a birthday or wedding, an accident or the funeral of a loved one). Dwell in the experience for a bit, observing how the memory appears to you. Do you experience colors? Tastes? Sounds? Is it as if you are actually reexperiencing the event from the first-person perspective, or is it more like watching a movie of someone else? Are you transported entirely to the past, or are you still experiencing the present while simultaneously experiencing the past?

As with our previous phenomenological investigations, it is worthwhile paying attention to your experience to see how well a theory accounts for the way things appear to you. Theoretical expectations shape our experience, but the nature of experience can also correct our theories. Moreover, there is a possibility that experiences differ. Everyone at some point wonders if the things that look yellow to me look blue to you. We learn common names for colors through social training, but what is to prevent our color experiences from being entirely different? One answer to this question was offered in Chapter 1: the physical nature of the represented properties combines with the structure of our sensory systems to prevent the possibility of wide divergences in human color experience. What looks yellow to me might look to be a slightly different shade to you, but it can't look blue (Clark 2000). The range of options is constrained by the nature of the properties we represent coupled with the way our visual system has evolved to represent them.

Some of the same constraints apply to conscious memory. The main claim in the chapter is that conscious memory represents past experiences as part of the experience of the present moment. If this is correct, then conscious memories must include some properties of the past experience and some structure by which those properties are represented *as past*. As I describe the theory in more detail and relate it to my own experience, continue to reflect on your own conscious memory to see how well the theory fits your experience and to what extent our experiences are similar.

## The Problem of Pastness

Go back to your memory again and ask yourself how you know the event is past. What about the experience distinguishes it from the present or the future? David Hume suggested vividness of the image as a guide. Perception is most vivid, memory somewhat less vivid, and imagination the least vivid of all (Hume 1739: Book I, Part I, §III). While this guide is somewhat useful, it does not adequately distinguish among these different sorts of experience. Sometimes a memory is particularly vivid, as it is in the tragic case of post-traumatic stress disorder. Flashbacks can be so consuming, the person loses touch with the actual environment. Moreover, perception can be quite fuzzy at times, as when you are just waking up or about to fall asleep.

The content of the memory can sometimes indicate the past, as when you remember your childhood home or a specific past event. Your memory of breakfast is not like that. Most likely you can conjure up a conscious memory of this morning's breakfast, and chances are that the event was nothing special. I ate the same sort of bagel I often eat with the same sort of coffee out of the same mug. So what about the memory indicates that it is this morning's breakfast as opposed to an imagination of a future breakfast?

The *problem of pastness* is the difficulty of identifying what it is about conscious memory that indicates it is past. It might seem that the simple ability to rely on learned knowledge is sufficient to represent the past. If I can remember that 2 + 2 = 4, I must have learned it in the past. However, this sort of factual memory is importantly different from conscious memory. Along with skill memories like riding a bike, factual memories rely on past experience but do not *represent* past experience. When you remember facts and skills, you do not reexperience the past learning, you just use the information and ability learned. In conscious memory, by contrast, the past experience itself is an essential aspect of the memory.[3]

Bertrand Russell noticed this important difference in his distinction between perception and recollection:

> What is called perception differs from sensation by the fact that the sensational ingredients bring up habitual associates—images and expectations of their usual correlates—all of which are subjectively indistinguishable from the sensation. The FACT of past experience is essential in producing this filling-out of sensation, but not the RECOLLECTION of past experience.
>
> (Russell 1921: 107, emphasis original)

In *recollection* a "memory image" or copy of the past experience accompanies present sensation. As Russell astutely observed, the problem of pastness in recollection is that there is no necessary connection between the memory image and the past experience that it is supposed to copy. My memory of breakfast might be false, perhaps the result of hearing about someone else's breakfast or being confused about which morning is which—was the bagel today and the oatmeal yesterday, or the reverse? So Russell suggested an extra bit of glue, a belief that "this existed," where "this" is the event depicted in the image—the bagel and coffee. The conviction that the event existed is based on a feeling of pastness combined with a feeling of reality (Russell 1921: 125–6). Since your memory image is a copy of your past sensation, recollection puts you directly in touch with the event that caused the sensation you remember.[4] The belief that "this existed" adds the important element that the event is past and actually occurred.

Russell's account fits well with the familiar idea that memory transports you back to the past, because copies of sensations serve as representations of those events. Marcel Proust famously described how his memories transported him back to the town of Combray where he had spent many summer days:

> And once I had recognised the taste of the crumb of madeleine soaked in her decoction of lime-flowers which my aunt used to give me ... immediately the old grey house upon the street where her room was, rose up like the scenery of

a theatre to attach itself to the little pavilion, opening on to the garden, which had been built out behind it for my parents ... ; and with the house the town, from morning to night and in all weathers, the Square where I was sent before luncheon, the streets along which I used to run errands, the country roads we took when it was fine.

(1928: 65–6)

As vivid as Proust describes the town and his exploits there, even he admits a tenuous connection to the past, noting the fragile quality of memory, its uncertainty, and its inventiveness (Proust 1928: 63). We don't simply reproduce a past event, we construct it anew from several sources. Some bits are certainly stored, and some means of connecting elements together is needed to form a plausible representation of the past experience. As has been noted, though, a belief that "this existed" may fail to accurately represent past events.

More to the point, the belief that "this existed" does not provide much help in solving the problem of pastness. While our beliefs about past and future, reality and fiction do differ, these differences beg explanation rather than offer it. *Why* are some images accompanied by a belief that "this existed," and what determines when that belief is *appropriately* applied? What exactly is a "feeling of pastness," and how does it come to be attached to an image when and only when that image was caused by the past event it depicts?

The next section will develop the Temporal Representation Theory solution to the problem of pastness. Let me just close this section by emphasizing the constructive nature of memory. Even when a person appears to remember every single detail of a past event, this is not a guarantee of perfect memory. John Dean, former counsel to President Nixon, delivered an impressively detailed testimony of events and conversations related to the Watergate scandal. Yet when Ulrich Neisser (1981) compared Dean's testimony to tape recordings, he found that details of one event were often mistakenly attributed to another event, and some statements were conflated together. Nonetheless, the general structure of events was accurate, and the testimony appropriately represented the basic substance of each person's contribution.

The features we remember from an event do not simply replicate the past, they are constructed due to their resonance with the present situation, either in response to a cue like Proust's tea and madeleine cakes or the relevance of the past event to something happening now. Memories serve to connect us to the past, and they can do that in many ways other than recording and replaying sets of sensations.

## The Embedded Theory of Conscious Memory

Return again to your own memory. Do you feel transported into the past, as if you are experiencing the past event itself? It may be that some memories feel that way, but my memories are never that vivid. As I sit here remembering that day last summer when we built sand castles, my memory seems to bring the past into the present. Rather than traveling back in time to North Carolina in August, the bright blue sky and grainy sand become part of my experience here on this cold Pennsylvania morning. The memory cheers me up, but even if I concentrate, I don't feel the warmth of the sun on my face. The swoosh of the waves and crunch of shovel in sand accompany my visual images, and I have some vague bodily sensations of floating on the surf to ease the stiffness in my back.

My experience is that the past is included in what is happening now, which would explain both the consciousness of memory and its pastness. Since on my view consciousness is a representation of the present moment, representations of the past that are embedded *into* the representation of what is happening now must be conscious. This simple explanation of why some memories are conscious strikes me as an advantage of the Temporal Representation Theory of consciousness. To understand how pastness is explained by the theory will be more complicated.[5]

Let's start with a schema to help think about the elements in a representation of the present moment. Here I sit, firmly entrenched in the present, looking out at the cold April rain.

{now, here} → <chair, window, April, rain>

The {} brackets indicate the time and space picked out by the representation. Thus far in the book I have emphasized the role of time in a conscious representation. That is because we specify a unique spatiotemporal position by time rather than space. In reality space and time change in tandem, yet experience and action rely on relatively stable spatial positions to navigate. Time is what changes in experience. The brackets specify the position in space-time that my consciousness represents. The <> symbols mark the contents of that conscious representation. What I am conscious of now and here are the comfy warmth of my chair and the gray-white streaks gusting past the window. For simplicity, we can leave aside any further details to consider just these elements as my representation of what is happening *now*.

To include a memory in this conscious representational moment we need to embed a representation of my past experience at the beach. That is, my representation of the August day in North Carolina needs to become part of the contents of the present moment.

{now, here} → <chair, window, April, rain, [past experience]>

    where [past experience] = [{past, there} → <sand, sea, August, blue sky>]

The first line in this schema is my conscious representation of the present moment. What I am conscious of now, here is the same as it was a moment ago with the addition of my beach memory, marked by the [] brackets. On the second line, the structure of the memory has the same form as a conscious representation, since it represents my past conscious experience.[6] Where consciousness represents the present moment, memory represents a past moment with its own particular contents. The image can give you a visual sense of the overlay effect that my memories give me. Is this something like the way memory appears to you?

**Figure 5.1** Depiction of a beach memory embedded in the present rainy day. Image by Paula Droege.

Perhaps your memories are more vivid, and it seems as if you are truly reexperiencing the past event. Even in this case, you represent the memory to be happening now. You experience the memory contents (the castle, sea, sky) as present.[7] On the Temporal Representation Theory, memories are conscious when they are experienced as occurring now.

Memories remain unconscious when past experience contributes to your performance of a skill or your ability to recall a fact without being embedded in a representation of the present moment. As noted earlier, you do not need to reexperience all the past events that made it possible for you to ride a bike. Nor do you need to produce a conscious image of your classroom and grade school teacher in order to remember that $2 + 2 = 4$. If you did produce conscious memories every time you remembered something, you would have difficulty doing anything.

Jill Price suffers from something like this. The description of her hair-trigger conscious memory brings home the functional value of the limits on what and when we consciously recall the past.

> At any given moment, anything at all that someone said to me, or some hurtful or ridiculous thing that I said to someone that I desperately wish I could take back, may pop into my mind and yank me back to that difficult day and exactly how I was feeling about myself. The emotional intensity of my memories, combined with the random nature in which they're always flashing through my mind, has, on and off through the course of my life, nearly driven me mad.
>
> (2008: 38, quoted in Bernecker 2010: 2)

Because consciousness is so amazing, it may be tempting to think that more consciousness is always better. Taking function into account reveals the error in succumbing to that temptation. Later in the chapter we'll consider exactly what function conscious memory and imagination serve. At this point it is useful just to be grateful that we are often blissfully unconscious of the past and future.

## Time for a Higher-Order Explanation

Look again at the schema for conscious memory:

{now, here} → <chair, window, April, rain, [past experience]>
    where [past experience] = [{past, there} → <sand, sea, August, blue sky>]

Notice that the structure of the memory is higher-order. A *higher-order representation* is a representation that includes another representation as part of its content. It is a representation of another representation, like a picture of a picture. According to the Embedded Theory, a conscious representation includes the memory as part of its content. I am now having a representation of my past representation. Or in more familiar terms, I am remembering my past experience.

We saw above that embedding memory into a conscious representation explains why it is conscious. This structure also solves the problem of pastness. Conscious memories feel past because they are *represented as past*. Just as presence is the content of conscious representations, the past is the content of memory representations. The function of consciousness is to represent what is happening now; the function of memory is to represent what happened then. Memories can fulfill this function even when they are vague and somewhat inaccurate. I remember the beach as sunny even though most days were overcast. A bit later in the chapter we will look at how memory can represent an event despite inaccuracy. (As a hint, this is another version of the problem of error in representation considered in Chapter 1.)

Recognition of the higher-order structure of conscious memory provides a good opportunity to contrast the Temporal Representation Theory of consciousness with another prominent philosophical view. On a *Higher-Order Theory* of consciousness a mental state is conscious when there is another mental state that represents it. The intuitive idea is that a person is aware of her sensations and thoughts when they are conscious, but not aware of them when they are unconscious. David Rosenthal describes the idea this way:

> It sometimes happens that one sincerely denies being in some mental state, even though one acts in a way that makes it plain that one is in that state. One's behavior may clearly show that one thinks or desires something or that one feels happy or sad, despite one's sincere, consistent denials. The natural conclusion is that one is in that state but the state isn't conscious.
>
> (2005: 3–4)

On a higher-order theory, an unconscious state is conscious when a person has a thought or sensation about it. There are a number of different higher-order theories depending on what sort of mental state is essential for consciousness and how the higher- and lower-order states are related (Gennaro 2018; Rosenthal 2004). The prime advantage of all higher-order theories is that they utilize the basic operation of unconscious sensation or thought in explaining consciousness. Once we have an idea about how sensation and thought work, we can simply apply that process to consciousness.

To take Rosenthal's Higher-Order Thought (HOT) theory as an example, the first stage of explanation is the acquisition of a sensation or thought about something, like a tree. This mental state remains unconscious unless I have a higher-order thought that I am seeing (or thinking about) a tree. According to the HOT theory, that sensation is conscious when there is a higher-order thought about it. What it is for a person to be conscious of seeing the tree is that she has the higher-order thought that she is seeing the tree.

There are important qualifications for the particular sort of higher-order thought that is necessary for consciousness, but the details are not critical in order to compare the HOT Theory with the Temporal Representation Theory of memory.[8] I have described conscious memory as a conscious representation of the present that includes a representation of the past. I am having a mental state that is about my experience last summer at the beach. There are all sorts of memories that are not conscious; only this beach memory is conscious due to the fact that I am representing it as part of my experience now. My beach memory is conscious because it is part of a higher-order representation. So it may seem that the Higher-Order Theory is reinforced by my account of conscious memory.

In the description of my beach memory, however, both my present experience *and* my past experience are conscious. On the Temporal Representation Theory, the past experience becomes conscious by being incorporated into a conscious state. On the HOT Theory, my past experience is conscious when I have a thought about it, but that higher-order thought is not itself conscious. If a higher-order thought is what explains how another state is conscious, then the HOT could only be conscious if there is another higher-order thought (HOT2) about *it*. This would result in an infinite regress—the conscious HOT would require another yet higher-order thought (HOT3), and so on. Since HOTs are not themselves conscious, according to HOT Theory, there is no regress (Rosenthal 2005: 48).

A consequence is that the higher-order structure of conscious memory does not offer added support to HOT Theory. A HOT account can explain how a past experience becomes conscious, but it cannot explain why conscious memory includes a feeling of pastness when other conscious experiences do not. If any mental state becomes conscious when there is a HOT about it, there is no reason that my memory of last year's beach vacation should appear any different than my sensation of the tree outside my window. A HOT theorist can cite other possible explanations, but there is nothing within the structure of HOT Theory itself to account for the feeling of pastness in conscious memory.

On the Temporal Representation Theory, by contrast, the higher-order structure of conscious memory is fundamentally different from the structure of a conscious representation of the present moment. What makes an experience conscious is its collection of sensations and thoughts that represent what is happening now. A memory is conscious when past representations are included in a present conscious experience.

On the other end of the temporal continuum is the ability to imagine the future. When these experiences are conscious, they are also higher-order. The capacity to imagine one's personal future is connected neurophysiologically and theoretically to memory of one's personal past. Structurally similar brain areas are utilized in both conscious memory and conscious imagining of the future, so damage to these areas affects both capacities (Addis, Knapp, Roberts, and Schacter 2012; Addis, Pan, Vu, Laiser, and Schacter 2009; Kwan, Carson, Addis, and Rosenbaum 2010). We think of amnesia as strictly a deficit of memory, yet it is equally a deficit of personal imagination. When memory researcher Endel Tulving asked K.C., who is severely amnesic, to describe his state of mind when thinking about the future, K.C. said that it is "blank." "Indeed, when asked to compare the two kinds of blankness, one of the past and the other of the future, he said that they are 'the same kind of blankness'" (Tulving 2005: 28).

The neural connection between past and future is related to the theoretical connection. Throughout this book I have emphasized the importance of function. To understand the mind, including consciousness, we need to understand its function in contributing to survival. On the Temporal Representation Theory, the function of consciousness is to represent what is happening now so as to determine the best action toward accomplishing goals. Consciousness becomes necessary when an animal is capable of switching direction or switching goals by evaluating how things are now. By considering the function of conscious memory, we can likewise gain insight into why it is advantageous, how it fails, and how it is connected to imagination.

## Extending One's Self in Time

In addition to conscious memory and imagination, introspection is another important type of higher-order state. As the name suggests, introspection is a looking inside, a way of identifying our own thoughts and feelings so as to better understand ourselves. Nicholas Humphrey (1983) has offered a just-so story about how these higher-order capacities might have originated.

In the beginning there were creatures capable of sensation and intelligent action, but without the ability to monitor their own mental states. Over the course of time some of these creatures discovered that forming social groups could be useful in defending themselves against predators, finding food, and generally having fun. One problem with being social, though, is that other creatures can be unpredictable. Suddenly one guy gets angry or another starts acting silly, and it is hard to understand why. To try to reduce some of this uncertainty, some of the creatures started to keep track of how different members of the group responded to different events in order to better anticipate what causes would bring on what sort of behavior from whom. After a while these clever creatures—which Humphrey calls 'nature's psychologists'—realized they could apply these same tracking abilities to their own reactions in order to understand themselves better.[9]

Just-so stories like this cannot be definitively proven; their value is in piecing together what we do know in a way that makes sense. The basic connection between social interaction and mind-reading skills is fairly well-established, although theorists disagree about *how* social interaction drives us to learn to interpret the minds of others (Goldman 2006). Humphrey's suggestion that we come to interpret ourselves as a result of understanding others is more controversial. A primary reason that explaining consciousness is so difficult is that we feel like we know our own minds better than anyone else does and better than we know anything else. Descartes' famous dictum *cogito ergo sum*, I think therefore I am, is compelling. I am my mind, my knowledge of my mind is the most certain knowledge I have. Humphrey's story and all of developmental psychology run counter to this intuition (Gopnik 1993).

This counter-narrative is that we are born oriented to the world, not ourselves, and other people are an important part of the world. So we come to learn about people and how they differ from things like stones and trees. Eventually, our interactions with other people push us to reflect on our own minds. Whether that process is a kind of inference from the minds of others or an exclusively inner developmental process, the reason to develop the capacity for introspection is social. A person needs to be able to manage her own thoughts and feelings in order to function in the context of a group.[10] The desert island dweller has no use for self-reflection, because there is no value in keeping track of her own states. Without an Other to react well or badly as a consequence of a happy smile or angry outburst, there is no need to regulate the thoughts and feelings that generate these behaviors. All she needs to do is act appropriately in relation to her mental states, to run when afraid, to relax when content; she does not need to represent her states as well. In a social environment, on the other hand, that angry outburst might have severe consequences. The capacity to reflect on her feelings can help a person control them and the actions that result from them.

Conscious memory and imagination are essential to both self-understanding and control. Remembering how hurt my friend was last week when I yelled at her can help me respond differently in the future. The conscious memory adds vividness and detail to the emotional valence, so the next decision to respond either by yelling or by restraint becomes weighted toward restraint. Given the complexity of human social interactions, natural selection would not likely favor fixed mechanisms for calculating fitness benefits. Instead, adaptive behavior is shaped by revisable concepts and motivations that tend to increase value (Boyer 2008). More fundamental than this pragmatic control function, conscious memory and imagination serve to connect experiences in the present with those in the past and future. On the Embedded Theory, past and future experiences are incorporated into a representation of the present. A single conscious memory, for example, includes representations of both present and past or future events, generating a link between experiences represented as occurring at different times.

The temporal connection of experiences from past to present to future extends the self I am right now to form a continuous self as the bearer of a relatively consistent set of experiences over time. The idea that memory is the glue that binds experiences together into a self was defended most forcefully by John Locke: "as far as this consciousness can be extended backwards to any past Action or Thought, so far reaches the Identity of that *Person*; it is the same *self* now it was then; and 'tis by the same *self* with the present one that now reflects on it, that that Action was done" (Locke 1689: Book II, Ch 27, §9).

Because my consciousness now includes a consciousness of the past, the two experiences can be attributed to the same person. The immediacy of conscious recollection supplies what William James called the "warmth" that constitutes the feeling of self. "Remembrance is like direct feeling; its object is suffused with a warmth and intimacy to which no object of mere conception ever attains" (1892: 158). Yet there are well-known problems with Locke's view that the self is composed *only* of experiences one can consciously remember. I don't remember when I was born, for example, but I do think that early part of my life is still mine, part of my self. Even more problematic for Locke's view, I regularly forget and reinterpret past experiences. Nonetheless, I remain the same person despite these changes.

On the other hand, the self cannot survive with no conscious memory or imagination at all. A tragic consequence of alcohol abuse is sometimes the onset of a chronic memory disorder known as Korsakoff's syndrome. Neurologist Oliver Sacks (1970) describes a particularly severe case of a man with retrograde and anterograde amnesia; that is, he cannot remember his past experiences and cannot form new memories. As a result, Mr. Thompson is confined to the present, even though he retains his knowledge of people and places from the past. Without conscious memory to form the sense of a life, Mr. Thompson is driven to confabulate a narrative in a desperate attempt to interpret an otherwise meaningless series of events. Sacks describes the case as a loss of "inner drama": "To be ourselves we must *have* ourselves—possess, if need be re-possess, our life-stories. We must 'recollect' ourselves, recollect the inner drama, the narrative, of ourselves. A man *needs* such a narrative, a continuous inner narrative to maintain his identity, his self" (Sacks 1970: 111).

Conscious memory supplies the experiential thread that strings the pearls of a life into the strand of a self. Without the conscious experience of one's past and future, information about oneself forms at best an inferential, third-person self. My parents told me that I was born in Chicago, but that part of my remembered self is an abstract part of my story. I know about my early life in the same way I know about lives of others, as a story that narrates a character. The "warmth" that James felt as essential to the self is missing without the conscious representation of time provided by my other conscious memories. Both sorts of memory are important to the story of my self. Locke's reliance solely on conscious memory is inadequate to maintain a stable identity given the gaps and shifts in conscious recollection. Nonetheless, conscious memory and imagination extend my experienced sense of myself backward and forward in time, animating the narrative elements with self-conscious identification and thereby making the story truly my own.

## To Err is Human

If the function of conscious memory is to provide an experiential connection between a present self and its past self, then memories only need to be accurate enough to serve this function. The goal is not to copy the past but to represent it in a way that is useful. As it happens, one of the ways memory is most useful is when it is accurate about how things were in the past. Remembering my friend's reaction last week will help me respond most effectively if my memory about that event is correct, at least for the most part.

One reason conscious memory and imagination utilize the same brain areas is that both processes involve constructing experiences from remembered elements (Addis et al. 2009). Memory does not record and replay past experiences, it creates them in much the same way as imagination creates new possible experiences. The difference is that memory aims toward the past while imagination aims toward the future, and those temporally opposing aims result in very different sorts of constructions.

Aiming backward, memory needs to construct experiences that form a stable narrative identity. Most often, stability is grounded in truth. Even if I'd like to remember myself as virtuous and successful and well-loved, that fantasy would not be of much use in daily life where I struggle to do the right thing, toil at my mediocre job, and face occasional rejection. Better to remember the bad and the good, roughly in the way it happened, so as to know how I fit into the world. In fact, people tend to remember bad things more often than good ones, possibly to avoid repeating past mistakes (Kensinger 2007). Overall, there is good reason to believe that memory is reliable in representing our past experiences in basically the way they occurred (Michaelian 2016).

Even so, everyone misremembers. I vividly remember attending a friend's birthday party, but I wasn't even there. The combination of photos and stories about the event made such a strong impression on me that I constructed a conscious memory of my own participation. This sort of wholesale confabulation is rare; everyday reconstructions involve minor changes like confusing the time order of events or conflating two similar events together. So long as the gist of the past experience is correct, memory can fudge the details and still do its job.

Even serious lapses are not problematic if the rememberer accepts correction when it is offered. Confabulated memory becomes pathological when the person persists in holding her own interpretation of the past in the face of contradictory facts and reports from others that counter her own (Droege 2015). Recall Humphrey's point that a central function of the temporally extended self formed by conscious memory is to aid in social interactions. I remember how things transpired in the past to better deal with people in the future. To be effective, my memory needs to be reasonably accurate about myself and about others. So if I maintain a grossly inaccurate memory, I disrupt my ability to deal with others and, critically, their ability to deal with me. My friends and family cannot rely on me if I entirely invent my past and refuse to accept any other version of events.

My own telling of the story of my self is continually in conversation with the stories others tell about me. As we all change over time, the stories we tell change accordingly to make sense of the course of events. Formerly prominent memories fade into obscurity and once-forgotten experiences gain new salience. An event that seemed disastrous can be reinterpreted in light of its positive consequences, or an action that seemed like the right thing to do at the time is later cause for regret. While our memories are grounded in evidence of the actual course of events, the significance of those events shifts over time, and our stories of ourselves shift as well.

These shifts are a very good thing, as we will see in the next chapter. The possibility of change as a result of reevaluating our selves, our beliefs, our values, is the source of a realistic, physics-compatible free will. Rather than think of freedom as a choice that breaks with history and material causes, I will suggest we embrace our history, in the form of our memories, and reflect on ways to better realize past achievements and improve upon past failures. Free will is the invaluable result of our capacity for memory and introspection.

## What about Goldie?

My dog Goldie is a beautiful mutt of indeterminate heritage. She is smart, obedient when it suits her, and affectionate to everyone but the mail carrier. Does Goldie remember me when I go away? Does she imagine how wonderful it would be to catch one of those squirrels that heckle her from the tree? The debate about animal memory has been a hot topic since researchers demonstrated that scrub jays can keep track of where and when they cached different types of food (Clayton and Dickinson 1998). If allowed to retrieve their cache after a short time, the jays will retrieve the tasty worms. If it's been a few days, however, they will choose to retrieve the longer-lasting albeit less tasty peanut cache. Since these birds can remember when they cached these different sorts of food, does this mean they have conscious memory?

I have argued that it does not (Droege 2012). The behavior definitely demonstrates flexibility and thereby provides evidence for consciousness (see Chapter 4), but more is required to demonstrate conscious memory. On the Embedded Theory, conscious memory involves a capacity to consciously represent a past experience. So evidence of higher-order representation is required to demonstrate conscious memory.

Further research with scrub jays does suggest they might have this more sophisticated capacity (Emery and Clayton 2001). When scrub jays have had the experience of stealing another bird's cache, they will re-cache their own food whenever another bird has observed their cache location. Scrub jays that have never stolen food do not exhibit this behavior, even when they have watched other birds cache food and when other birds have watched them.

Imagine the mental process that might motivate the scrub jays to move their food cache. First, the bird draws on its own experiences as a thief to recognize the value of thievery, and transfers this insight to other birds. Further, the scrub jay realizes that when another bird has seen the location of its cache, that bird could return to steal the food. Most significantly, the jay thwarts the potential thief by moving the food, so the other bird now has a false representation of where the food is located. If this description is correct—which it may not be, since each element is controversial—then the scrub jay utilizes higher-order representations to deceive other birds.

Even conceding the possibility of higher-order representation, the capacity for conscious memory and imagination may require additional mental abilities. Humphrey's just-so story provides a social motivation for keeping track of our selves in time, but it does not give a full explanation. We need to keep thinking about how conscious memory functions and how it relates to other higher-order representational abilities like linguistic self-reference and false belief. Although these higher-order capacities develop together in humans, animals may be capable of one or another ability without being capable of them all.

No animal exhibits the communicative complexity of human language, and theories vary about the relation between complex thought and the evolution of language (Corballis 2017). Conscious memory may require language, or social interaction may be sufficient, as with deception. As argued earlier, the ability to keep track of oneself and others in time clearly serves a social function, suggesting it could develop with similar socially useful capacities such as deception. On the other hand, a representation of past events as past requires a concept of linear time that organizes events in a rough sequence. While my memory may be sketchy about exactly when I took that trip to the Grand Canyon in my youth, the event is definitely earlier than the trip to Maine, and both trips occurred before I went to college. This autobiographical timeline may require language to solidify the concepts of individual events in sequential order. If so, then conscious memory is a more sophisticated capacity than deception or even introspection.

The takeaway from this chapter is that questions about conscious memory are best addressed by looking for biological function and then figuring out how that function is performed. I have argued that conscious memory represents a person's past experiences in order to tell a story of her self. That story also projects forward by imagining future experiences. Past and future are represented as part of the present, giving the story an immediacy and sense of personal ownership that is missing from stories told by others. My conscious memories feel like *mine*; they form the foundation of my self on which other information about me rests. Even though my story, and my memories, change over time in response to conflicting accounts, my sense of a self extended in time depends on bringing past and future experiences into the present moment, into consciousness.

# How Free Are We?

*My first act of free will shall be to believe in free will.*

William James, Letters

"Free will has been debated since the beginning of time." This canard of introductory philosophy essays is all I had written after staring at a blank page and dreading the fast-approaching end of summer. So I adopted another trick of introductory philosophy students and googled "free will." Following the usual definitions and a Wikipedia article, I found an essay by Stephen Cave (2016) in *The Atlantic*: "The sciences have grown steadily bolder in their claim that all human behavior can be explained through the clockwork laws of cause and effect. This shift in perception is the continuation of an intellectual revolution that began about 150 years ago, when Charles Darwin first published *On the Origin of Species*." If Cave is right,[1] everything I have said so far about materialism and the importance of biological function in understanding the mind implies that we have no free will. Our actions are governed by "clockwork laws." Cave's article jolted me out of my writer's block by reminding me how common and how misguided this view is.

Free will is not undermined by the recognition that the mind is material. Quite the opposite, this chapter will argue, free will is enhanced by an understanding of material causal forces. The better we understand how we function and fail to function in the world, the more control we can exercise over our future interactions. The oft-repeated claim that free will is an illusion stems from a faulty idea about the role of the conscious mind in decision-making. We imagine we can choose ex nihilo whether to resist that chocolate cake or succumb to the temptations of its delicious evil. We can't. A good mind, like a good body, requires training. The true power of free will lies in how we think about our past and future selves to develop available mental and physical skills to become the sort of person we want to be.

# The Classic Problem

*Determinism*[2] is the philosophical view that all events, including human actions, are fully specified by the original conditions at the Big Bang and the laws of physics.[3] This view of universal causal determination means that every event, including my decision to have a bagel for breakfast, necessarily happened in the exact order that it happened. A consequence of Determinism is that there is no possibility that I might have chosen granola instead.

There are two traditional responses to Determinism. First, *Incompatibilism* is the immediately obvious position that Determinism rules out free will. For incompatibilists, free will is a choice that falls outside universal determinism. *Libertarians* are incompatibilists who believe that free will nonetheless exists; conscious decisions can intervene in the causal order by means of some mysterious mental force, perhaps connected to a fundamental indeterminacy at the quantum level of reality (Robinson 2012). At breakfast this morning I could have disrupted the physical causal order and chosen granola instead of the bagel by consciously willing to eat one rather than the other.

*Hard determinists* are also incompatibilists, but they believe free will does not exist. Indeterminism, quantum or otherwise, is simply randomness, not free will. If my action fails to be governed by the physical causal laws that determine all physical effects, hard determinists say, then that action is arbitrary, not the result of a free choice. The conscious feeling we have of choosing what to eat, whom to marry, where to live is all an illusion. Adopting this illusion might be a useful fiction in order to give people a sense of self-control and to maintain social order (Smilansky 2000). Nonetheless, all our actions are caused by physical forces beyond our control.

A less obvious but more palatable response to Determinism is to view it as consistent with free will. *Compatibilism* rejects the idea that free will intervenes in the causal order. According to compatibilists, any action based on our beliefs and desires, that is not either restrained or coerced, counts as free. Even though physical causal laws have determined since the Big Bang that I would eat a bagel this morning, that choice was still free, according to compatibilists. No one forced me to eat the bagel, it was what I wanted, and I was satisfied. Moreover, there is no way for me or others to know what I will choose at any given future moment. Too many microphysical interactions are occurring every microsecond for anyone but an omniscient mind to be able to calculate exactly what events will take place in the future. Consequently, we all inevitably think of the future as open, deliberating breakfast and career choices as if anything might happen.

Since we cannot know what will happen, it is appropriate (and unavoidable) to make decisions in just the same way we would if the outcome were not already fixed by causal law.

Compatibilism has the twin virtues of preserving the sense of our selves as agents in control of our actions while acknowledging the physical reality of the causal context of our decisions. Even so, I find Compatibilism unsatisfying. My ability to choose my own future still seems illusory if that future is already determined. While it's great that my beliefs and desires are part of the causal force that brings about my behavior, those beliefs and desires also were determined to be what they are. So long as every event is fixed from the beginning of time, there is no possibility for me to truly change my future. Things will necessarily unfold in the way determined by the Big Bang.

My response to this brief trip down the rabbit hole of the free will/determinism debate is to reject the terms. Both incompatibilists and compatibilists accept that physical causation is subject to universal determinism, and they disagree only on whether and what kind of free will we might have as a result. But physics does not demand a binary choice between determinism and randomness. Physical causation is multilayered and its dynamic interactions continue to surprise. I suggest that this interactive way to view causation is more productive than strict Determinism.

The philosopher's job is not to dictate the terms of scientific investigation into causal processes. What we can do is to articulate possibilities that integrate considerations from disparate sources, such as ethics, psychology, motor control theory, and consciousness studies. My goal in this chapter is to articulate the possibility that free will is part of the physical causal world, not as a cog in the relentless machinery of Determinism, but as one of the many interacting causal forces that change the course of events over time. The next section will describe a way of thinking about causation as probabilistic rather than determined, dynamic rather than hierarchical. The following section will show how free will fits into this reframed causal order.

## Causation under Control

Universal determinism is a theoretical posit, a hold-over from the heyday of Newtonian physics in the seventeenth and eighteenth centuries. This was an age when the powers of God, logic, and the forces of nature battled for control over the sublime mind. The great philosophers of the day—Spinoza, Leibniz,

Kant, Hegel—took turns grappling with the necessities of universal religious and moral law in competition with universal natural law. Each of these philosophers developed ingenious systems to reconcile the world of reason with the world of causation in an attempt to carve out some form of free will as the ground of human action and moral responsibility.

Then in the early twentieth century, Albert Einstein threw a quantum wrench in the clockwork of natural law. Underlying the apparently unexceptioned regulation of Newtonian physics is the probabilistic churning of quantum mechanics. According to Einstein, swirls of subatomic particles interact with one another according to a non-deterministic yet statistically calculable probability function.

Though physicists don't have a fully worked out theory about the relation between quantum physics and Newtonian physics, it is important to note that Newton's laws still hold at the macro level. Objects in motion remain in motion. Force still equals mass times acceleration. For every action, there is an equal and opposite reaction. Engineers are well-advised to build their buildings and airplanes with these laws in mind. Quantum physics does not overturn Newtonian physics; it overturns universal determinism. Or at least it opens up the possibility that causation is ultimately probabilistic rather than deterministic.[4]

Determinism might be true, in which case free will is an illusion, and we just have to live with that, one way or another. My point is that evidence from physics does not compel us to decide for deterministic and against probabilistic causation. Both views are consistent with all the facts and the basics of physical theory. Everyone agrees that physical interactions cause change and that change follows an arrow of time—causes precede effects, never the other way around. The only question is whether those changes are determined from the Big Bang or whether there is wiggle room in the course of events due to the probabilistic interactions of subatomic particles over time.

I am in favor of wiggle room. Thinking of causation as probabilistic is best suited to address the forms of change a mind needs to understand and control. Climate change, for example, is the result of the ongoing dynamics of the excavation and use of fossil fuels, the depletion of forests, and the intricate web of environmental relationships among temperature rise, polar ice melt, sea level, and extreme weather. The multitude of events involved in climate change means that scientific theories rely on statistical models to understand its causes and consequences. These models are critical to proposals for reducing the carbon dioxide that is driving climate change and for mitigating the damage that has already been done.

Statistical models are also essential to understanding how the interactions between genes and environment lead to differential health outcomes. The deterministic picture of genetics as a blueprint for development has been replaced by probabilistic models of epigenetic evolution. In the same way that Newton's laws structure physical causation at a macro level, genes form the biological structure of an organism. Yet that structure is not fixed. Over time, genetic processes are modified by innumerable influences such as nutrition, stress, pollution, exercise, social relationships, and so on. Even though headlines continue to announce the discovery of a gene for cancer or alcoholism, careful attention to the actual scientific results shows that the presence of particular genes increases the risk of health problems but rarely determines them with 100 percent certainty.

The upshot of these considerations about probability is that an understanding of causal interactions is a means to gain control over the future. What science tells us is that given particular conditions, the probability of particular results can be calculated. Particular changes in conditions lead to particular changes in probabilities. These calculations are not always correct; science doesn't yet have all the answers. But where we do have good evidence of cause and effect, the information is empowering, not paralyzing. Data on the spread of infectious disease can recommend best practices for hygiene and quarantine precautions. Analysis of climate change can mobilize global cooperation to reduce carbon emissions (we hope). By taking the long view offered by the statistics of large populations, we gain more effective means of creating a desirable future.

## A Will Worth Wanting

An understanding of probabilistic causal relations is also a means of gaining control over our personal futures. On the classic determinist view of causation, advocates of free will are forced to squeeze self-control into the machinery of history. Either free will is a magical intervention of conscious decision weight the scales of quantum indeterminacy, as the libertarian proposes. Or decisions are part of the causal process determined from the beginning of time, as the hard determinist and compatibilist suggest. Probabilistic causation offers an alternative option: beliefs and desires are part of a vast dynamic neural network that can alter itself by means of self-reflection.[5]

To better see how these traditional options structure the contemporary debate, I'll look at how the Libertarian view of free will has been challenged by evidence from neuroscience. Though it is popular among neuroscientists to conclude that free will is an illusion, I think the results point to the opposite conclusion. Free will is embodied in the physical interactions that constitute our sense of our selves over time.

Just as the problem with Determinism is a faulty view of physical causation, the problem with Libertarian free will is a faulty view of the mind. On this view, an action is freely willed only if conscious decision intervenes at a particular point in the causal order. Various events happen in the world that require a decision: you are graduating from college, you need to order dinner at a restaurant, you want to cheat on your lover. These events form the input to the mind where conscious deliberation takes place. Your conscious mind weighs pros and cons, takes into account your beliefs and values, and comes to a decision. Once this conscious decision takes place, an order for action is sent to the body to implement. You take steps to fill out job applications, tell the server you'll have spaghetti, agree to an adulterous tryst.

Neuroscientists have adopted this picture in their research on free will in the brain. Their assumption is that conscious decision must come *before* brain activity initiates action in order to be free. On this way of thinking, free will requires that you feel yourself making a decision, this feeling causes your brain activity, and your brain activity causes your action.

In opposition to this picture, evidence suggests that the brain activity that initiates action begins *before* conscious decision. A famous and controversial experiment by Benjamin Libet (1983) measured the onset of motor cortex activity prior to a hand movement, and compared that time with the time subjects report consciously deciding to move their hand. Libet discovered that the brain activity began a half second prior to the conscious decision. So the actual order is: brain activity, then the feeling of deciding, then the hand movement. If free will requires that the conscious feeling of willing to move your hand must occur before brain activity initiates movement, then the Libet result shows free will is an illusion.

Note that this conclusion follows even on my probabilistic version of physical causation. The problem here is not that the action has been determined since the beginning of time; the problem is that the action has been determined by the brain instead of conscious decision. Because free will is limited to the direct causal power of the conscious feeling of willing, on this view, brain activity prior to conscious decision pre-empts free will. If the conscious feeling of will has no power to directly cause action, the conclusion must be that free will is illusory.

As with determinist causation, the solution is to throw out this definition of free will and reconsider the role consciousness plays in decision-making. This book proposes that consciousness represents the present moment in order to track progress toward goals. As discussed in Chapter 3, what is represented as *now* is actually a rough estimate of current events based on available input ±100 ms from the time of the representation vehicle. Since that input took time to process from the stimulus source through the sensory system to whatever global brain process constitutes consciousness, the representation of *now* lags a bit behind the event at the source.

Consequently, it is not surprising to find neuroscientific evidence that consciousness is too late to be effective in direct control of immediate action. The basic processes of action and decision are unconscious, as reviewed in Chapter 2. The job of consciousness is not to micromanage—or even manage— the complex processes that run our daily lives. Consciousness simply keeps track of what is happening now to supply the rest of the system with the information needed to function properly.

So, here comes the part that will probably be the hardest to accept. You are the whole system. You (and your free will) are not limited to your consciousness; you include much, much more than that. To begin, when the unconscious decision-making processes of your brain come up with a conclusion, *you* made that decision. When your unconscious action-generating processes swing a tennis racquet and hit a sweet drop in back court, *you* deserve to be awarded the point. You are your brain. You are your body. Free will should not be restricted to actions directly caused by consciousness. Free will includes all actions attributed to your self (more will be said later about this mysterious entity). A will worth wanting is one that causes your actions to conform to your beliefs and values. Restricting free will to the direct control of consciousness over immediate action completely obscures the potential of free will to control the direction of your future self.

## Who Am I?

Wait a minute, you say. How can I control my future if all my decisions and actions are generated by unconscious processes? Even if I am my brain and body, where does the control come in? To answer these questions, recall the role of memory and imagination in producing a story of the self, described in Chapter 5. The ability to extend consciousness in time means that imagined future events can be part of the decision-making equation that determines action.

To have control over the future requires the capacity to reflect on the past. Humans can remember the consequences of their past actions and compare them with one another to assess which actions were better or worse, all things considered. We can think about whether actions conform to our beliefs and values, whether decisions are reasonable, whether strategies for change are effective. All of these reflections feed into the unconscious decision-making system that calculates the best response to life's ongoing challenges (Proust 2014).

Who I am, then, is in good part who I think I am. The story I tell myself about my past and future is the basis of my capacity to create the future I want for myself. Obviously, there are limits. If my own story about my past deviates too widely from the story others tell, then I am either lying or delusional. The same holds for my future projects; if my imagined prospects are unrealistic, they will fail to materialize.

The most important limit on my story is my causal history. Not only does my story need to be true enough to actual events to be an effective guide to action, the way I think about the past and the future and everything else has been shaped by my causal interactions with the world. As we saw in Chapter 1, a mind is a device for representation. It functions to aid me in navigating my environment. My cup representation means "cup," because this representation has been successful in my past interactions with cups. I speak English with a Midwest accent, because I grew up in Indiana. The fact that my father was a college professor was undoubtedly a causal factor in my eventual choice to pursue the same career.

Two of the titles in this chapter were caused by my reading of other sources: *How free are you?* is the title of a book by Ted Honderich, and "The varieties of free will worth wanting" is the subtitle of Daniel Dennett's book *Elbow room*. When I originally came up with these titles, I didn't recall their causal history. Only after writing the chapter did I notice my unintentional plagiarism. Since I have been reading about free will and determinism for years, I undoubtedly ran across the titles in the past. This unconscious reproduction nicely illustrates the way we are influenced by events even when we are not aware of that influence.

All our ideas and actions have a causal history. They are part of the physical causal flux that is reality. Far from dooming us to life as a cog in the wheel of history, this fact reveals how our ideas can actually change history. Think about that phrase, "change history." We change history by doing things today that are influential in producing the future. Free will does not require that we disavow the causal antecedents of our actions, it involves leveraging those influences to provide sufficient torque to sway the course of events.

## The Causes Lie in the Future

When I was originally trying to work through these ideas (Droege 2010), I was in the lucky position of Visiting Lecturer at the Humboldt University in Berlin, Germany. A friend recommended a new exhibit on the work of Joseph Beuys at the nearby Hamburger Bahnhof Museum für Gegenwart.[6] Beuys was a mid-twentieth-century German artist in the avant-garde art movement. As I began to browse and read about the art, I became intrigued by the resonance between Beuys' view of creativity and my own thoughts on free will.

Beuys considered art to be an expression of the creative power to overcome dualisms such as mind/matter, individual/social, humanity/nature, poverty/wealth. He believed that the physical environment impels the production of meaning. In order to live, everyone must create a world with a safe place to sleep, food to eat, a community to share life's burdens and joys. With the slogan, "everyone is an artist," Beuys opened the concept of art to include all of the ways we participate in the processes of change and transformation that occur each day. "If creativity relates to the transformation, change, and development of the substance, then it can be applied to everything in the world, and is no longer restricted to art" (quoted in Tisdall 1979: 10).

The interaction of mind and body in creative activity has the power to organize spiritual and physical forces toward a better future. Thinking, for Beuys, structures the energy of things into patterns. "When I speak about thinking I mean it as **form**. Ideas should be considered in the way the artist considers sculpture: to seek for the forms created by **thinking**" (quoted in Tisdall 1979: 20, emphasis original). Beuys considered his work to be "social sculpture" and encouraged everyone to adopt this view as well. In the catalogue introduction for his 1979 Guggenheim exhibition, one of his last and most famous exhibits, Beuys dramatically draws the connection between thoughts and things:

> My objects are to be seen as stimulants for the transformation of the idea of sculpture, or of art in general. They should provoke thoughts about what sculpture **can** be and how the concept of sculpting can be extended to the invisible materials used by everyone:

| | |
|---|---|
| **Thinking Forms—** | how we mould our thoughts or |
| **Spoken Forms—** | how we shape our thoughts into words or |
| **SOCIAL SCULPTURE—** | how we mould and shape the world in which we live: |

**Sculpture as an
evolutionary process;
everyone is an artist.**

That is why the nature of my sculpture is not fixed and finished. Processes
continue in most of them: chemical reactions, fermentations, colour changes,
decay, drying up. Everything is in a **state of change**. (quoted in Tisdall 1979: 7,
emphasis original)

The processes of nature are shaped by human thought, not by opposing mind
and matter, but by recognizing that mind is one of the material processes of
evolution. Thought provides a means of creating the future by recognizing and
sculpting physical interactions.

My title for this section, "The causes lie in the future," is from Lukas
Beckmann's chapter in *Joseph Beuys: Mapping the Legacy* (2001). Beckmann
traces the history of Beuys' activism on environmental, economic, and social
justice issues. The source of hope for progress toward a sustainable and just
society, according to Beuys, is the human ability to conceive it. As Beckmann
explains, thought inverts the rule that a cause must be in the past. If we have a
goal, pursue an end, the effect influences the cause. That is how human activity
works. The human being performs an action that he has envisioned. From this
envisioned future, he causes it to happen. How else, Beuys asked, could the
future be created at all? (Beckmann 2001: 111)

Thoughts cause the realization of goals by operating within the causal order,
drawing on past influences to effect future outcomes. Our ideas do not come
out of thin consciousness; their history is the foundation for our knowledge of
how to bring about our goals. Who we are, what we create, and what we value
are woven into the fabric of our physical and social reality. Artists develop
their skills through years of training and their vision in the context of a culture
of art. Using a format borrowed from Beuys, Peter Davies colorfully connects
artists, materials, and ideas that he suggests is art history "as close to science
as it gets."[7]

Art is not opposed to science; free will is not opposed to physical causation.
By reflecting on past interconnections among things, we can determine the
most effective means to bring about the sorts of things we desire and avoid
the things we dread. Art contributes to this process by opening thought to
possible connections that might otherwise have been overlooked. It also allows
us to explore possible futures through imagination that can serve as models or
cautionary tales.

## The Moral of the Story

What I am suggesting is that the story we tell ourselves about our selves through memory and imagination is the source of free will. An understanding of the causal forces, both mental and physical, individual and social, gives us the capacity to create the future out of the material of the past and present. An understanding of causality also reveals the constraints on our capacity to create the future. The tendency of both advocates and opponents of Materialism is to focus on these constraints. In his book *Incognito: The secret lives of the brain*, David Eagleman reviews all the ways that human behavior can be traced to biological function: brain damage, neurochemistry, hormones, bacteria and viruses, genes. Given these causal influences, Eagleman concludes that "criminals should always be treated as if incapable of acting otherwise ... So culpability appears to be the *wrong question to ask*" (Eagleman 2012: 177, emphasis original). Instead of asking whether a person is to blame for committing a crime, Eagleman proposes the correct legal question is what can be done to prevent crimes in the future. In some cases punishment might have the right causal effect, in others drug treatment is appropriate, and in a few cases of severe psychopathy, a life sentence may be the only way to protect society.

While I agree with Eagleman's recommendation of a forward-looking legal system, it rests on an inconsistent position. If none of us is capable of acting otherwise, how could we choose to change the legal system? Presumably the causal process of reading Eagleman's book and reflecting on the material basis of thought and action results in a new way of thinking about crime and punishment. The ideas in the book are part of the causal process of social change. This is a reasonable assumption, but it runs counter to the claim that criminals are incapable of altering their actions. If external ideas like reading a book can have causal force, there is good reason to think internal ideas can be causally effective as well. Given that the mind is material, our own ideas should be able to affect our own future as much as or more than the ideas of others.

This means that the question of culpability—and morality in general—is entirely appropriate. We simply need to widen our view of the time course and form of responsibility. First, the timing of self-control is a life-long process, not an instant of conscious decision. Consciousness plays a role in attending to the results of actions, thereby initiating self-conscious reflection of factors that bring about wonderfully good or terribly bad outcomes. By means of this sort of reflection, actions with positive consequences become more likely and actions with negative consequences become less likely. The neural process of reflective reasoning is fundamentally the same as classic pleasure/pain conditioning except that the moral evaluation of good and bad generates the relevant changes in the brain (Doris 2018).

Second, the form of responsibility shifts away from an assessment of conscious intent as the immediate cause of action. A person's entire history should figure in the assignment of blame. Of particular concern is whether a person was given the resources to develop the skills necessary for self-reflection and self-control. *Agency* and *autonomy* are terms often used to characterize a person's ability to act within the context of environmental forces. By talking about agency instead of free will, the aim is to avoid the classic opposition with Determinism. Since my goal is to reframe both concepts of free will and determinism, I will use "agency," "autonomy," and "free will" interchangeably.

Most human brains have the capacity for autonomous decision and action, but like all capacities, the proper conditions are required for its development. From the very beginning of life, sufficient food, adequate health care, and a safe place to live are minimum conditions for the brain and body to thrive. In addition to the basic biological requirements for development, a person needs to learn how to think about her self and her capacities. A public education should include instruction in self-reflection and critical thinking skills to give students a sense of how they fit into the world. Reading novels can help them imagine the world from different perspectives as well as imagine entirely different worlds. The study of science offers insight into the natural processes of the environment and how causes of various kinds generate their effects. Finally, the most obvious condition for autonomy is the ability to act. All the skill in the world amounts to nothing if that skill cannot be put to use. The availability of jobs that pay a living wage and safe, affordable childcare are a couple of the resources that allow people to exercise control over their lives and to plan for their future.

In other words, true freedom is not independence from the forces of causation and other people. We all depend on one another to provide the conditions for the development and exercise of our agency. True freedom is the power to act in a way that is responsive to and responsible for the well-being of our selves and our world.[8]

## How Free Are We?

Here at the end of the chapter it seems appropriate to return to the causal force that propelled me forward at the beginning. In another article on free will,

Stephen Cave (2015) answers the question "how free are we?" with a numerical scale he calls "The Freedom Quotient." Cave describes various skills that give animals the capacity to decide what food to eat, when and how to escape a predator, which behavior is appropriate with friends, lovers, and leaders. Animals, including humans, have evolved "an entirely natural free will, one that we need precisely because we are not rocks. We are complex organisms actively pursuing our interests in a changing environment."[9]

The Freedom Quotient scale fits nicely with the conditions for autonomy I described in the previous section. First, a capacity to generate options is important. Without at least two possible choices, there is no decision and no free will. More options are generally better, though there is a point where more choices simply overwhelm—how many cereal options does a person really want? Especially useful is the capacity to construct options that are not immediately obvious. By attending to and rearranging the particular variables in a situation, new ways to resolve conflicts can be discovered. The tendency toward dualist opposition extends well beyond the mind-body problem to frame nearly every decision we make: public or private school, Democrat or Republican, vanilla or chocolate. Whether it is because humans have two hands or because the philosophical/political culture of debate trains us to think oppositionally, we often have a hard time thinking of more than two options. We would more successfully maximize our interests and navigate a complex environment if we developed our capacity to think beyond two.

The second variable in Cave's Freedom Quotient is the ability to make meaningful choices among the options we have. Finding the best course of action requires skills such as reflection on our beliefs and values, empathy for others, understanding of consequences, ability to gather and assess relevant information. Skills such as these form the core of *autonomy competency*, the ability to act in ways that satisfy our needs and desires. This is not to say that acting autonomously is selfish. Evolutionary psychology has shown that social animals both need and desire to be part of a group. Good decision-making involves considering others in the group as well as oneself. Prosocial behavior is evolutionarily valuable for the species, and usually for the individual as well. The tit-for-tat strategy—variously configured as the Golden Rule, karma, what goes around comes around—is a good way to ensure that I'll get help when I need it, since I've been helpful to others in the past.

One significant difference between the sorts of autonomy skills found in many animals and human decision-making is the capacity for self-conscious reflection. Because humans have language, the capacity for abstract reasoning, and an extended sense of self,[10] we have the unique ability to formulate moral principles and evaluate actions by means of moral judgment. As discussed earlier, conscious memories of negative and positive consequences of action provide a kind of biofeedback effect to influence the likelihood of similar actions in the future. When things go dreadfully wrong or delightfully right, reflecting on the reasons for the outcome boosts the chances that better decisions will be made in the future. This sort of reflection can only be done self-consciously, showing that consciousness is indeed important to free will even if it is not a micro-manager of action.

Finally, the third variable in the Freedom Quotient is that no one *else* is the micro-manager of action. While it may seem obvious, it bears repeating that a person obstructed from action or coerced into action is not free. Social structures should facilitate rather than restrict autonomous action. Those of us living in democratic nations might be tempted to gloat about our freedoms, but no one should take them for granted. There always seem good reasons to restrict speech, assembly, voting rights, and so forth in order to protect security or social values or political institutions. We should be very circumspect of any restrictions to ensure the gain is worth the cost.[11]

More proximate restrictions on autonomy are even more common. Every app on our phones requires we "choose" to surrender personal information in exchange for the convenience of technology. Accepting a job means submitting to an employer's decisions about clothing, work hours, health care, and even whether or not to have children.[12] A spouse may dictate what a person eats and with whom, what she does for fun, and how she spends money. Unless these restrictions are recognized, a person is likely simply to narrow her consideration of options. *Preference deformation* occurs when a person changes what she wants on the basis of what is available (Nussbaum 1999).

Cave emphasizes an individual's capacity for willpower and self-control in overcoming obstacles to autonomous action. These are certainly important skills that can be improved through training. Given the historical treatment of free will as an individual conscious act, however, it is important to recognize that willpower develops primarily through social instruction and requires social support to maintain. Moreover, there are biological factors that can undermine a person's willpower. Addiction, for example, disables the reward system in a way that distorts a person's assessment of the relative value of things (Montague 2008). Drugs become more valuable than life, gambling more valuable than home and family, alcohol more valuable than school or work.

All of these issues need to be taken into account in considering how free we are. They should also be taken into account in considering how we might change social and political institutions to enable everyone to gain greater autonomy. Free will is a basic good, and people have a right to exercise our will to the maximum of our ability, provided our actions do not infringe on others. Far from eliminating free will, an understanding of our biological capacities and limits provides the means of enhancing the ability of everyone to pursue the life we have chosen.

# What Next?

*This is dizzying. It may be like trying to find your way
in a strange house, in the middle of the night, when you
are not enough awake to realize you are not at home.
So you blink and bump your head.*

O.K. Bouwsma *Philosophical Essays*

With all the cards in place, we have seen how the Temporal Representation Theory offers useful ways of thinking about difficult problems such as animal consciousness, free will, memory, and imagination. Even so, you may not be convinced. As Bouwsma observes, philosophy is dizzying. The attempt to connect mind and body requires wandering through strange, dark concepts like representation, consumer function, flexibility, and neural timing. This book is meant to be a guide, to lead you through the house until you can find the way on your own. Once you become more familiar with its structure, my hope is that you will find it generally sound. Perhaps some reconfiguring is needed here or there. Almost certainly additional cards will be required to secure this strange house against all conditions. This concluding chapter anticipates some of the additional cards that might be needed: further research into neurobiological mechanisms, an understanding of the role of emotion in consciousness, what would be involved in creating an artificial consciousness, and an investigation into alternative forms of consciousness such as delusion, hallucination, and meditation. There is a great deal of work yet to be done. In the end, I do not claim to have solved the problem of consciousness. My aim has been to show the structure of a possible solution.

## Explanatory Gap 2.0

Recall the explanatory gap from the Introduction. Nagel argued that the subjective experience of consciousness cannot be explained by any objective scientific theory. The experiences of a bat can only be known by the bat. Chalmers further argued that the explanatory tools of science—structure and function—do not apply to consciousness. Because we can imagine a zombie that has no conscious experience but is physically identical to a human, he claimed that no physical explanation of consciousness is possible. The explanatory gap is the Hard Problem of how consciousness could possibly be physical; it is the gap between the mind as we experience it and the body that houses it.

Chapters 1 through 3 argued that the explanatory gap can be bridged by thinking of the mind and consciousness in terms of biological function, contra Chalmers; and Chapter 4 considered objective ways to determine when this function is performed, contra Nagel. A mind has the function of representing the world, and consciousness has the function of representing the present moment. While each mind is unique in the details of what and how it represents, the general theory of mental representation applies to all minds. The relation is analogous to the unique genetic material that composes each body, and the general theory of genetics that applies to all biological organisms. All minds function by representing the world in order to better utilize its resources. Conscious minds have the particular function of representing the present moment in order to respond flexibly to shifting situational demands.

If strong enough, this bridge across the conceptual gap between mind and body solves the Hard Problem. Consciousness can be explained in terms of its function. Yet there remain several "easy" problems to be solved. Call this next set of issues the *Explanatory Gap 2.0*. While the Explanatory Gap 1.0 is the problem of how consciousness could *possibly* be physical, the Explanatory Gap 2.0 is the problem of how *exactly* consciousness is physical. This is a problem about the neurobiological mechanisms that instantiate consciousness. Until we bridge this second gap, it will likely be difficult to find widespread consensus that the first gap has truly been bridged.

Again, a comparison with genetic theory is fruitful. When Darwin and others proposed evolution by natural selection, the theory encountered significant public resistance even though the scientific community fairly quickly accepted the basic idea of evolution. Not until the mechanisms of genetics were discovered was evolution by natural selection widely understood as the explanation of diversity and adaptation. A materialist explanation of consciousness will face a similar public rejection without a more comprehensive understanding of the mechanisms by which a brain produces consciousness.

Think for yourself about what it would take for you to be thoroughly convinced that we understood how consciousness works. Already neuroscientists can manipulate consciousness in various ways. Tweaking the environment produces illusions; drugs generate feelings of euphoria or remove consciousness altogether. Brain stimulation treats pain and depression or disrupts visual awareness ('Brain Stimulation Therapy' 2019; 'Deep Brain Stimulation' 2019). Some neuroscientists claim to be able to read your mind by looking at brain imagery ('"Mind Reading" Technology Decodes Complex Thoughts' 2017), although there is reason to be skeptical (Resnick 2016).

Perhaps the only way to convince you is the ability to create an artificial consciousness. Some argue that you don't really understand something until you can build it (Biever 2013; F. Dretske 1994). I'll consider the prospects for that achievement later in the chapter. For this section, the point is simply that understanding the mechanisms of consciousness can be convincing in a way that no theoretical explanation is. A look at the last twenty years of consciousness research confirms this point. Neuroscience theories have advanced significantly in number, evidential support, and explanatory power, while philosophical theories have changed little. Higher-order Theory remains the dominant view, despite objections and challenges over the years. Until a philosophical theory can capture both the intuitive appeal of Higher-order Theory and the empirical confirmation of neuroscience, it is unlikely that any solution to the Explanatory Gap 1.0 will be accepted. (So, please, any neuroscientists out there who like the Temporal Representation Theory, come to my aid!)

## Emotions and Other Minds

The next outstanding issue to consider is the role of emotion in consciousness. Unconscious emotion appeared in Chapter 1 as a test case for the Representational Theory of the mind. There I argued that emotions represent bodily states in order for an organism to respond more effectively to the world. Joy reinforces action; anger motivates aggression. Emotion functions as a more refined regulator than pain and pleasure to determine the valence of a situation. Recent work by animal researchers suggests that emotions are part of a core affective structure that serves as a common currency for decision-making (Mendl, Burman, and Paul 2010). In order to weigh the fear of an electric shock against the desire for a food reward, an animal needs to be able to compare the value of these different emotions to determine appropriate action.

Since consciousness represents the present moment to assess appropriate action, according to the Temporal Representation Theory, emotions are clearly central to consciousness. Weighing fear against desire is necessary for evaluating goals. But how are emotions involved, exactly, given that they can be unconscious as well? This is the question that needs further research to answer. One possibility is that emotions allow for more fine-grained representations—distinguishing between fear and anxiety, for example—that are necessary for flexible decision-makers. A bi-valent good/bad measure may be sufficient for an organism like *C. Elegans* that responds in a fixed way to stimuli. For pushmi-pullyu animals like this (see Chapter 2), a calculus of nutrients and toxins determines the direction of motion. No further information about hopes or fears is needed. The practical animal, on the other hand, needs to evaluate a wide variety of elements in the current situation. Recall the cleaner wrasse (Chapter 4) who determines whether to do its duty in biting off only parasites or whether to cheat and take a bit of tasty flesh. These fish assess the situation based on past experience with individual fish, whether it is a predator or prey fish, and how many other fish are watching. A fish in such a predicament needs to weigh fear and anxiety against hunger and desire.

The emotional variety demanded by mutual exchanges between cleaner wrasse and clients is further expanded in social interactions among complex groups with structural hierarchies, affiliations, and division of labor. In Humphrey's story from Chapter 5 about "nature's psychologists," animals learn to read the emotions of other group members in order to better anticipate their behavior. Neuroscientists have been exploring the role of a particular neural circuit known as the *mirror neuron network* in facilitating the sort of mind-reading Humphrey proposes. The same mirror neurons are activated both when an action is performed and when that action is seen being performed by someone else. For example, your mirror neurons would be activated both by reaching for food and by seeing someone else reach for food. Researchers hypothesize that mirror neurons aid in the interpretation of what action is being performed and also in understanding why the action is being performed (Acharya and Shukla 2012).

Interpreting the emotional motivation behind social action is essential to negotiating intricate group dynamics. By simulating the actions seen, such as smiling or frowning, the mirror neuron network generates the intentions and emotions associated with that action (Lehrer 2019). In other words, we share the feelings of others when we see them expressing emotion. This research suggests that our private emotional experiences are not that private after all. Our brains come equipped to simulate and thereby share the emotions of people we see.

Returning to the question of how emotions relate to consciousness, I see two areas for further investigation. (1) A better understanding of the relationship between conscious emotions and flexibility would be useful. Is there evidence to suggest unconscious emotions lead to fixed or habitual responses whereas conscious emotions allow for alternative actions? Do practices designed to make people more conscious of their emotions help them respond more effectively in their social environment, as Chapters 5 and 6 propose? (2) Earlier in this section I suggested that more fine-grained emotional representations aid flexible decision-making. This hypothesis should be developed and tested as part of the research on consciousness in non-human animals. Chapter 4 developed a general framework for investigating animal consciousness, and social/emotional capacities would figure within that framework. Tests for differential response or appropriate action in novel situations could include social and emotional factors such as predators, rivals, and potential mates. Evidence for a mirror neuron network may be part of an anatomical explanation of empathetic action in animals.

Research already suggests that emotions are embodied and essential motivators of action (Barrett and Lindquist 2008; Price and Harmon-Jones 2015; Prinz 2004). Emotions bind us to the world and to one another. Further research can deepen our understanding of how emotions influence the nature and development of consciousness, and how consciousness affects the function of emotion.

## Artificial Consciousness

Reflecting on the role of emotion in consciousness is an appropriate preface to consideration of artificial consciousness. This book has framed emotions within a biological context: emotions serve the biological function of drawing us toward good and away from bad situations, people, actions. The increasing complexity of emotions arguably correlates with the increasing complexity of possible responses to nuances in our physical and social environments. In the context of artificial consciousness, the value of emotion raises the question of what would be necessary to manufacture emotion. Because the basic level of emotion—pleasure/pain, good/bad—involves representations that can occur unconsciously on my view, we can separate the question of emotion from the question of consciousness.

This separation is useful in avoiding the conflation of artificial consciousness with artificial intelligence (AI). Since AI research is the original and most prominent approach to machine minds, it is important to begin here before we get back to emotion and consciousness. AI was born at a time when the Computational Theory of mind was in its heyday (see Chapter 1). Consciousness was considered a distraction or a fiction that hard-minded scientists should avoid. If we could build a system that models all the input-output relations of a mind, that system would be a mind, according to the Computational Theory. AI research focused on creating systems that could do the sorts of computational thinking that human minds do: play chess, have conversations, reason logically. The result of research over a half-century is the variety of amazing computers, such as IBM's Jeopardy-winning Watson. Arguably, however, the Computational Theory has not produced intelligence, much less consciousness. In Chapter 1 we saw how Searle argued that a central failure of AI is that its representations have no meaning other than their value for the programmer and the user. The machine itself does not understand the words it processes or experience the joy of winning at chess. It simply computes the output based on the input and its code.[1]

So what would it take to produce a real artificial intelligence, with representations meaningful for the system itself? This question is fundamental to both intelligence and consciousness. Until we understand what is necessary for a machine to have genuine representations, for it to be a mind at all, it is premature to ask what would be required for a machine to be conscious. On the Consumer Theory that I recommended in Chapter 1, representations serve a biological function. Minds represent things in the world due to the evolutionary pressure to satisfy needs and desires. This biological basis provides explanatory power in situating minds in a physical causal context but threatens to make artificial consciousness impossible as a matter of definition. Anything that is not biological, it seems, cannot have a mind or be conscious. To rule out artificial consciousness in this way is problematic. Whether the prospects of artificial consciousness are bleak or promising, the issue is empirical, not logical.

That said, the empirical and logical may be deeply entwined in this case. Consider research on the question of artificial life, which primarily involves models and simulations of evolutionary processes. While this research informs our understanding of biology, there is no more reason to believe a model of life actually produces life than a model of a mind produces a mind (or a model of a tornado produces a tornado). In contrast, development of synthetic biology manufactures actual genetic material. By recoding the arrangement of the basic molecules in DNA, researchers are able to produce forms of life that are not the products of natural evolution (Zimmer 2019). If this new form of life can survive and reproduce, I would be inclined to count it as alive. While both the simulated organism and the synthetic organism survive and reproduce in their environments, only the synthetic organism would count as alive, because it survives in the physical rather than the virtual world.

More to the point, a living synthetic organism would have a mind, on the Consumer Theory. The reproductive demands coded into its DNA would determine the needs and desires that drive its representational system. The organism would need some way to represent the nutrients to pursue and toxins to avoid by means of simple pushmi-pullyu representations, similar to those of *C. Elegans*. The possibility of artificial life brings with it the possibility of an artificial mind.

Even with an artificial mind, synthetic biology does not get us much closer to artificial consciousness. Millions of years and an untold number of evolutionary accidents would likely be required for natural selection to produce the peculiar pressure for behavioral flexibility and the consciousness it demands, according to the Consumer Theory and the Temporal Representation Theory. Programs for modeling evolutionary processes of random mutation and selection in various environments might provide insight into the dynamic processes of speciation and adaptation that could speed up development, but evolving consciousness would still be an extended and fraught undertaking. Might there be a way to bypass evolution and build a conscious, non-biological robot in the next decade or so? In the absence of the life/mind connection provided by natural or synthetic biology, this question becomes how to ensure the needs and desires that drive a robot are meaningful *for the robot*.[2]

A clear initial condition for genuine representation on the Consumer Theory is interaction with the physical environment. Recent advances in AI and robotics capitalize on the value of interaction to move beyond the fixed algorithms of computational systems. *Connectionism*, for example, models information processing with *artificial neural nets* rather than lines of code. A simple artificial neural net has three layers: an input layer, a hidden layer, and an output layer. The input layer is equivalent to sensation; the nodes in this layer are fed the information that the system needs to process. Say we want to sort apples and bananas. We would feed photographs of apples and bananas into the network and the input layer would translate those images into pixels or whatever format is appropriate for that system. The hidden layer is where the work happens. Initially, the nodes in this layer are activated based on randomly weighted connections to the input layer, and they in turn randomly activate the output nodes. If that output happens to be correct—an apple image is fed into the system and the output node for "apple" is activated, the connection strengths between input, the hidden layer, and the output nodes are reinforced. If the output is incorrect, the connections are reweighted to produce a different output. After training the system with many different images of apples and bananas, eventually new photos will be accurately sorted (Rescorla 2017).[3]

This simple neural network can be made more sophisticated by adding layers and providing internal feedback mechanisms between layers. The details and differences among these systems are beyond the scope of this book, which is why it is included in the chapter on future developments in consciousness research. The point to highlight here is the fundamental difference between a connectionist system and a computational one. The difference isn't the machine, since connectionist programs are run on standard digital computers. The difference is the relationship between the system and the world. A computational system processes input from the world according to a set of algorithms coded into the program. The information input may be changed in various ways by the interaction of algorithms, but the system itself does not change. A connectionist system, on the other hand, fundamentally changes how it processes input based on its previous interactions. The weights of the nodes change in response to input-output feedback. Consequently, even the programmers of connectionist systems cannot say exactly how the system works. Nor are two connectionist systems identical, even if they are trained to process the same information.

These two features of a connectionist system—opaque and unique functional relations—are similar to brains and part of the reason they are called "artificial *neural* networks." Yet there are many dissimilarities between connectionist systems and brains, so caution is warranted. Even the most sophisticated artificial neural network is dwarfed by the complexity of the brain, and neurons operate in different ways than the nodes of a connectionist network (Rescorla 2017). The promise of Connectionism, in relation to the Consumer Theory, is the way that an artificial neural net represents[4] the world—apples and bananas— by interacting with it.

Despite the interaction in a connectionist system, its representations are not meaningful to the system itself on a Consumer Theory. The very simple network that sorts apples and bananas arguably does not care about the difference between these two sorts of fruit. Successfully sorting images is valuable for designers and users, not for the system itself. What more might be required? Returning to the issue that began this section, emotions are a likely candidate for making representations meaningful. At the most basic level, emotions determine what counts as good and bad for a system. In biological systems, good and bad are tied to survival and reproduction. While these may not be necessary conditions to meaningful representation, it is unclear what would serve their normative function in an artificial system. It seems inadequate to say the connectionist system *wants* to distinguish between apples and bananas. Yet I do not have a theory of artificial emotions to offer. What might be required for a system to care about its environment in a meaningful way is one of the problems to be solved next.

Say someone does solve that problem, and emotions can be wired into an artificial system in the way that human infants come wired with emotions as a result of natural selection. Given that needs and desires ground the artificial representations, they are meaningful on the Consumer Theory. What additional features would that system need to have in order to be conscious? According to the Temporal Representation Theory, the system would also need to have representations of the present moment. Consciousness evolved to track the present in order to respond flexibly to alternative possibilities. One open question is whether consciousness is the *only* way for a mind to perform the function of flexible response. Animals have evolved different ways to walk—on two, three, or four feet—and different ways to communicate. Could there be different ways to respond flexibly?

I think not. As just discussed, meaningful representations require emotional valence. Moreover, there is good reason to think that the complex representations needed for flexible behavior require a comparable emotional complexity to evaluate the affective salience, motivations, and goals of the situation. Luiz Pessoa (2017) has argued that cognitive and emotional systems must be deeply integrated in any intelligent architecture in order to perform executive functions such as inhibiting irrelevant information, updating working memory with task-appropriate contents, and shifting tasks to better fulfill overall goals. Emotions affect perception, attention, cognition, and action selection. If this is correct, then any system capable of behavioral flexibility will need representations of the present moment to perform the functions that consciousness performs in biological systems like ours. That is, any artificial system will need to keep track of what is happening now in order to determine the appropriate action in relation to its goals. Like ours, its representations must be selected in relation to its goals, unified with one another, and flow one after the other. These are the aspects of representations that constitute consciousness, according to the Temporal Representation Theory.

This does not mean that an artificial consciousness will be exactly like human consciousness, any more than fish consciousness, presuming they are conscious, is exactly like human consciousness. Precisely what is represented and how it is represented determines the quality and quantity[5] of consciousness. Differences between individuals, species, and origins (natural or artificial) are to be expected even while structural commonalities can be identified. Careful attention to both differences and similarities is needed to answer the ongoing questions raised by the prospect of artificial consciousness.

The key features that must be similar among all forms of consciousness, according to the Temporal Representation Theory, are: (1) the content of representations is determined through interaction with the world, (2) emotions give the representations meaning for the system itself, and (3) cognitive and emotional complexity requires representations of the present moment. If any of these features is absent, a system is not conscious. In particular, it is insufficient to program a system simply to represent the present. The only sort of representation adequate for consciousness is interactive and meaningful. There are no shortcuts to consciousness.

## Alternative Forms of Consciousness

Another area for further investigation is the vast terrain of altered states of consciousness. By and large this book has focused on everyday situations of walking, driving, remembering, and decision-making. These situations form the support beams of the theory, because they determine the functions of the representational system that is the mind. A living being needs representations to get resources for survival and to avoid threatening dangers. This smoothly functioning system is not the end of the story though. As discussed in Chapter 1, one hallmark of representation is error. Sometimes things go badly, and misrepresentation occurs. Sometimes things go very badly, and misrepresentation overwhelms the system in delusion and pathology, to be discussed soon.

Hallucinations also involve total misrepresentation, which may or may not indicate that things are going badly. Dreams and drug-induced hallucinations offer examples where misrepresentations may have functional value. Meditative and mystical states also present a challenge to the claim that conscious states represent the present moment. Meditators and mystics often describe these states as absent of contents, with no representations at all, not even a representation of the distinction between self and other. Similarly, descriptions of near-death experiences suggest that consciousness may continue after the physical system ceases to function. If true, then the explanation given in this book is incomplete.

All of these cases are fascinating and complicated. Only in the last decade have researchers begun connecting consciousness theory with previous work on these topics. In this section I will provide a sketch of the relations between altered states and the Temporal Representation Theory. As with the other issues in this chapter, this sketch will need to be filled in, and possibly redrawn, by future research. These are exciting times, filled with the potential to synthesize and advance our understanding of unusual forms of experience.

## Delusion and Pathology

The first form of altered state to consider is delusion. I occasionally joke about having delusions of grandeur that my theory of consciousness will revolutionize how we think about the mind. This is a joke, both because it is exceedingly unlikely and because I know it is exceedingly unlikely, as evidenced by calling the idea a *delusion*. People who are clinically delusional hold their false beliefs even in the face of counter-evidence. Currently prominent *Two-factor Theories* explain delusion in terms of a failure to properly evaluate faulty beliefs. The first factor in pathology is a malfunctioning perceptual or cognitive system that produces the mistaken belief. The second factor is a malfunctioning belief-monitor that fails to revise the mistaken belief (Bayne and Fernández 2009).

People who have Capgras syndrome, for example, believe that imposters have taken the place of loved ones. They persist in this belief despite photographic and fingerprint evidence, knowledge of personal information by the presumed imposter, and recall of shared events. In this case the first factor is the failure of a mechanism that connects face identification systems and affective systems (Pacherie 2009). Though the person looks just like the loved one, the appropriate emotion of familiarity and love is not activated. What makes the error delusional is the second factor; the belief evaluation system resists evidence against the conclusion that the person is an imposter.

Thinking about the function of the mind is a good way to differentiate simple error, structural malfunction, and delusion (Droege 2015). Simple errors happen all the time. A bush in the dark appears to be a threatening person lurking ahead. The sound of a flycatcher appears to be the elusive Buff-collared Nightjar (Pieplow 2009). Of course, the structural malfunctions produced in Capgras syndrome are persistent and debilitating. Even so, adjustments to these malfunctions can be made within an otherwise functional system. Second factor malfunction, on the other hand, prevents the system from correcting itself. Delusion is appropriately restricted to this sort of malfunction, because it constitutes a fundamental break with rationality. Making mistakes does not make a person irrational, they make a person human. Or more generally, to make mistakes is to be *alive*. A person is irrational when those mistakes are not acknowledged. Without a recognition of error, a person cannot compensate for or correct the error. In the case of Capgras syndrome, the result is pain and alienation for both the delusional person and her loved ones.

The overall point is that a theory of the mind grounded in function can also provide a useful account of *malfunction*. In fact, a functional account is far more likely to explain delusion and pathology than a computational account. If we think of the mind in terms of algorithms processing inputs into outputs, it is unclear how or why some minds make mistakes. Algorithms simply calculate an output based on input. Garbage in, garbage out. So where is the garbage in Capgras syndrome? The perceptual system and the affective system are both functional; the failure is in connecting them. Possibly a hardware problem accounts for the first factor error, but what about the second factor? Why would an algorithm fail to calculate the input that constitutes counter-evidence? It is difficult enough to develop AI that successfully processes information; it is unclear what it would mean for AI to be delusional. Of course we wouldn't want delusional AI, but we should be able to say what would be involved. An adequate theory of mind needs to account for every kind of mental state.[6]

## Hallucinations

One missing feature in my considerations about delusions is the role of consciousness. Capgras syndrome was described in terms of perceptual and belief system malfunctions without any mention of a malfunction of consciousness. To correct that omission, let me begin this section with a discussion of hallucinations that occur in schizophrenia. *Hallucinations* are sensory representations of things that do not exist. They are represented as occurring now, that is, according to the Temporal Representation Theory, they are consciously experienced, but the person does not realize that the things experienced are not really happening. In schizophrenia, auditory hallucinations often appear in the form of voices. The voices seem real and seem to be produced by someone else. One reason schizophrenia patients have difficulty believing that they are not real is the vividness and urgency of the experience. As with Capgras syndrome, a possible explanation for these hallucinations is a failure of self-monitoring. The voices are internally generated thoughts that are not recognized as internal and so interpreted as coming from an external source (Waters et al. 2012). On a Two-factor Theory, schizophrenic hallucinations are delusional, because the person refuses to accept that the voices are symptoms of illness rather than the genuine speech of God, the devil, or an unknown person. The schizophrenia sufferer misrepresents both the source of the sounds and their reality by taking the voices to be produced externally. If patients can accept that the sounds are self-generated, they are in a better position to recognize the hallucinations and deal with them.

A more familiar experience of hallucination is dreaming. Jennifer Windt (2018) describes dreams as immersive experiences of the here and now. Though we often associate waking states with consciousness and sleep states with unconsciousness, Windt argues that this strict division fails to account for the ways some waking states, like mind wandering, are similar to unconscious states, and sleep states, like dreaming, are similar to conscious states. In terms of the Temporal Representation Theory, dreams represent the dream world as present, and so dreams are conscious. Of course the dream world is not real, so dreams are also hallucinations, representations of things that do not exist. Upon waking, we immediately realize that the flight across the field and the swimming kittens were not real. During the dream, though, all these strange events are accepted as happening now in the hallucinated world.

Drug-induced hallucination is another form of consciousness where strange events are experienced as real and present, even though they are not. People experiencing this form of hallucination usually recognize the world of the hallucination as unreal once the effect of the drug has worn off. After all, escaping reality is often why people take hallucinogens. A very different reason to take hallucinogens is to provide access to an alternate reality. These cases are challenging to a materialist theory of consciousness, because they suggest that the mind is capable of transcending the physical world to make contact with a world beyond the bounds of science.

If the mind did travel to an actual world inaccessible to scientific study, this would indeed imply that science and Materialism cannot explain all conscious experience. So in the remainder of this section and the next section on mystical states and meditation, I'll say a bit about why I think that the value of these sorts of experiences is better incorporated within Materialism than as an exception to it. To begin, notice how difficult it is to articulate the nature of a non-physical world. All the familiar colors and shapes of the physical world are found in hallucinations. Basic structures like spirals, gratings, and cobwebs are called "form constants," because they occur regularly in visual hallucinations. The next stage past random colors and shapes is the appearance of complex images of fantastic cities and mythical beasts. All of these are constructed by combinations of things in the world. Unsurprisingly, the more inclined a person is to interpret a hallucination as reality, the closer to physical reality the experience is (Blackmore and Troscianko 2018: 383).

The sort of hallucination that seems most real is one that proves meaningful in a person's post-hallucination physical life. These often occur as part of a spiritual practice, such as the use of peyote to induce hallucinations in the shamanic traditions. People who undergo these experiences report a sense of connection with all things, increased empathy, and a reduced fear of death. Even in a laboratory setting, people who try the hallucinogen psilocybin for the first time maintain a sense of personal well-being and feelings of altruism long after the experience (McGreal 2012).

These effects are profound and call for further examination. In particular, more investigation is needed of the role of context and interpretation in producing the benefits of hallucinations. Though there are common features among all hallucinatory experiences, the nature and impact of a person's hallucination is shaped by her religious and cultural beliefs as well as her expectations about what the experience will reveal. If, for example, a person expects spiritual guidance to appear in the form of an animal, she will interpret her experience differently from a person who expects spirituality will manifest in light.

In other words, the reality of hallucinations is firmly linked to the reality of the physical world. The biology and beliefs we take with us into the hallucination shape the experience, and the way we incorporate the experience into our lives after the experience is grounded in material existence. The hallucinated world need not be an actual non-physical realm in order for the experience to be real and true. Like any other truths, those revealed through hallucinations are tested by the ongoing struggles of life. The mundane belief that my coffee cup is in the dishwasher is true, because I can find my cup there when I go look for it. The spiritual belief that all things are connected is confirmed in acts of altruism that bring joy to everyone involved.

## Mystical States and Meditation

The sort of drug-induced hallucination that yields spiritual insight is one form of the general category of mystical states. Fasting and meditation are other ritual practices that are designed to generate mystical states. The goal of these practices is to experience a sense of unity with the universe, similar to the connection with all things found in psychedelic hallucinations. By extreme discipline of the body, the mind is channeled into an altered state of consciousness.

In his work cataloguing forms of religious experience, William James identified four markers of mystical states (1902: 299–300). (1) They are *ineffable*: people have difficulty describing the nature of the experience and often say that you need to have the experience in order to understand it. (2) They are *noetic*: the experience yields knowledge or enlightenment. (3) They are *transient*: the experience passes quickly and the vivid quality fades. (4) They are *passive*: the person is not in control of the experience or her body or mind.

These four features of mystical states are connected to the loss of a sense of self. The experience of an infinite cosmos puts the daily concerns about career advancement and family squabbles in perspective. As an individual, each person is insignificant, but as part of a vast web of being, life takes on transcendent meaning. Though not in control of this powerful force of existence, a person who has a mystical experience comes to understand herself in relation to it. After returning to her normal state of consciousness, however, it is easy to slip back into familiar patterns of thought. Language designed for normal living fails to capture the quality of mystical experience. The self and its interests resume control. Even though the exhilaration of transcendence passes away, people who have had this experience are profoundly changed and seek to return to the mystical state.

All of the features of mystical states combine to sharply separate these experiences from everyday experience and give the impression that transcendent consciousness is the purest form. If this were the case, my evolutionary approach in this book is a mistake. I have concentrated on the sort of consciousness humans share with mammals and possibly other animals such as fish, and the everyday experiences we have while driving or hiking in the woods. An examination of the structure of these familiar experiences resulted in the definition of consciousness as the representation of the world at the present moment. In mystical states, on the other hand, the loss of the self breaks down the division between subject and object, and the experiences are often described as timeless. If this is the true or pure form of consciousness, it would seem to make more sense to begin with an explanation of mystical states.

The problem with flipping around the order of explanation in this way is that we lose the tools of science and history. By taking the evolutionary approach, I have been able to place consciousness within a functional theory of the mind. Conscious representations evolved as necessary for flexible behavior. Animals need to represent the present moment as distinct from not-yet-realized goals in order to monitor progress toward those goals or to switch goals as opportunities and dangers arise. If we start with a feeling of timeless unity, on the other hand, it's not clear to me what else there is to say. When an experience seems to be outside of the physical and temporal boundary formed by language and explanation, these tools are little help in developing theory.

One response to this disconnect is to conclude that the real nature of consciousness is actually non-physical and non-temporal, and mystical states prove Dualism is true. If you are inclined to draw this conclusion, remember the difficulties with Dualism from Chapter 1. A radical distinction between mind and body fails to address phenomena such as emotion that merge mental and physical. More fundamentally, the mind must be physical in order to have causal effects. Dualism may satisfy the subjective experience of our sensations and thoughts as distinct from our experience of tables and chairs. Yet it fails to explain how a table causes a perception and a thought moves a body to sit in a chair.

An alternative response is to look for reasons to explain why and how mystical states *seem* to transcend space and time. As with all the topics in the chapter, what follows is just an outline of this position. More work needs to be done to see how well Materialism can satisfy the inclination to believe in a non-physical reality.

To begin, the brain chemistry of neurotransmitters along with patterns of neural activation can account for how psychedelic drugs and sensory manipulation generate states structurally similar to forms of consciousness such as hallucinations. Scientific study of drug-induced states is an area of renewed interest after a long dormant period following the initial excitement about mystical experience in the 1960s and 1970s (Bayne and Carter 2018; Calvey and Howells 2018; Carhart-Harris et al. 2014). Even so, the empirical research results will be unconvincing without an account of the deep spiritual transformation that people undergo in these states.

Scientists tend to avoid comment on spirituality, for very good reasons. The way we interpret our experiences as transcendent or divine is beyond the scope of scientific inquiry. As just noted, science can explain how we come to have these experiences, but it cannot explain why we seek them or why they are so meaningful. Philosophy or religion can more appropriately address the issue of meaning.

So why might we seek to transcend the spatial-temporal confines of everyday experience? The answer I find compelling comes from the Lutheran theologian, Paul Tillich. In his small gem of a book, *Biblical Religion and the Search for Ultimate Reality* (1955), Tillich describes the desire for an answer to the existential question: why is there something and not nothing? Once language and culture freed the human mind to think beyond space and time, an understanding of finitude and death came along with the package. Remember the tree of the knowledge of good and evil from the Garden of Eden? Adam and Eve learned that knowledge and paradise are incompatible. We now all live with the knowledge that our lives are limited, and so the choice of what to do with this one and only life is urgent and immediate. We are filled with anxiety about whether our choices are good ones, whether our lives have purpose, and ultimately, why we were even born.

Given this anxiety, the loss of self in mystical states can be an enormous relief. The pressure for me to make sense of my life disappears when my life is seen as a small part of an ultimate reality. This realization can lead to faith, but it can also lead to despair. Faith results when the sense of connection to forces beyond the self brings a feeling of power and purpose. Despair results when the feeling of insignificance leads to resignation. There may seem to be no point to living, if no life ever amounts to much in the scheme of things. These disparate responses signal the importance of interpretation in the psychophysical response to altered states, particularly those induced by psychedelic drugs (Hartogsohn 2016).

Though meaning and value have a physical basis, as this book has argued, a full explanation requires an appreciation of their function in human life. Because humans are social, linguistic beings with a cultural history, we interpret our experiences within these contexts. Work needs to be done to draw connections between these interpretive contexts and the neurophysiological basis of mystical states. The prospects for a fully satisfying materialist theory of consciousness can only be assessed given this broader account.[7]

One particular challenge for the Temporal Representation Theory of consciousness is raised by the mystical states experienced by advanced meditators. The claim is sometimes made that the pure consciousness of meditation is an experience without any content whatsoever, no representation of sensation, thought, or even the distinction between subject and object. If this sort of state is possible, then consciousness is more than its representational function.[8]

Though I have trouble imagining what a content-less state could be like, it would be poor phenomenology to simply deny the experience of others. In any case, the topic deserves further investigation. I see three ways this study could go: (1) Advanced meditative states are more appropriately described as representations where the only content is the present moment. (2) The Temporal Representation Theory is proven wrong and is replaced by a theory that captures the essence of consciousness underlying both content-less meditative states and all other sorts of conscious states. (3) Content-less meditative experiences involve a different use of consciousness than the use everyday experiences evolved to perform. For obvious reasons, I would opt for the first or third option, due to the power of the Temporal Theory to place consciousness within an evolutionary story about the mind.

Think of consciousness as a tool, like a screwdriver. It was designed to do a particular job, but once it was invented, it can be used to do all kinds of things. A screwdriver *is* a driver of screws even if it can also be used as a weapon, a doorstop, a paint can opener, or any number of other uses. Likewise, consciousness *is* a representation of the present moment even if it can be used for dreaming, spiritual enlightenment, or meditation. These other forms of consciousness are different from yet depend upon the function of consciousness to facilitate flexible action in a physical world of opportunities and dangers.

## Near-Death Experiences

The last sort of altered consciousness that I will discuss may be the last sort of consciousness any of us experiences, after which we may know whether or not anything I have said in this book is correct. People who have had near-death experiences offer remarkably similar descriptions of reviewing major life events, traveling down a dark tunnel toward a light, and being greeted by friends and loved ones (although in some cases, the friends are replaced by demons and a hellscape). As with mystic states, near-death experiences are transformative. People become more calm and less concerned with fame and monetary success; they are more kind and report greater life satisfaction (Lichfield 2015).

The challenge of near-death experiences to a materialist theory is the possibility of consciousness after the body ceases to function. As with mystical states, the scientific response needs to be coupled with a spiritual response. A scientific explanation of the life review, tunnel, and heaven (or hell) involves euphoria-inducing endorphins that flood the neural system as well as widespread brain activation in response to the trauma of near death (Timmermann et al. 2018). There is no evidence (and probably could never be evidence) that the experience occurs in the absence of brain activity, since all descriptions of these experiences occur after the person has recovered waking consciousness.

A spiritual explanation draws attention to the individual differences in experiences. Which events you will experience—whether you will be greeted by Jesus or Krishna or Muhammed, or whether you will be faced with eternal damnation—these variations are meaningful based on personal and cultural history. Likewise, how the experience transforms a life is determined by its meaning within that life. Even after we account for the physical causes of near-death experiences, we still need to understand the various ways in which these experiences are interpreted. The temptation to dismiss their spiritual significance should be resisted; these events have deep and lasting effects that demand an account.

## The End of Consciousness

If we can give a satisfying account of near-death experiences in physical terms, does that mean there is no life after death? Does a materialist theory of consciousness mean that consciousness will end when the physical body ends? Yes and no. The Temporal Representation Theory explains how consciousness comes to be part of the world. So yes, on this theory the consciousness that we experience in the world ends when the parts of the world that support it—the brain and body—end. However, the theory does not claim that the brain and body are the only possible support for consciousness. Given the right conditions, machines might someday be conscious. There might be some way to transfer human consciousness to an artificial medium, sometimes called "uploading" consciousness. So no, the Temporal Representation Theory does not rule out the possibility that there is some unknown medium, even possibly an immaterial medium, that supports consciousness after death.[9]

That's the thing about death, there is no way to know what happens. There isn't even a good way to predict what happens after death other than to extrapolate based on what happens in life. If we limit our predictions to physical processes and explanations, consciousness and the self end with death. As a materialist, must I accept this conclusion? Ludwig Wittgenstein put it best at the end of the *Tractatus Logico-philosophicus*: "Whereof one cannot speak, thereof one must be silent" (1922, §7) Wittgenstein's point is that language, and science, should restrict its claims to what it knows. While the impulse to point beyond what we can say and study is the human drive toward the mystical, we can only speak about the impulse, not about what lies beyond. The challenge of the mind-body problem is precisely to account for what seems mystical about the mind in terms of what we can say and study. This book accepts that challenge and makes no claims beyond it.

Reviewing the central claims of the Temporal Representation Theory shows how much there is to say within the bounds of mortal existence. In the Introduction we saw that the mind seems non-physical because representations are the content that physical vehicles carry. The pages and ink of the book (or the pixels on the screen) are the vehicles for the story, yet the content is what the story is about, dragons and fairies, or lovers, or warriors. Because our mind's representations are about things that go beyond our brains, it is difficult to see how neural systems could possibly explain the marvelous shapes and colors and smells and tastes that the mind represents. Chapter 1 offered a theory of representation in terms of function. A neural vehicle has the content it does, because it has been useful to other parts of the neural system, and consequently useful to you or me. A bit of my brain represents bananas to help my arm, hand, and fingers reach out and grab a banana when I'm hungry.

Much of this representational system does its work unconsciously, as Chapter 2 argued. I don't have to consciously direct my muscles to contract and extend appropriately; I simply pay enough attention to my movement to keep it on track. If I am particularly occupied with a demanding task, like writing a book, the process of grabbing, peeling, and eating the banana may be almost entirely unconscious. Consciousness is difficult to study, in part because the gradations from clearly conscious to clearly unconscious shade imperceptibly together. Even from the first-person point of view it is often impossible to say definitively whether or not a particular sensation, thought, or action was conscious.

The limits of first-person authority on the contents of consciousness reinforce the importance of a materialist theory. Because introspection is not a perfect source of information about consciousness, our bodies can provide an alternate reliable source. If there were a unique neural signature for consciousness, then we could determine whether patients in a coma are conscious and which sleep states are conscious. We could say what exactly a distracted driver is conscious of on a long-distance drive.

My claim has been that the key to finding a unique neural signature for consciousness, to bridging the explanatory gap, is to define consciousness in terms of function. If the mind could function exactly the same way without consciousness, there would have been no evolutionary advantage to being conscious. While this might be the case, a more satisfying theory gives a reason that natural selection favored organisms with consciousness. Chapter 3 argued that flexible behavior is the function consciousness serves. To be flexible means the ability to switch actions in order to reach a goal or to switch goals in light of new opportunities or dangers. Consciousness facilitates flexibility.

According to the Temporal Representation Theory, conscious processes select and coordinate representations into a representation of the world at the present moment. Given the time it takes for a stimulus to travel from source to sensory organ, and from early sensation to whatever process culminates in consciousness, conscious states include representations of stimuli that occur slightly earlier. Likewise, in order to anticipate world events like a moving ball, conscious states include representations of stimuli that are likely to occur but have not yet occurred.

Furthermore, conscious states combine representations appropriate to goals. Presumably, one of your goals right now is to read these words, and so they are part of your representation of the present moment. As much as I'd like to believe you are so engrossed in this book that nothing else occupies your consciousness, realistically and practically, you are probably also conscious of notifications on your phone, people walking by or in the next room, bodily sensations of hunger or sleepiness. A practical animal such as yourself needs to keep updated on changes in the world over time in order to monitor progress on goals (just a few more pages) or change course (oh, an invitation to lunch just popped up).

The most important contribution made by the Temporal Representation Theory, I believe, is this connection between the phenomenology of consciousness (the experience of consciousness *as now*) and the function of consciousness (flexible action). Consciousness keeps track of the world *now* in order to respond effectively to variable situations.

The test of the theory is twofold. (1) Is the phenomenology correct? You conduct this test yourself. Pay attention. Does consciousness always represent the present moment, even when it also represents the past or future? (2) Is the function correct? Is consciousness necessary for flexible behavior? The test of function is a more complicated, interdisciplinary project. Chapter 4 described some elements of that project by applying the theory to the question of animal consciousness. Part of the project is philosophy: reasons connect temporal representation to flexible action. Part of the project is cognitive ethology: tests for flexibility move beyond arguments by analogy to determine when an animal is conscious.[10]

The remaining three chapters situated the Temporal Representation Theory of consciousness within a larger context. Chapter 5 considered conscious memory, that is, how a representation of the present moment could also represent a past moment. Phenomenology again proves essential. Conscious memory is always represented in some way as present; the sensations and thoughts of the past event are experienced as occurring now. By embedding a representation of the past event within a representation of the present moment, we gain an explanation of both the pastness of memory and its consciousness. Since an embedded representation is higher-order—a representation of a representation—it makes sense that the capacity for conscious memory appears developmentally at the same time other higher-order representational capacities appear, such as imagination and deception.

Chapter 6 took on the controversial topic of the role of consciousness in free will. One of the consequences of the Temporal Representation Theory is that consciousness is less influential in directing behavior than we might have thought. Because a representation of the present moment takes time to be produced, it is usually too late to cause immediate action. Nonetheless, conscious reflection can shape future action by influencing our thoughts and habits. By paying attention to the relation between cause and effect, a person can learn what sorts of behavior produce positive and negative results. This information feeds into the decisions we make about what sort of person we are and want to be. As the artist Joseph Beuys said, "the causes lie in the future." Humans are capable of imagining a future, and that conception operates as a cause of actions we make in the present. The capacity to be conscious (to represent the present) and to be self-conscious (to represent the future in the present) is fundamental to the capacity for purposeful change.

And finally, considerations in this chapter point us toward that future change. However compelling the Temporal Representation Theory is in bridging the explanatory gap, there remain many challenges ahead. We still need to understand how the brain produces consciousness, the role of emotions, what might be involved in creating an artificial consciousness, and how alternative forms of consciousness are related. These are all difficult and exciting puzzles. Each one has the potential to reveal new discoveries that overturn previously held views of ourselves and our world.

That's the great thing about explanation: There is always more to explain! Anyone who fears that a theory of consciousness will suck the mystery out of life need only reflect on the miracle of birth. We know pretty much everything there is to know about where babies come from, yet each birth is a miracle. The same could be said of the growth of a tree from an acorn or the movement of waves with the tide.

As I gaze at the birds pecking at the sun-dappled lawn, my consciousness is representing the colors and shapes and objects of the world for me at the present moment. My firm conviction that this experience is the result of evolutionary processes shaped by my lifelong interaction with the environment enhances rather than diminishes its beauty. I appreciate the complexity and expanse of nature's operation that has resulted in this moment. To be a small element in a vast network does not bring me despair, but peace.

# Appendix: *On Temporal Consciousness*

*That great mystery of TIME, were there no other;*
*the illimitable, silent, never-resting thing called Time,*
*rolling, rushing on, swift, silent,*
*like an all-embracing ocean-tide,*
*on which we and all the universe swim*
*like exhalations, like apparitions*
*which are, and then are not.*

Thomas Carlyle

Temporal consciousness is the experience we have of the rolling, rushing, swift, and silent progress that Carlyle describes. While it might seem that temporal consciousness is integral to the Temporal Representation Theory (TRT), much of the debate in this field runs orthogonal to my claims. This Appendix will discuss how the TRT figures in relation to the main theories: the Cinematic View, Retentionalism, and Extensionalism. Theorists working on temporal consciousness ask: *given consciousness, how is temporal content experienced?* As Barry Dainton puts it, "we seem to be directly aware of change, movement, and succession across brief temporal intervals. How is this possible?" (Dainton 2018)

In contrast, my question has been: *given unconscious representational capacities, why did conscious representations evolve?* The answer is that conscious representations evolved to facilitate flexible action. Consciousness represents the present moment, which allows the conscious animal to track progress toward its goal and shift its goals in response to the current situation. My aim is to clarify how these questions differ, and how answers to them can be mutually informative. Most pointedly, I will argue that the Temporal Representation Theory illuminates some problematic assumptions underlying the temporal consciousness debate.

## Motion, Change, Succession

In keeping with the emphasis throughout this book on phenomenology, let's begin by examining the experience of temporal phenomena at issue. Look at something moving—the leaves and branches of a tree, your fingers waggling in front of you, an animal meandering from one point to the next. What is the movement like? How does it differ from the experience of something still? I find it difficult to focus on the movement per se. As I watch the leaves wave up and down on this windy day, I keep getting distracted by my own eye movements in a way that does not happen when I focus on the solid oak trunk. Watching my fingers gives me the impression of a time-lapse photo where the images blur into one another, with the front fingers in greater detail. The waving leaves move more smoothly, despite the occasional distraction.

Now listen to the movement of sounds and feel the movement of textures. I hear the harmonic chant hold one note and then smoothly introduce another so the first sounds both same and different from one moment to the next. Running my fingers across the desk, I notice the tiny irregular bumps of the wood grain. Getting up for another cup of coffee, I again find it difficult to pay attention to my bodily movement as it is drawn to tasks I am doing and away from the actions to accomplish them.

Keep these experiences in mind as we consider the three types of theory to account for temporal consciousness. One question is whether experiences of movement, change, and succession[1] are illusory and what that might mean. Do you really experience temporal relations, or is the sense of change a kind of judgment or inference? Another issue is how to think about the temporal parts of experience, the earlier and later elements that result in the sense of movement. Do the different positions in a movement need to unfold over time or can they be represented together? A final consideration involves the relation between the experience of temporal relations and the objective events that occur in time. When one event occurs and then another event, does experience necessarily present the one and then the other, or might experiential order differ from objective order? The fault lines that divide the theories of temporal consciousness are set by the way they address these puzzles.

## Cinematic, Retentional, and Extensional Theories

This section will introduce the three main approaches to temporal consciousness. The broad overview of the positions given here is primarily to show how issues that arise in the debate about temporal consciousness connect to the claims of TRT. A full examination of the arguments and objections in the debate can be found in several excellent collections (Arstila, Bardon, Power, and Vatakis 2019; Arstila and Lloyd 2014; Phillips 2017), see also the comprehensive article in the *Stanford Encyclopedia of Philosophy* (Dainton 2018). On the *Cinematic View*, the experience of change is an illusion. Strictly speaking, temporal experience is composed of a series of snapshots that are then interpreted as moving and changing. *Retentional Theories* are similar in taking experience to be composed of momentary episodes, but they claim that each episode in some way retains the recent past and anticipates the future. *Extensional Theories* hold that experience itself must be temporally extended in order to accommodate the immediate awareness of movement and change.

The first question about temporal experience—whether experiences of movement, change, and succession are illusory—sets apart the Cinematic View from its opponents. According to the Cinematic View, the impression of movement and change is a kind of illusion. The contents of each experience are limited to a single instant, like a still from a film. These stills occur rapidly one after the other without a break, generating the connections that we interpret as temporal extension. Christof Koch describes these perceptual moments like this: "Within one such moment, the perception of brightness, colour, depth and motion would be constant. Think of motion painted onto each snapshot" (Koch 2004: 264). The primary objection to the Cinematic View is that temporal phenomena seem to be part of perceptual experiences themselves rather than inferences or judgments about their relations. Go back to your experiences of motion and change. For me, waggling my fingers did seem somewhat like a series of snapshots, but my experience of the music did not at all. Both the continuity and the tonal changes seemed incorporated as part of the experience. There is a unity to the experience of change that the Cinematic View fails to capture.

Yet the most pressing difficulty with the Cinematic View, I think, is the problem of individuating the temporal bounds of a snapshot. Phillip Chuard (2011) suggests temporal content could do this work, so for example each tonal change would count as a different experience. Yet the ongoing, dynamic neural processes that produce temporal experiences do not allow conscious content to be individuated this finely. Say I am watching my fingers waggle as I listen to the music. To have successive representations for each finger position that precisely matched the harmonic chord at that instant would require visual and auditory signals to be integrated with millisecond accuracy. This seems both physiologically implausible and unnecessary.[2]

Valtteri Arstila (2018) argues that the contents of experience are "punctate," which makes even less neurological sense. The production of a representation takes time due to sensory latencies, neural integration, and modulation processes. Evidence suggests that conscious representation takes even longer to reach neuronal adequacy than unconscious forms of representation (Boly et al. 2013; Bor and Seth 2012; Mashour, Roelfsema, Changeux, and Dehaene 2020). Abstractions such as a time-slice of a world line may be useful for theorizing about the nature of time in metaphysics (Deutsch and Lockwood 2016), but a knife-edge instant is not an appropriate unit for theorizing about the individuation of mental contents. On the Consumer Theory discussed in Chapter 2, the temporal relations required for representation extend well past sensory stimulation and integration to include the history and effectiveness of environmental interaction. While it may be possible to distinguish between the temporal-causal conditions for representation from its momentary instantiation, it is unclear what the motivation for such a distinction would be.

Though *Retentionalist* Theories are also committed to the claim that experience itself is instantaneous, the analysis of the content of experience is fundamentally different. Husserl developed one of the most influential Retentionalist accounts of temporal consciousness, in addition to its influence on the Temporal Representation Theory, as discussed in Chapter 3. According to Husserl, the now-point of the present includes the content of the just-past, *retention*, and the anticipated future, *protention*. So the experience of temporal breadth is explained in terms of the breadth of the temporal contents of each instant. As the now-point recedes into the past, it is retained in the next now-point, and so on as experienced time flows toward the future.

The second issue of temporal consciousness demarcates Retentional Theory from its competitors: how the temporal parts of experience unfold over time. For the Retentionalist, past, present, and future occur all at once, so to speak. A single representation includes the temporal parts that account for the experience of movement, change, and succession. On the face of it, this seems contradictory. How can different times occur at a single time? Dainton calls this the *Retentional Simultaneity Problem*: "how is it possible for a collection of contents which occur simultaneously to seem successive?" (2018) This paradox is related to the *Problem of Surplus Content*: if each instant represents a span of time and the next instant represents roughly the same span of time, it seems that the experience of any given interval would be crammed with indefinitely many representations of the same set of events. For example, if I hear *do-re-mi*, then on the Retentional account *do* is represented at least three times, by the initial note and retained in the experiences of the next two notes. Multiply this by the number of instantaneous representations required for the duration of each note, and *do* appears in experience an unreasonable number of times.

The Extensionalist solution to this problem is to extend experience to include its temporal parts. For an Extensionalist, hearing the notes *do-re-mi* is one experience that contains each successive item in the order that it appears. Thus we come to the final issue that divides theories of temporal consciousness: the relation between the experience of temporal relations and the objective events that occur in time. Extensionalists are committed to what Ian Phillips calls the Inheritance Principle: "for any temporal property apparently presented in experience, our experience itself possesses that temporal property" (2014: 137). So you really experience change over time by virtue of having experiences that themselves change over time, as you hear music or watch the leaves swaying in the breeze.

Because of their claim that experiences themselves are extended in time, Extensionalists face what Dainton calls the *Extensional Simultaneity Problem*: "how is it possible for contents which are (i) experienced together, and (ii) experienced as present, to be experienced as anything other than simultaneous?" (2018) To experience the leaves swaying requires that all the parts of the motion are included in a single experience, otherwise the theory would be a Cinematic one. Yet if the parts are included in a single experience, it seems that they must appear at the same time. An Extensionalist cannot explain the extension of experience in terms of the different times represented, or the theory would be a Retentionalist one.

Temporal illusions present an additional problem for the Extensionalist, as pointed out by Rick Grush (2016). In the well-known illusion called the Phi Phenomenon, a stimulus presented quickly following and at a slightly different location from an initial stimulus will appear to move from one location to the next. However, if the first stimulus is presented alone, it will appear stationary. The movement cannot be represented in experience until the second stimulus appears, so it seems the mind somehow reinterprets the temporal relation after it has occurred. Extensionalists maintain that experience unfolds in a way that matches the unfolding of events, so it is unclear how later events could affect the experience of earlier events without making use of the Retentionalist distinction between the order of events and the order of representation.

Each type of theory is committed to a position that distinguishes it from the others. Cinematic Theories claim that the experience of temporal phenomena is a kind of illusion based on inference or judgment; movement and change are not perceivable phenomena. Retentional Theories propose that a single representation can include a representation of past and future for an extended interval. Extensional Theories tie the temporal relations of events firmly to the temporal relations within an experience to account for the perception of succession, change, and movement. Yet each theory has counterintuitive implications.

## Reframing the Paradox of Temporal Awareness

Dainton sums up the theoretical conundrum in his description of the *Paradox of Temporal Awareness*: we seem to be aware of things moving and changing, but "if our awareness is confined to the present, our awareness must itself lack temporal depth" (2018). The paradox is that we seem to be aware of things as both present and temporally extended, but these are contradictory.

As I mentioned earlier, my concerns in this book have been different but related to the debate about temporal consciousness. My question has been, *given unconscious representational capacities*, why did conscious representations evolve? This section will draw on the resources used to answer this question in order to reframe the Paradox of Temporal Awareness. By looking more carefully at the function of consciousness and the function of temporal representation, we may gain some perspective on what it is to be conscious of temporal phenomena and how the paradox might be resolved.

This book has considered several ways in which time figures in the minds of animals. At the most basic representational level, inflexible pushmi-pullyu representations track change (Chapter 2). A stimulus leads to a response in the appropriate temporal relation to accomplish some adaptive function. When an animal is able to flexibly respond to a situation based on multiple possible actions and goals, it needs a more advanced representation of the present moment to track opportunities and obstacles as it makes its way through the world (Chapter 3). According to TRT, consciousness is the representation of what is happening now and includes the temporal phenomena of movement, change, and succession. Any account of the human experience of these phenomena should be applicable to animals (Chapter 4), keeping in mind that differences in sensory equipment and ecological demands translate into differences in the kinds of temporal relations represented. What movement means to a hummingbird and a sloth is certainly not the same. Their representations are nonetheless similar to one another and to ours in being conscious representations of something moving *now* (presuming these animals indicate behavioral flexibility as described in Chapter 4).

Where representations of time by humans may diverge from other animals is with the development of meta-representations (Chapter 5). The ability to embed a representation of the past within a representation of the present may be unique to humans. Self-conscious forms of memory and imagination allow humans to develop a sense of self over time, which is useful in negotiating the particular demands of complex human communities.

The evolutionary value of all of these forms of representation is their ability to aid the animal in exploiting objective temporal relations. To understand how temporal representation accomplishes its various functions, three types of temporality need to be considered: (1) objective time, (2) time of vehicle, and (3) time of content.

(1) Objective time: This is the actual temporal structure of events in which an animal lives. Change, succession, and movement are temporal relations that every living organism must represent in order to survive. Note that no commitment to a particular metaphysics of time[3] is implied by calling it "objective time." Whether all times exist (Eternalism) or only a knife-edge instant (Presentism), the spatiotemporal relations of events is the reality within which minds operate.

(2) Time of vehicle: Representations are instantiated in some way, most likely by patterns of neural activation in the brain. The timing of these neural vehicles is essential to understanding how different sensory signals are integrated, and why the time of the vehicle may be behind or in advance of the objective time of events represented.

(3) Time of content: The three theories of temporal awareness focus on this type of temporality. A particularly stark way to state the Paradox of Temporal Awareness is: if consciousness represents the present, how can it also represent the past and future events included in succession, movement, and change? Each type of theory tries to resolve the paradox by tweaking the contents of temporal representation. Cinematic Theories restrict perceptual content to the present and explain temporality as cognitive inference. Retention Theories expand the representational breadth of the present to include past and future. Extension Theories expand consciousness itself so that multiple temporal contents are experienced together.

It seems to me that the focus on the contents of consciousness is needlessly restrictive. Resources other than introspection and logic are needed to resolve the Paradox of Temporal Awareness. By expanding our theoretical scope to include objective time and the time of the vehicle, and thinking about how these types of temporality interrelate to serve various representational functions, it may be possible to reframe the debate about temporal awareness.

The first tool to bring to bear on this issue is the time of the vehicle of representation. Rick Grush (2016: 13–14) demonstrates the power of distinguishing vehicle from content in his defense of Retention Theory from the Problem of Surplus Content. Grush's Trajectory Estimation Model (TEM), described in more detail in Chapter 3, proposes that each neural vehicle represents an approximately 200 ms temporal interval. If each vehicle lasts for 20 ms, then there would be fifty representations over the course of a 1 sec interval of objective time. Since each representation carries 200 msec of content, that seems to add up to 10 sec of content for each 1 sec of objective time. This is the Problem of Surplus Content. Grush's reply is the same one I made to a similar objection to the Overlap Model in Chapter 3. Though each vehicle carries 200 ms of content, only one vehicle at a time is representing that content, and content is not additive. In the *do-re-mi* example, there may be three vehicles that carry the *do* content, but the same note is represented by each vehicle. So, actually a 1 sec interval of objective time is represented by 1 sec of content, not 10 sec.

But without a theory of consciousness and its function, Grush assumes that the timing of experience has to conform to the timing of objective events with millisecond accuracy in order to be causally effective. In objecting to a move by Extensionalists to account for temporal illusions by delaying the onset of an experience, Grush argues that even a 100 ms delay would come with significant behavioral cost (17–18). In contrast, TEM posits that each representation overwrites the previous one as the perceptual system gains new information. To use the Phi Phenomenon as an example, the TEM account is a conscious experience of the first stimulus as stationary which is quickly replaced by it as moving to the position of the second stimulus.

However, this explanation does not fit the phenomenological sense that the first stimulus was never stationary. It may be the case that consciousness is continually presenting slightly different interpretations of events that are immediately forgotten when replaced. But a better explanation would allow for temporal adjustment prior to consciousness.[4]

According to TRT, adding a delay of 100 ms need not involve a behavioral cost, because fine-grained action-guiding processes are unconscious. Consciousness represents the present moment in order to keep track of how action is progressing toward goals, not to initiate action. Consciousness is an orchestra director rather than a player. As Chapter 6 argues, the role of orchestra director is an important causal force in formulating, assessing, and selecting goals. There is no need for consciousness to direct action within milliseconds for it to do this job.

Ultimately, the question of how vehicle timing best serves its function of representing content is an empirical question. One of the reasons I favor TEM is its foundation in the science of neural processing. I also agree with the proposal to represent a 200 ms interval with each vehicle. This Retentionalist account of a brief moment of temporal consciousness in terms of representational content fits neatly with the TRT account of "now." Consciousness itself does not need to be extended in time to carry the content of change, movement, and succession.

As an empirical matter, though, longer time frames than 200 ms might be better explained by the Extensionalist Theory. Again, a theory of consciousness and its function is needed to say what exactly it might mean that "consciousness itself" is extended to include multiple temporal parts. Carlos Montemayor and Marc Wittmann (2014) argue that there is no single way to relate the psychological present with the objective present. They propose a hierarchical, three-level analysis of the present in terms of simultaneity, the presence of experience, and the mental presence of a narrative self.

The first level, *simultaneity,* ranges from 2 to 300 ms where events are perceived as simultaneous. At the shortest time frame, simultaneity can be detected prior to distinguishing temporal order. At the longest time frame within this range, cross-modal temporal integration occurs. Events within this interval are perceived as co-temporal units (329–330). Though Montemayor and Wittmann call these units "static snapshots," the ability to detect simultaneity and temporal order within this range suggests they are neither static nor snapshots. According to the TRT, these are the basic units of consciousness, where representations are selected to form a representation of the present moment.

The second level, *the presence of experience,* is the range Montemayor and Wittmann take to be fundamental to temporal consciousness. Spanning from 300 ms to 3 sec, the presence of experience consists of parts that are temporally ordered, such as when perceiving music and language. We experience a song or a sentence as one extended experience composed of elements unfolding over time. I have described this time frame as *the specious present,* and I agree that conscious experience is composed of a series of "now" representations that dynamically interact to provide a continually updated picture of the world in flux.[5]

This longer unit of time seems to fit Extensional Theories. If each "now" representation is a temporal part of a specious present, it might well be the case that the representation of succession is usually a matter of successive parts.

Though temporal phenomena are represented by a "now" representation, they are rarely if ever isolated within such a narrow unit. The movement of the leaves waving and my fingers waggling continues on far longer than the 200 ms interval of a single conscious representation. Empirical support for this hypothesis would be if temporal illusions at intervals longer than 300 ms only involve duration. Motion and succession illusions should be limited to the "now" moment, whereas duration illusions would involve the perception of relations among multiple moments. Unlike brief motion and succession illusions, Extensionalist Theories can explain duration illusions as an error in estimating the length or number of temporal parts in a specious present.

The third level of temporality, *the mental presence of a narrative self*, applies to much longer time frames where metacognitive abilities are required. According to Montemayor and Wittmann, experience at this level involves the sense of oneself in time. Episodic short-term memory appears in the context of autobiographical memory to "form the impression of a stable self that endures through time as part of the experience of reminiscing about the past and planning for the future. That is, the contents of autobiographical memory are instantiated within the boundary of the mental present defined as the temporal window of working memory" (Montemayor and Wittmann 2014: 333).

As discussed in Chapter 5, temporal errors at this level are confabulations rather than illusions. When non-delusional, these errors are part of the process of formulating a coherent narrative self. Out of fairness, I would like to say the Cinematic View describes this level of temporality, due to the way episodic "snapshots" are strung together by cognitive processes akin to inference or judgment. However, I doubt that advocates of the Cinematic View would appreciate my generosity here. They intend the theory to account for the sense that we directly experience temporal phenomena such as motion and change, and these phenomena are better explained by the Retentional Theory.

## The Reality of Consciousness

So in the end, the theory of consciousness provided by the TRT endorses aspects of the Retentional and Extensional Theories of temporal awareness, and only rejects the Cinematic View entirely. This result is not surprising given the rejection of phenomenology as illusory by the Cinematic View and its foundation for the other theories. One of my guiding principles in thinking about consciousness follows Husserl's edict to return to the "things themselves," meaning the way things appear in consciousness (Husserl 1900: 168). Our experience fudges, misrepresents and lags behind reality, but it is not an illusion. The world as it appears *now* is fundamental to how we think about reality and ourselves.

Yet we cannot understand the nature of consciousness if we limit ourselves to the tools of introspection. Though we *know* the world through our conscious investigations, the world *exists* outside of and prior to those investigations. Every scientific theory confirms this humbling fact. I may be the center of my universe, but I am not the universe itself. Therefore, an adequate theory must explain why consciousness came into being, which is to say what evolutionary function consciousness provides. This book has presented the theory that consciousness represents the present moment, and it serves the function of facilitating flexible action.

Consciousness tells me how the world is now and now and now and now. Now always involves some element of change and duration. The leaves are *now* *swaying* in the breeze, anchored by the enduring oak. These temporal elements are represented *as now* by each conscious representation and are collected together into a specious present by their interconnections over time. Existentially, this moment places me in the context of a life somewhere between its beginning and (hopefully much later) end. This ultimate timescale gives me the perspective needed to respond to the world, not just flexibly, but also ethically. The power of *now* is the power of choice.

# Notes

## Introduction

1   William Lycan calls this the "stereoptic fallacy". The brain of someone having a sensation looks nothing like the experience of that sensation, so it seems no amount of information about the brain could be informative about the experience. As Lycan points out, no materialist claims that brains are qualitatively similar to experiences. The fallacy confuses the subject having the experience with the subject viewing that person's brain (Lycan 1996: 47–8).

2   There are many attempts (Chalmers 2010; Koons and Bealer 2010; Robinson 2018). Since my objective in this book is to provide an alternative to Dualism, I will not provide a full argument against Dualism. Other books admirably take on that task (Kirk 2017; Papineau 2002; Perry 2001). Thanks to Anna Strasser for suggesting I address Dualism right at the beginning.

3   "Default mode" is a problematic term in the context of evolutionary explanation. As I will argue in Chapter 5, self-conscious reflection requires representational capacities beyond phenomenal consciousness. Why humans tend toward self-consciousness in the absence of other tasks is a question beyond the scope of this book.

4   For other variations, see the useful collection of essays in *Higher-order Theories of Consciousness* (Gennaro 2004).

5   By "sensation" I mean a sensory representation, that is, a vehicle that represents a sensory stimulus. Each sensory organ evolved to represent specific stimuli. For example, sounds represent auditory stimuli with features such as frequency, pitch, timbre. (Note that "sound" is ambiguous between the representation and its object. Here "sound" means the representation.) Technically, a "perception" involves the classification of a sensation under a concept, such as the sound of a bell. I will generally use "sensation" broadly to refer to either sensations or perceptions unless the distinction is relevant. Neither sensations nor perceptions are essentially conscious, in my view. A "thought" is a conceptual representation and is also not essentially conscious. For further discussion of the contentious issue of unconscious sensations and thoughts, see Chapter 2.

6   Not just any higher-order thought is sufficient, it must be occurrent, non-inferential, and assertive (Rosenthal 2005).

7   This brief discussion is autobiographical rather than analytical. Even so, I am grateful to Michał Klincewicz for encouraging me to be more precise in describing HO Theory. Brevity entails inadequate exposition, but I have tried to be true to the

theory in outline. For a more precise development of an argument against HOT Theory and Dretske's Representational Theory, see Chapter 2 of Droege (2003).

8 See Chapter 3 for a response to those who argue that the unity of consciousness is an illusion.

9 In comments on a recent article submission, one reviewer objected that all forms of associative conditioning are conscious, and the other reviewer objected that no forms of associative conditioning are conscious. There is little consensus on what constitutes consciousness, yet firm convictions nonetheless. These convictions need to be loosened to make any conceptual progress.

10 My rhetorical position is similar to Gerald Edelman's Feasibility Argument (Edelman 1990).

11 "Feeling," like "sensation" and most other words used to describe mental states is often taken to imply consciousness. Unlike "sensation," which I will not take as implying consciousness (see Footnote 5), I will honor that implication for "feeling," so "conscious feeling" here merely emphasizes and clarifies that feelings are conscious.

12 The descriptions in this section apply to both unconscious and conscious sensations. See Footnote 5 for the distinction between sensation and perception. Chapter 1 will discuss the difference between types of sensations, e.g., between visual and kinesthetic representations. Chapter 2 will argue that unconscious sensations maintain their representational content when they become conscious.

13 As William Robinson correctly pointed out to me, "heavy," "light," and "animated" are metaphors rather than literal descriptions of bodily states. See Chapter 1 section "Joy" for how these metaphors can be cashed in representational terms.

14 Ginsburg and Jablonka (2019) offer a similar view of the co-evolution of mind and life.

15 Higher-Order theorists should not read this as begging the question. In HO terms: the target is state consciousness rather than introspective consciousness.

16 See Footnote 5 for the definitions of "sensation" and "thought."

17 Thanks to Keya Maitra for help in characterizing meditation. I am a novice, however, and still may not have gotten it quite right.

18 While exercises such as this one are common, my phrasing has likely been influenced by repeated exercises using Jon Kabat-Zinn's guided meditation practice (Kabat-Zinn 2006).

19 Bodily sensations and emotions do not involve self-consciousness, as I am using this term. It is of course reasonable to characterize these states as self-conscious because they constitute what Thomas Metzinger would call the *phenomenal self-model* (Metzinger 2004, 2010). For rhetorical reasons, I think it is important to draw a sharp and clear line between consciousness as first-order and self-consciousness as second-order. Centuries of confusion in philosophy of mind rest on conflating first- and second-order forms of consciousness, as we will see in Chapter 2.

20  Some features of biological organisms are not determined by function; *spandrels* are the result of genetic mutations that survive by accident rather than natural selection. While it is possible that consciousness is a spandrel, one of the central arguments of this book is that a functional explanation of consciousness is more plausible.

21  While I will draw on insights from the phenomenological tradition, problems with its complete reliance on introspection were noted earlier. Introspection is an essential but unreliable means of investigating consciousness. The results of phenomenological investigations must be integrated with neuroscientific studies and evolutionary explanation. This interdisciplinary method is the one I adopt in this book.

22  In the freezing rotation illusion, words rotate steadily but appear to freeze when the background rotation is in synch (http://www.vertigocenter.ch/duersteler/). Max Dürsteler, who designed that illusion, suggests that the visual system ignores the regular motion of the smaller object in order to treat it as part of the larger surround. Motion representation is suppressed when the figure matches the ground.

23  Tool use will be discussed in more detail in Chapter 4. It is a good example both of the tendency to anthropomorphic definition and the ways functional analysis can provide cross-species comparison of capacities.

24  The rule in animal cognition research, known as Lloyd Morgan's canon, is to always opt for less complex psychological explanations when possible. Reasons that this rule conflicts with other principles of effective scientific theory will be discussed in Chapter 4.

25  Whether the same physical structure can serve different representational functions will be considered in Chapter 1.

# Chapter 1

1  Plato's views can be found in *The Republic* (Plato 375 AD), and Aristotle outlines his view on the soul in *De Anima* (Aristotle 350 AD). For an illuminating review of the subtlety of Aquinas's position, see Sect 8 "Body and Soul" of Ralph McInerny and John O'Callaghan's entry in the *Stanford Encyclopedia of Philosophy* (2015) http://plato.stanford.edu/entries/aquinas/#BodSou

2  The logical positivists adopted a principle of verificationism that grounded knowledge in sensation; sense-datum theorists such as C. D. Broad (1923) reified sensation into particulars that appear immediately before the mind and are taken to represent external objects.

3  As I am using the terms, "sensation" refers to sensory processes prior to the formation of concepts; "perception" refers to sensation that is conceptual. Even

though sensation is nonconceptual, the attentional processes that guide sensation are often informed by beliefs and goals. Neither sensation nor perception implies consciousness.

4  https://www.youtube.com/watch?v=vJG698U2Mvo

5  This failure would not concern a dualist like Locke, since impressions are pictures in the mind and not the brain on his view. Here we are looking for a theory of representation adequate for Materialism. Thanks to William Robinson for defending Locke on this point.

6  These two objections against Picture Theory have been most forcefully waged by Dennett (1991) against what he calls "Cartesian Materialism." While I agree that consciousness does not produce a movie in the mind in the way the Picture Theory suggests, I disagree with Dennett's conclusion that the only alternative is to give up the idea that conscious contents are unified. For a full argument to support this position, see Droege (2003: Ch 5). Thanks to Anna Strasser for reminding me to credit Dennett here.

7  Another version of Reductive Materialism, called *Eliminativism*, claims that a full understanding of neuroscience would replace the current tendency to think of mental processes as different from and additional to brain processes. This position underestimates the value of distinct levels of explanation, including explanation in terms of mental states and processes. A theory that can bridge the explanatory gap is preferable to a theory that simply tries to demolish it.

8  See the Introduction for more on Dualism and zombies.

9  If you do understand Chinese, pick a language that you do not understand for the experiment, preferably one with a script you do not understand for maximum thought experimental effect.

10  The statement is ambiguous about the nature of the quantification claim, which as it turns out is one of the problems with this way of determining content.

11  Either the banana content is *caused by* or *has the function of varying in accord with* that set of stimuli, depending on whether we adopt the Causal or Consumer Theory. The details for these theories will be discussed shortly.

12  As circular as that sounds, the reasons are in the form of a *reductio* and so do not assume what needs to be proved. Assume Externalism: if I am in a vat, then there would be evidence of the vat, because my representations are determined by the vat. There is no evidence that I am in a vat, so I am probably not in a vat. Assume Internalism: if I am in a vat, there may be no evidence of the vat, because my representations are determined by internal relations. There is no evidence that I am in a vat, so there is no way to say whether or not I am in a vat. Of course, the argument is not a *reductio* for someone who is happy to be in a vat (Chalmers 2016).

13  "Perception" is usually taken to be a success word among philosophers. Any perception is a veridical one. Since representations maintain their content even

when they fail, on my view, I will use the word "perception" interchangeably with "sensory representation." Veridicality is not implied.

14 On this point I agree with enactive theories of perception. For several points of disagreement, see Objection 2 below.

15 The number of ways theories are the inverse of one another points to the struggle in reconnecting mind and world after Descartes set them in opposition.

16 Enactive theories take Direct Realism to be entirely nonrepresentational. In the sense that "representation" refers specifically to items in abstract computational systems (Frith et al. 2016), I agree. As I argue in Objection 2 below, even the Enactive View must make use of representations in the sense I have defined. Thanks to Anna Strasser for help in clarifying my position here.

17 This rather vague characterization indicates the limitation of a biological theory to specify representational content in a particular case. What do I mean by "banana" right now? The answer depends on past and current uses of my banana representations. The Consumer Theory explains the process of content determination, but it cannot as it were, read content off a vehicle. This limitation points to a flaw in mind-reading claims by some neuroscientists more than a flaw in the Consumer Theory (Droege 2019).

18 In hallucination the representation fails because there is no object to fulfill the required function. For internalists there must always be an object, either an actual object or a "mere intentional object" to be the thing pictured in the representation. The metaphysical status of these nonexistent mental objects is a puzzle the Consumer Theory avoids. Hallucinations are representations that fail to fulfill their functions, not relations to nonexistent objects.

19 Swampman is usually attributed to Davidson (1987), although Millikan also discussed a version (Millikan 1984: 93), see also her recent (Millikan 2017: 95–6).

20 For fans of thought experiments, consider the difference between you and SwampYou in a vat. Since your representations are all meaningful, they are all mistaken in the vat until you interact with the vat world. Over time your representations come to represent the vat world rather than the real world, since your needs are met by vat objects rather than real objects. SwampYou, on the other hand, starts out with no representations, so interacting with the vat world immediately produces representations about that world.

21 Though Alva Noë also calls the theory "actionist" (2004), the "Enactive View" seems to be more widely adopted to describe the sensorimotor approach to mind and consciousness (Gallagher 2017; Stewart, Gappene, and Di Paolo 2011; Thompson and Stapleton 2009)

22 Philosophers may recognize this as the Kripke-Wittgenstein problem of rule-following (Kripke 1982). If everything you do counts as an exercise of sensorimotor contingencies, then there is no way to make an error.

23 Anil Seth (2014, 2015) supplements the Enactive View with models that predict the causes and consequences of sensory input. This move is a good one; however, both

the Enactive View and Seth's Predictive Processing Approach face a third problem to be discussed in Chapter 3. Neither theory explains the distinction between unconsciousness and consciousness.

24 See the Wikipedia entry "Color" for good illustrations of this phenomenon and the color space mentioned earlier. https://en.wikipedia.org/wiki/Color

25 Even after-images are represented externally, as occupying a particular spatial location in the visual field.

26 The objective nature of sensory systems and behavioral discrimination addresses another long-standing puzzle about the mind and consciousness: inverted spectrum. Everyone loves to contemplate the possibility that bananas really look blue to you even though we both use the word "yellow" to describe them. The answer to this puzzle will be discussed in Chapter 5.

27 For more argument that qualitative character can be explained in terms of representation, see Lycan (1998); Rosenthal (1991); Tye (2000).

28 Thanks to Dorit Bar-on (in conversation) for raising this objection.

29 In relation to the epistemological interlude earlier, Externalism also applies to emotions. Though emotions are *internal* in the sense that they represent states inside my body, the content of an emotional representation is nonetheless determined *externally*, that is, by factors other than the representation itself. On the Millikan formula for representation: emotions vary in accord with particular bodily states, because these variation relations have been useful in the past.

30 Other reasons to believe that emotions can be unconscious will be considered in Chapter 2.

# Chapter 2

1 A seven-letter word for dream is "imagine."

2 See Blanke and Metzinger (2009); Metzinger (2014). Though Metzinger agrees that the weak 1PP is unconscious, he reserves the term "subjectivity" for the conscious sense of self.

3 The following evidence is based on the previous argument that qualitative character (e.g. colorQ) is the property of sensations in virtue of which they represent physical properties (e.g. colorP). As William Robinson objects, this evidence fails if sensations have all their representational capacities in the absence of qualitative character.

My point here is not to prove that qualitative character must be representational; it is the more modest goal of supporting the overall explanatory structure. The coincidence of behavioral and neural evidence for qualitative character and emotion suggests that unconscious and conscious representations are relevantly similar. This similarity, together with arguments in Chapter 3 about differences between unconscious and conscious representations, provides good explanatory reasons to accept both accounts. They are not the only possible accounts.

4   http://neurochannels.blogspot.com/2009/09/consciousness-7-more-ambiguous-figures.html

5   There is some debate about exactly how blind the lesion field is, since there are some reports of motion awareness. More fine-grained responses are also elicited with a range of categories from "no experience" to "clear experience" (Overgaard 2011). Despite this controversy, evidence of stimulus identification in the absence of subjective report of consciousness contributes to the overall support for unconscious sensory processing.

6   Another study (Tooley, Carmel, Chapman, and Grimshaw 2017) showed that some physiological responses to emotional stimuli are similar when unconscious (such as skin conductance response, or SCR), and others differ (such as heart rate changes). This research underscores the complexity of emotion and the need for further investigation of unconscious processing.

7   See Kouider and Dehaene (2007) for a critical review of this research.

8   The classic work on race bias in job applications is Bertrand and Mullainathan (2004). Recent work on gender bias looks at differential ratings of competence and suitability (Foschi and Valenzuela 2012). A new study showing no bias in hiring (Darolia, Koedel, Martorell, Wilson, and Perez-Arce 2016) may reflect flaws in the procedure or the positive effect of training procedures to address implicit bias in the workplace. More research is needed to assess these unconscious sources of discrimination.

9   See Block (2014); Tsuchiya, Wilke, Frässle, and Lamme (2015) for evidence against subjective report as criterial for consciousness and the proposal of alternate no-report paradigms for research.

10  Only very sophisticated systems are able to represent without any immediate use for the representation. In the beginning, all representations are either good or bad in relation to their function. Thanks to Anna Strasser for pressing this point.

11  Eventually the demand for self-conscious representation emerges, a point that will be discussed in Chapter 5.

12  As I will argue in Chapter 4, conscious memory and future imagination are also represented as *now*.

13  (Hoerl and McCormack 2019) make a similar distinction when they argue that animals and infants have a sense of time (temporal updating) without a capacity to represent time (temporal reasoning). There are important terminological and substantial differences between their view and mine, however. On the Temporal Representation Theory, temporal reasoning involves higher-order temporal representations (see Chapter 4), and there are two developmentally prior ways representations utilize temporal relations: tracking change and representing the present moment.

14 Cf. John Searle's (1983) discussion of "direction of fit" for beliefs and desires. These simple associations are not full-fledged beliefs and desires; even the language of "description" and "direction" might sound too cognitive. As with "representation," the terminology captures the appropriate relation and highlights the continuity in function from basic to sophisticated forms.

15 For more explanation of pushmi-pullyu representations and how they individuate content, see Millikan (2004: Ch 6 and 13).

16 Gibson's insistence on the necessity of action in perception led him to reject any talk of representation as a component of perception. I will make use of Gibson's insightful notion of "affordance" without adopting his restrictions on representation or other more controversial Gibsonian views.

17 Foremost, explicit representation sometimes is taken to imply conscious representation but does not do so here. The psychological literature often refers to unconscious processing, such as in the priming studies discussed earlier, as "implicit perception." I am not using the explicit/implicit distinction to make any implications about consciousness except in the specific ways described. (Dienes and Perner 1999) discuss the explicit/implicit distinction in terms of knowledge acquisition. (O'Brien and Opie 1999) focus on the way a representation is coded, as physically discrete (explicit) or logically implied (implicit). In keeping with the evolutionary explanation provided, my use of the distinction is based on functional considerations.

18 This description of implicit representation roughly follows Millikan's description of "tacit suppositions" (1993: 104–5).

19 The importance of misrepresentation was discussed in Chapter 1, and the way time can be misrepresented will be discussed in Chapter 3.

20 The hierarchy of representational capacities I describe in this chapter—pushmi-pullyu animals, practical animals, and theoretical animals—follows Dennett's Tower of Generate-and-Test (1995). See also Chapter 4.

21 Millikan (2004: 169) cites Daniel Dennett (1984) as the popular source for this example. For more information on this amazing insect, see insectidentification.org.

22 Nicholas Shea and Cecilia Heyes propose a similar condition on when metamemory indicates consciousness: it "can be tokened in a variety of different situations and can be deployed to control a range of different actions" (2010: 106).

23 An amusing example is Millikan's description of the elaborate method followed by a squirrel in developing its plan to assault a bird feeder (Millikan 2004: 204–6).

24 More technically, sensations are sensory representations, and thoughts are conceptual representations.

25 For more on the connection between an abstract representation of time and language, see Droege (2012).

# Chapter 3

1   As you might have guessed, Einstein's space-time relativity only creates more metaphysical questions than it solves.

2   Some of the metaphysics appears in the Appendix, where I will consider how the Temporal Representation Theory of consciousness relates to theories about how time is represented in consciousness.

3   The counterintuitive corollary that conscious representations of past and future also represent the present will be discussed in Chapter 5.

4   Recent arguments that the flow of consciousness is illusory point to the inability of the perceptual system to distinguish between competing metaphysical theories of consciousness (Gruber, Bach, and Block 2015; Prosser 2016). Regardless of whether external events actually flow, my claim is that, phenomenologically, consciousness flows. On a Consumer Theory, representations are reproduced because they prove effective, not because they mirror or picture reality. This does not mean that there is no evidence about reality that can be gained from representations. See Millikan (2017) for a description of the way the mind organizes reality into structures that license inductive inferences.

5   See Chapter 1 for reasons that Cartesian Dualism is problematic.

6   "World" here includes bodily states and mental states like thoughts.

7   The role of top-down and bottom-up processes in producing a representation of the present moment will be discussed in more detail later in the chapter.

8   For an excellent analysis of the unity of consciousness, see (Bayne 2012).

9   Some other binding problems include general coordination and binding of variables prior to the specification of their values (Feldman 2013).

10  Though not discussed here, Gerald Edelman's Neural Darwinism (Edelman 1990) bears striking similarities with TRT. Space constraints prevent a full review of every related theory, so I have chosen those that best illuminate contrasts.

11  The mathematical complexity of IIT has been radically simplified here to convey the general theoretical claims. For more detail, a good source is Tononi and Koch (2015). For all the mathematical complexity, see Oizumi, Albantakis, and Tononi (2014); Oizumi, Tsuchiya, and Amari (2016).

12  This problem also applies to the Enactive Theory discussed in Chapter 1, and the more recent Predictive Processing Model (Hohwy, Paton, and Palmer 2016; Seth 2015).

13  The phenomenal/access debate is connected to the earlier debate about the unity of consciousness, because phenomenal consciousness is claimed to unify contents accessible to subjective report.

14  One advocate of the Spare View, David Rosenthal, uses the connection between consciousness and reportability to 'fix the extension of' consciousness (Rosenthal 2005: 291).

15 In the Myth of the Cave, people are only able to see shadows of objects reflected on the cave wall. They don't realize their error because they have never seen the real objects or the light of day (Plato 375 AD Bk. VII, 514a–517c).

16 Dehaene argues that computers are limited by their modularity. Information processed in one module is not available to other modules (Dehaene 2014: 168). While this is true, it is unclear why information transfer in itself constitutes consciousness unless consciousness just is information transfer. At this point, the distinction between the conscious access of subjective report and the simple availability of information to a processing system becomes obscure.

17 In earlier work (Droege 2003: Appendix) I speculated that attentional mechanisms perform the selection and coordination function necessary to produce consciousness. This account still seems roughly correct, given refinements described in this chapter.

18 See Chapter 2 for an explanation of pushmi-pullyu representations and how they come apart to form descriptive and directive representations.

19 See Siegel (2010) for a defense of the claim that visual experience includes a representation of kind properties.

20 To get a good sense of the debate about cognitive phenomenology, see Bayne and Montague (2011). My remarks here are unlikely to be satisfying to partisans on either side of the debate. As with many of the deep and fraught issues entwined with consciousness theory, a full development of this position would require long and technical arguments and would not contribute substantial explanatory support to the theory.

21 The scare quotes around "now" are designed precisely to scare you into noticing that the word indicates the content represented as now. Though not quite a case of mentioning a word, I am definitely not using it.

22 Andy Clark (1997) talks about the value of externalizing thought processes in writing as *scaffolding*. The physical symbols constitute new input that sparks new thought. I am suggesting that conscious thought plays a similar role, not unlike Julian Jaynes' (1976) description of the origin of consciousness. Where Clark tends to underplay the role of internal conscious processes, Jaynes tends to underplay the role of sensory conscious processes. TRT claims that both forms of self-stimulation involve a representation of one's thought or action *as present*.

23 See the Appendix for further discussion of the puzzles of temporal consciousness and the central theories for solving them.

24 Richard Gregory (1998) has argued that consciousness serves the function of "flagging the present" in order to distinguish past memory from present sensation. While there are important points of connection in our views, Gregory's emphasis on the vividness of consciousness is mistaken. Focal conscious contents are vivid, but peripheral ones may not be.

25  Thanks to Anna Strasser for prompting me to clarify the relation between consciousness and decision-making.

26  Predictive Processing Theories analyze "best" in terms of probabilistic inference about external causes (Seth 2014). Like IIT, these models offer an account of mechanisms of representation but do not adequately account for content.

27  ±100 ms is shorthand for the 0–200 ms range of stimuli represented as "now." A neural vehicle potentially incorporates 0–100 ms of stimulus input (-100 ms) and anticipates the next 100–200 ms of input (+100 ms). Thanks to William Robinson for suggesting this clarification.

28  Wittman (2011) calls this the "experienced moment" and refers to the 100–300 ms range as the "functional moment." Recall that Prinz calls this the "present." I will follow James and call it the "specious present." Physically speaking, the present is an instant; thus the extension in time is "specious."

29  These are *episodic memories*, "recollection" in Husserl's terminology, and will be discussed along with future imagination in Chapter 5.

30  Similar diagrams appear in Tye (2003: 93) and Gallagher (2003: 11).

31  In the same year another research group (Campbell and Bryant 2007) studied temporal estimates of novice sky-divers. They found that the experience was estimated longer in proportion to the amount of fear experienced.

32  To view a number of motion illusions, including this flash-lag illusion, go to Michael Bach's website (http://www.michaelbach.de/ot/).

33  Meditation within a religious context also involves spiritual goals, such as oneness or enlightenment.

# Chapter 4

1  Look at these videos for some remarkable animal cognition demonstrations: primate sign language (https://www.youtube.com/watch?v=SNuZ4OE6vCk), dolphin cognition (https://www.youtube.com/watch?v=qn41Uim8PA0), archerfish (https://aeon.co/videos/what-the-spitting-archerfish-might-tell-us-about-small-brain-intelligence), bee training (https://www.theverge.com/2016/10/5/13171714/bee-trained-skills-teach-other-bees).

2  We even ascribe emotions to geometric figures. Watch this classic video from Heider and Simmel and see if you don't think that poor circle was scared (https://www.youtube.com/watch?v=VTNmLt7QX8E).

3  Or, as William Robinson suggests, agnosticism about consciousness in others logically follows from the lack of evidence. No one adopts this position either.

4  Elliot Sober (2000) argues that *genealogical justification* favors anthropomorphic inferences over skeptical ones when theorizing about the minds of animals

that share a common ancestor. He usefully notes that the absence of this form of justification in the case of extraterrestrials and computers means that these inferences are fundamentally different and more tenuous.

5    In Edelman, Baars, and Seth (2005) the authors assert that "it is not likely that the question, 'what is it like to be an octopus tentacle?' will ever be posed by any rational philosopher" (178). They seriously underestimate the rigors of the profession!

6    There are regular challenges to this exclusive status, although so far no conclusive results. While some primates have learned sign language, as I mentioned in the beginning of this chapter, their use of it is narrowly restricted to expressing current needs and desires.

7    While attention is neither necessary nor sufficient for consciousness (see Chapter 3), it is the primary means by which representations are selected to represent the present moment. In the context of a novel situation, attention is needed to determine the appropriate action *now*.

8    See Chapter 2 for the importance of *goal-state representation* to the evolution of consciousness from pushmi-pullyu to practical animal. "Explicit" goal representation indicates that the goal state is separate from the representation of the current situation.

9    View the video of crow problem-solving here: https://www.youtube.com/ watch?v=AVaITA7eBZE

# Chapter 5

1    Many thanks to William Doan for help constructing this memory sequence and for permission to use the epigram quote.

2    Unless otherwise noted, this chapter will focus on conscious memory and imagination. When unconscious forms of memory and imagination are considered, they will be identified as unconscious states.

3    My terminology intentionally differs from the standard terms in psychology, because I am interested specifically in the difference between conscious memory and unconscious memory. Though *episodic memory* is often taken to be equivalent to conscious memory, it is also used to refer to memory of specific episodes whether or not those episodes are consciously reexperienced. For a discussion of how the Embedded Theory of memory relates to some standard distinctions in psychology, see Droege (2013).

4    For Russell, sensations are not representations of external phenomena, they actually *are* the objects you sense. So you are as directly connected to past events as you are to present events; both are constituted by what he called "sense data."

5    There is a rapidly expanding literature on memory and the feeling of pastness that I will not engage here for reasons of space. My aim is to demonstrate how the

Temporal Representation Theory deals with conscious memory and imagination rather than to develop a full-bodied theory of memory. Additional resources include: (Bernecker and Michaelian 2019; Macpherson and Dorsch 2018; Michaelian, Debus, and Perrin 2018; Michaelian and Sutton 2017).

6    Self-reference may need to be included so as to identify the memory as *mine*. It would be fairly easy to add another component if one belongs, but that complication can be saved for another day.

7    In this case, the schematic of your memory would look more like this: {now, here} → <[past experience]> where [past experience] = [{past, there} → <sand, sea, August, blue sky>]. A more extreme case involves "flashbulb" memories where one feels entirely transported into the past. Here the indexical indicator for {now, here} would map the representational contents from the past event. Such a representation would not be higher-order, nor would there be a "feeling of pastness." In such a case, the experience misrepresents the past event as now. One reason traumatic memories are so disruptive is that the person fails to realize that the experience is a memory and responds as if the terrifying event is happening all over again.

8    For a full explanation and defense of HOT Theory, see Rosenthal (2004, 2005). For a sampling of objections to the theory, see Block (2011b); Dretske (1993); Droege (2003).

9    This is a retelling of Humphrey's story from Droege (2013: 187).

10   William Robinson (2018: Ch 8) reasonably argues that thoughts and feelings are not under a person's control, only the expressions of them. This point fits well with my view that consciousness does not have immediate causal relevance, but I will argue in Chapter 6 that introspection does shape one's future self.

# Chapter 6

1    Later in the article Cave rejects this skepticism about free will and adopts a view similar to the one I advocate in this chapter.

2    Philosophers are likely to be frustrated by my treatment of the issues in this chapter. I will characterize the central positions in very broad strokes, overlooking the many subtle distinctions and arguments in this tricky debate. My aim in this chapter is to sidestep all of these thorny issues by reframing the classic problem in a way that makes sense of how minds work in the world. I do not claim to solve the classic problem; I hope to dispense with it.

3    A more technical way to put the point: "a complete description of the state of the world at any time *t* and a complete statement of the laws of nature together entail every truth about the world at every time later than *t*" (Vihvelin 2015).

4    Philosophers might argue that probabilistic causation is still a variety of Determinism and so my view counts as a kind of compatibilism. If so, I accept

the terminology so long as physical causation allows for an open future. Thanks to William Robinson for help in clarifying the distinction between probabilistic causation and complex determinist interactions.

5   While this chapter considers only neural processes, dynamic causation operates across many levels of interaction: neuro-chemical, bio-chemical, and microbiological, to name a few.

6   One translation in keeping with the theme of this book might be "Museum for the Present," or more prosaically "Museum of Contemporary Art."

7   Peter Davies. Fun With the Animals: Joseph Beuys Text Painting. 1998 www. saatchi-gallery.co.uk/imgs/artists.

8   See Baumeister, Crescioni, and Alquist (2011) for research supporting the evolution of free will as a resource by which individuals more effectively pursue their own and their social group's best interests.

9   Cave considers this sort of freedom "completely compatible" with Determinism. Given how Determinism is classically defined, it is not. The conclusion, in my view, is to reject the classical definition and reframe Determinism as "an entirely natural physical causation."

10  See Chapter 5 for an explanation of how human memory and imagination provides a sense of self extended in time.

11  The overwhelming amount of false and misleading information on social media platforms makes me think that restrictions would be worth the cost to free speech. Even in this case, though, we should tread very carefully before allowing Facebook and Twitter to determine what counts as "false."

12  A job that requires lots of travel, long hours and little vacation time is incompatible with child care.

# Chapter 7

1   The internet is also simply an input-output calculator with no mind of its own. The vast complexity of information in cyberspace merely increases the calculus without making the qualitative difference necessary for meaning.

2   (Ginsburg and Jablonka 2019) make a similar argument about the role of biology in producing consciousness.

3   Thanks to William Robinson for clarification of connectionist systems.

4   Connectionists often claim that their networks are not representational (Brooks 1991), because they do not have the symbolic representations that structure computational systems. This is one of the cases where "representation" has significantly different meanings in different research contexts. Here "represents" is used neutrally as "standing for," and in this case the representation relation is secured by the designers that trained the system.

5   That there can be more or less consciousness is controversial. The Temporal
    Representation Theory is committed to a kind of all-or-nothing claim: if there
    is a representation of presence, there is consciousness; if not, not. Still, there can
    be levels of consciousness from drowsy to alert, simple to complex, depending
    on factors such as arousal and modality. A variety of levels and contents of
    consciousness is not inconsistent with my view, a point of connection with
    Information Integration Theory (Chapter 3).

6   Most science fiction stories about the robot apocalypse imagine a hyper-rational
    intelligence rather than a delusional one.

7   My next project will undertake this task in a blog, provisionally titled: *In search of a
    material soul.*

8   Note that this description of advanced meditative states is only one among many.
    Mindfulness meditation, for example, confirms the Temporal Representation
    Theory by reducing self-reflective thoughts about past and future by redirecting
    focus to the "now" (Kabat-Zinn 2005).

9   My claims are firmly grounded in consciousness as it appears in the world and do
    not aim beyond the world. I do not consider possible world scenarios, because I
    rarely find them helpful in explaining features of the actual world.

10  Another part not discussed in Chapter 4 is neuroscience: neuroanatomical evidence
    and neural correlates for consciousness confirm the coincidence of flexibility and
    consciousness (Boly et al. 2013; Kanai et al. 2019; Mashour, Roelfsema, Changeux,
    and Dehaene 2020; Pennartz, Farisco, and Evers 2019).

# Appendix

1   I take movement, change, and succession to be the exemplary forms of the
    temporal phenomena at issue. Duration also involves temporal relations, but it
    raises different sorts of issues that need not be addressed for a general comparison
    of the theories. For the sake of brevity, one or the other of these forms of
    temporality occasionally stand in for all three phenomena.

2   Chuard (2011: 9) suggests that the unit of perception might be "a short-lived event,"
    but that only makes the question of individuation more puzzling. Is the event an
    element of waggle, of music, or of the combination? These would each deliver
    different units, facing different issues of integration in consciousness.

3   Other metaphysical commitments are implied, such as the commitment to an
    objective reality, but no particular metaphysics of time is implied.

4   For those familiar with Dennett's (1991) distinction, Grush is offering an Orwellian
    account and mine is Stalinesque. Dennett would argue that there is actually no
    difference, since subjective report is the same in both cases. Grush and I agree with

Dennett that there is no difference between Orwellian and Stalinesque accounts within a representation of a 200ms interval.

5   See Chapter 3 for a description of how "now" representations are related to this longer specious present.

# References

Acharya, S. and Shukla, S. (2012), "Mirror Neurons: Enigma of the Metaphysical Modular Brain," *Journal of Natural Science, Biology, and Medicine*, 3 (2): 118–24. https://doi.org/10.4103/0976-9668.101878

Addis, D. R., Knapp, K., Roberts, R. P. and Schacter, D. L. (2012), "Routes to the Past: Neural Substrates of Direct and Generative Autobiographical Memory Retrieval," *NeuroImage*, 59 (3): 2908–22. https://doi.org/10.1016/j.neuroimage.2011.09.066

Addis, D. R., Pan, L., Vu, M.-A., Laiser, N. and Schacter, D. L. (2009), "Constructive Episodic Simulation of the Future and the Past: Distinct Subsystems of a Core Brain Network Mediate Imagining and Remembering," *Neuropsychologia*, 47: 2222–38.

Akins, K. A. (1993), "A Bat without Qualities?" in M. Davies, and G. W. Humphreys (eds), *Consciousness*, 258–73, Oxford: Basil Blackwell.

Anwar, Y. (2010), "An Afternoon Nap Markedly Boosts the Brain's Learning Capacity," http://news.berkeley.edu/2010/02/22/naps_boost_learning_capacity/ (accessed April 12, 2016)

Aristotle (350 AD), *De Anima*, trans. H. Lawson-Tancred, New York: Penguin Classics. 1987.

Aronson, L. R. (1951), "Orientation and Jumping Behavior in the Gobiid Fish, *Bathygobius Soporator*," *American Museum of Novitates*, 1486: 1–22.

Aronson, L. R. (1971), "Further Studies on Orientation and Jumping Behavior in the Gobiid Fish, *Bathygobius Soporator*," *Annals of the New York Academy of Sciences*, 188: 378–92.

Arstila, V. (2018), "Temporal Experiences without the Specious Present," *Australasian Journal of Philosophy*, 96 (2): 287–302. https://doi.org/10.1080/00048402.2017.1337211

Arstila, V. and Lloyd, D. E. (eds) (2014), *Subjective Time: The Philosophy, Psychology, and Neuroscience of Temporality*, Cambridge, MA: MIT Press.

Arstila, V., Bardon, A., Power, S. and Vatakis, A. (eds) (2019), *The Illusions of Time: Philosophical and Psychological Essays on Timing and Time Perception*, Palgrave Macmillan. https://doi.org/10.1007/978-3-030-22048-8

Axelrod, V., Bar, M. and Rees, G. (2015), "Exploring the Unconscious Using Faces," *Trends in Cognitive Sciences*, 19 (1): 35–45. https://doi.org/10.1016/j.tics.2014.11.003

Baars, B. J. (1988), *A Cognitive Theory of Consciousness*, Cambridge: Cambridge University Press.

Baars, B. J. (1997), *In the Theater of Consciousness: The Workspace of the Mind*, Oxford: Oxford University Press.

Baars, B. J. (2003), "The Global Brainweb: An Update on Global Workspace Theory," *Science and Consciousness Review*. http://cogweb.ucla.edu/CogSci/Baars-update_03.html (accessed November 19, 2012)

Backus, B. T. and Oruç, i. (2005), "Illusory Motion from Change over Time in the Response to Contrast and Luminance," *Journal of Vision*, 5 (11): 1055–69. https://doi.org/10.1167/5.11.10

Baker, L. R. (2009), "Non-Reductive Materialism," in A. Beckermann, B. P. McLaughlin, and S. Walter (eds), *The Oxford Handbook of Philosophy of Mind*, 109–27, Oxford: Oxford University Press.

Barrett, L. F. and Lindquist, K. A. (2008), "The Embodiment of Emotion," in G. R. Semin, and E. R. Smith (eds), *Embodied Grounding: Social, Cognitive, Affective, and Neuroscientific Approaches*, 237–62, Cambridge: Cambridge University Press.

Barron, A. B. and Klein, C. (2016), "What Insects Can Tell Us about the Origins of Consciousness," *Proceedings of the National Academy of Sciences*, 113 (18): 4900. https://doi.org/10.1073/pnas.1520084113

Baumeister, R. F., Crescioni, A. W. and Alquist, J. L. (2011), "Free Will as Advanced Action Control for Human Social Life and Culture," *Neuroethics*, 4 (1): 1–11. https://doi.org/10.1007/s12152-010-9058-4

Bayne, T. (2012), *The Unity of Consciousness*, Oxford: Oxford University Press.

Bayne, T. and Carter, O. (2018), "Dimensions of Consciousness and the Psychedelic State," *Neuroscience of Consciousness*, 1. https://doi.org/10.1093/nc/niy008

Bayne, T. and Fernández, J. (eds) (2009), *Delusion and Self-Deception: Affective and Motivational Influences on Belief Formation*, East Sussex: Psychology Press.

Bayne, T. and Montague, M. (eds) (2011), *Cognitive Phenomenology*, Oxford: Oxford University Press.

Beckmann, L. (2001), "The Causes Lie in the Future," in G. Ray, L. Beckmann, and P. Nisbet (eds), *Joseph Beuys: Mapping The Legacy*, 91–111, New York: D.A.P./Ringling Museum.

Bernecker, S. (2010), *Memory: A Philosophical Study*, Oxford: Oxford University Press.

Bernecker, S. and Michaelian, K. (eds) (2019), *The Routledge Handbook of Philosophy of Memory*, New York: Routledge.

Bertrand, M. and Mullainathan, S. (2004), "Are Emily and Greg More Employable Than Lakisha and Jamal? A Field Experiment on Labor Market Discrimination," *American Economic Review*, 94 (4): 991–1013. https://doi.org/10.1257/0002828042002561

Biever, C. (2013), "Consciousness: Get with the Programs," *New Scientist*, 218 (2917): 40–1. https://doi.org/10.1016/S0262-4079(13)61259-2

Blackmore, S. and Troscianko, E. T. (2018), *Consciousness: An Introduction, Third Edition*, Oxon: Routledge.

Blake, R., Brascamp, J. and Heeger, D. J. (2014), "Can Binocular Rivalry Reveal Neural Correlates of Consciousness?" *Philosophical Transactions of the Royal Society B: Biological Sciences*, 369 (1641): 20130211. https://doi.org/10.1098/rstb.2013.0211

Blanke, O. and Metzinger, T. (2009), "Full-body Illusions and Minimal Phenomenal Selfhood," *Trends in Cognitive Sciences*, 13 (1): 7–13.

Block, N. (1995), "On a Confusion about a Function of Consciousness," *Behavioral and Brain Sciences*, 18: 227–87.

Block, N. (2011a), "Perceptual Consciousness Overflows Cognitive Access," *Trends in Cognitive Sciences*, 15 (12): 567–75. https://doi.org/10.1016/j.tics.2011.11.001

Block, N. (2011b), "The Higher Order Approach to Consciousness Is Defunct," *Analysis*, 71 (3): 419–31.

Block, N. (2014), "Rich Conscious Perception Outside Focal Attention," *Trends in Cognitive Sciences*, 18 (9): 445–47. https://doi.org/10.1016/j.tics.2014.05.007

Boly, M., Seth, A. K., Wilke, M., Ingmundson, P., Baars, B., Edelman, D., Laureys, S., Tsuchiya, N. (2013), "Consciousness in Humans and Non-Human Animals: Recent Advances and Future Directions," *Frontiers in Psychology*, 4. https://doi.org/10.3389/fpsyg.2013.00625

Bor, D. and Seth, A. K. (2012), "Consciousness and the Prefrontal Parietal Network: Insights from Attention, Working Memory, and Chunking," *Frontiers in Psychology*, 3. https://doi.org/10.3389/fpsyg.2012.00063

Boyer, P. (2008), "Evolutionary Economics of Mental Time Travel?" *Trends in Cognitive Sciences*, 12 (6): 219–24. https://doi.org/10.1016/j.tics.2008.03.003

"Brain Stimulation Therapy," (2019), https://www.psychologytoday.com/therapy-types/brain-stimulation-therapy (accessed June 5, 2019)

Braithwaite, V. A. (2010), *Do Fish Feel Pain?* Oxford: Oxford University Press.

Broad, C. D. (1923), *Scientific Thought*, London: Routledge and Kegan Paul.

Brooks, R. (1991), "Intelligence without Representation," *Artificial Intelligence*, 47: 139–59.

Brown, D. (2006), *Descartes and the Passionate Mind*, Cambridge: Cambridge University Press.

Bshary, R. and Grutter, A. S. (2005), "Punishment and Partner Switching Cause Cooperative Behavior in a Cleaning Mutualism," *Biological Letters*, 1: 396–9.

Caliskan, A., Bryson, J. J. and Narayanan, A. (2017), "Semantics Derived Automatically from Language Corpora Contain Human-Like Biases," *Science*, 356 (6334): 183–6. https://doi.org/10.1126/science.aal4230

Calvey, T. and Howells, F. M. (2018), "An Introduction to Psychedelic Neuroscience," *Progress in Brain Research*, 242: 1–23. https://doi.org/10.1016/bs.pbr.2018.09.013

Campbell, L. A. and Bryant, R. A. (2007), "How Time Flies: A Study of Novice Skydivers," *Behaviour Research and Therapy*, 45 (6): 1389–92. https://doi.org/10.1016/j.brat.2006.05.011

Carhart-Harris, R. L., Leech, R., Hellyer, P. J., Shanahan, M., Feilding, A., Tagliazucchi, E., Chialvo, D., Nutt, D. (2014), "The Entropic Brain: A Theory of Conscious States Informed by Neuroimaging Research with Psychedelic Drugs," *Frontiers in Human Neuroscience*, 8. https://doi.org/10.3389/fnhum.2014.00020

Carruthers, P. (2000), *Phenomenal Consciousness: A Naturalistic Theory*, Cambridge: Cambridge University Press.

Carter, G. G. and Wilkinson, G. S. (2013), "Cooperation and Conflict in the Social Lives of Bats," in R. A. Adams, and S. C. Pedersen (eds), *Bat Evolution, Ecology, and Conservation*, 225–42, New York: Springer Science & Business Media.

Cave, S. (2015), "Free Will Is back, and Maybe This Time We Can Measure It," *Aeon*, October 19. https://aeon.co/essays/free-will-is-back-and-maybe-this-time-we-can-measure-it (accessed December 7, 2017)

Cave, S. (2016), "There's No Such Thing as Free Will," *The Atlantic*. https://www.theatlantic.com/magazine/archive/2016/06/theres-no-such-thing-as-free-will/480750/ (accessed December 7, 2017)

Cellini, N., Torre, J., Stegagno, L. and Sarlo, M. (2016), "Sleep before and after Learning Promotes the Consolidation of Both Neutral and Emotional Information Regardless of REM Presence," *Neurobiology of Learning and Memory*, 133: 136–44. https://doi.org/10.1016/j.nlm.2016.06.015

Chalmers, D. J. (1995), "Facing Up to the Problem of Consciousness," *Journal of Consciousness Studies*, 2 (3): 200–19.

Chalmers, D. J. (2010), *The Character of Consciousness*, Oxford: Oxford University Press.

Chalmers, D. J. (2016), "The Matrix as Metaphysics," in S. Schneider (ed), *Science Fiction and Philosophy*, 35–54, Hoboken: John Wiley & Sons, Inc.

Chuard, P. (2011), "Temporal Experiences and Their Parts," *Philosopher's Imprint*, 11 (11): 1–28.

Clark, Andy (1997), *Being There: Putting Brain, Body and World Together Again*, Cambridge, MA: MIT Press.

Clark, Austen (2000), *A Theory of Sentience*, Oxford: Oxford University Press.

Clayton, N. S. and Dickinson, A. (1998), "Episodic-like Memory during Cache Recovery by Scrub Jays," *Nature*, 395 (6699): 272–4. https://doi.org/10.1038/26216

"Color" (2016, March 30), in *Wikipedia, the Free Encyclopedia*, https://en.wikipedia.org/w/index.php?title=Color&oldid=712745722 (accessed April 5, 2016)

Corballis, M. C. (2017), "Language Evolution: A Changing Perspective," *Trends in Cognitive Sciences*, 21 (4): 229–36. https://doi.org/10.1016/j.tics.2017.01.013

Cowey, A. and Stoerig, P. (2004), "Stimulus Cueing in Blindsight," in *Progress in Brain Research*, 144: 261–77, Amsterdam: Elsevier. https://doi.org/10.1016/S0079-6123(03)14418-4

Csikszentmihalyi, M. (2008), *Flow: The Psychology of Optimal Experience*, New York: Harper Perennial Modern Classics.

Dainton, B. (2018), "Temporal Consciousness," in E. N. Zalta (ed), *The Stanford Encyclopedia of Philosophy*, Stanford: Metaphysics Research Lab, Stanford University. https://plato.stanford.edu/archives/win2018/entries/consciousness-temporal/ (accessed May 7, 2020)

Damasio, A. (2012), *Self Comes to Mind: Constructing the Conscious Brain*, New York: Vintage.

Darolia, R., Koedel, C., Martorell, P., Wilson, K. and Perez-Arce, F. (2016), "Race and Gender Effects on Employer Interest in Job Applicants: New Evidence from a Resume Field Experiment," *Applied Economics Letters*, 23 (12): 853–6. https://doi.org/10.1080/13504851.2015.1114571

Davidson, D. (1987), "Knowing One's Own Mind," *Proceedings and Addresses of the American Philosophical Association*, 60 (3): 441–58. https://doi.org/10.2307/3131782

Dawkins, M. S. (2012), *Why Animals Matter: Animal Consciousness, Animal Welfare, and Human Well-Being*, Oxford: Oxford University Press.

"Deep Brain Stimulation" (2019), https://www.aans.org/ (accessed June 5, 2019)

Dehaene, S. (2014), *Consciousness and the Brain: Deciphering How the Brain Codes Our Thoughts*, New York: Penguin Books.

Dehaene, S. and Changeux, J.P. (2005), "Ongoing Spontaneous Activity Controls Access to Consciousness: A Neuronal Model for Inattentional Blindness," *PLOS Biol*, 3 (5): e141. https://doi.org/10.1371/journal.pbio.0030141

Dehaene, S. and Changeux, J.P. (2011), "Experimental and Theoretical Approaches to Conscious Processing," *Neuron*, 70 (2): 200–27. https://doi.org/10.1016/j.neuron.2011.03.018

Dennett, D. C. (1984), *Elbow Room*, Cambridge, MA: MIT Press.

Dennett, D. C. (1991), *Consciousness Explained*, Boston: Little, Brown and Company.

Dennett, D. C. (1995), *Darwin's Dangerous Idea: Evolution and the Meanings of Life*, New York: Simon & Schuster.

Dennett, D. C. (2006), *Sweet Dreams: Philosophical Obstacles to a Science of Consciousness*, Cambridge, MA: Bradford.

Dennett, D. C. (2018), *From Bacteria to Bach and Back: The Evolution of Minds*, New York: W. W. Norton & Company.

Dennett, D. C. and Kinsbourne, M. (1992), "Time and the Observer: The Where and When of Consciousness in the Brain," *Behavioral and Brain Sciences*, 15 (2): 183–247.

Descartes, R. (1641), *Meditations on First Philosophy, 3rd edition*, trans. D. A. Cress, 1993, Indianapolis: Hackett Publishing Company.

Deutsch, D. and Lockwood, M. (2016), "The Quantum Physics of Time Travel," in S. Schneider (ed), *Science Fiction and Philosophy: From Time Travel to Superintelligence*, 370–83, Hoboken: Wiley-Blackwell.

Dienes, Z. and Perner, J. (1999), "A Theory of Implicit and Explicit Knowledge," *Behavioral and Brain Sciences*, 22: 735–808.

Doris, J. M. (2018), "Précis of Talking to Our Selves: Reflection, Ignorance, and Agency," *Behavioral and Brain Sciences*, 41: 1–51. https://doi.org/10.1017/S0140525X16002016

Dretske, F. (1981), *Knowledge and the Flow of Information*, Cambridge, MA: MIT Press.

Dretske, F. (1993), "Conscious Experience," *Mind*, 102 (406): 265–81.

Dretske, F. (1994), "If You Can't Make One, You Don't Know How It Works," *Midwest Studies In Philosophy*, 19 (1): 468–82. https://doi.org/10.1111/j.1475-4975.1994.tb00299.x

Droege, P. (2003), *Caging the Beast: A Theory of Sensory Consciousness*, Amsterdam: John Benjamins Publishing.

Droege, P. (2009), "Now or Never: How Consciousness Represents Time," *Consciousness and Cognition*, 18 (1): 78–90. https://doi.org/10.1016/j.concog.2008.10.006

Droege, P. (2010), "The Role of Unconsciousness in Free Will," *Journal of Consciousness Studies*, 17 (5-6): 55–70.

Droege, P. (2012), "Assessing Evidence for Animal Consciousness: The Question of Episodic Memory," in J. A. Smith, and R. W. Mitchell (eds), *Experiencing Animal Minds: An Anthology of Animal-Human Encounters*, 231–45, New York: Columbia University Press.

Droege, P. (2013), "Memory and Consciousness," *Philosophia Scientiae*, 17 (2): 171–93.

Droege, P. (2015), "From Darwin to Freud: Confabulation as an Adaptive Response to Dysfunctions of Consciousness," in R. J. Gennaro (ed), *Disturbed Consciousness: New Essays on Psychopathology and Theories of Consciousness*, 141–65, Cambridge, MA: MIT Press.

Droege, P. (2019), "Not by Data Alone: The Promises and Pitfalls of Data Analysis in Understanding Consciousness," *European Review*, 27 (3): 341–56. https://doi.org/10.1017/S1062798719000036

Droege, P. and Braithwaite, V. A. (2014), "A Framework for Investigating Animal Consciousness," in G. Lee, J. Illes, and F. Ohl (eds), *Ethical Issues in Behavioral Neuroscience*, 79–98, Berlin, Heidelberg: Springer.

Droit-Volet, S. (2014), "What Emotions Tell Us about Time," in V. Arstila, and D. E. Lloyd (eds), *Subjective Time: The Philosophy, Psychology, and Neuroscience of Temporality*, 477–506, Cambridge, MA: MIT Press.

Dunlap, J. C., Loros, J. J. and Decoursey, P. J. (eds) (2003), *Chronobiology: Biological Timekeeping*, Sunderland: Sinauer Associates Inc.

Eagleman, D. (2012), *Incognito: The Secret Lives of the Brain*, New York: Vintage.

Edelman, D. B., Baars, B. J. and Seth, A. K. (2005), "Identifying Hallmarks of Consciousness in Non-Mammalian Species," *Consciousness and Cognition*, 14: 169–87.

Edelman, G. M. (1990), *The Remembered Present: A Biological Theory of Consciousness*, New York: Basic Books.

Edgley, M. (2015), "What Is *C. elegans*? | College of Biological Sciences," https://cbs.umn.edu/cgc/what-c-elegans (accessed October 13, 2015)

Emery, N. J. and Clayton, N. S. (2001), "Effects of Experience and Social Context on Prospective Caching Strategies by Scrub Jays," *Nature*, 414 (6862): 443–6. https://doi.org/10.1038/35106560

Feldman, J. (2013), "The Neural Binding Problem(s)," *Cognitive Neurodynamics*, 7 (1): 1–11. https://doi.org/10.1007/s11571-012-9219-8

Foschi, M. and Valenzuela, J. (2012), "Who Is the Better Applicant? Effects from Gender, Academic Record, and Type of Decision," *Social Science Research*, 41 (4): 949–64. https://doi.org/10.1016/j.ssresearch.2012.02.001

Frankish, K. (ed) (2017), *Illusionism: As a Theory of Consciousness*, Exeter, UK: Imprint Academic.

Frege, G. (1948), "Sense and Reference," *The Philosophical Review*, 57 (3): 209–30. https://doi.org/10.2307/2181485

Frith, C., Menary, R., Verschure, P. F. M. J., Seth, A., Blanke, O., Butz, M. et al. (2016), "Action-Oriented Understanding of Consciousness and the Structure of Experience," in A. K. Engel, K. J. Friston, and D. Kragic (eds), *The Pragmatic Turn: Toward Action-Oriented Views in Cognitive Science*, 261–81, Cambridge, MA: The MIT Press.

Gallagher, S. (2003), "Sync-Ing in the Stream of Experience: Time-Consciousness in Broad, Husserl, and Dainton," *Psyche*, 9 (10): 1–14.

Gallagher, S. (2017), *Enactivist Interventions: Rethinking the Mind*, Oxford: Oxford University Press.

Gallistel, C. R. (1990), *The Organization of Learning*, Cambridge, MA: MIT Press.

Gennaro, R. (ed) (2004), *Higher-Order Theories of Consciousness*, Amsterdam: John Benjamins.

Gennaro, R. (2018), "Representational Theories of Consciousness," in R. Gennaro (ed), *The Routledge Handbook of Consciousness*, 107–21, Routledge. https://doi.org/10.4324/9781315676982

Gibson, J. J. (1986), *The Ecological Approach to Visual Perception*, Hillsdale, NJ: Lawrence Erlbaum Assoc.

Ginsburg, S. and Jablonka, E. (2019), *The Evolution of the Sensitive Soul: Learning and the Origins of Consciousness*, Cambridge, MA: MIT Press.

Godfrey-Smith, P. (2016), *Other Minds: The Octopus, the Sea, and the Deep Origins of Consciousness*, New York: Farrar, Straus and Giroux.

Goldman, A. (2006), *Simulating Minds: The Philosophy, Psychology and Neuroscience of Mindreading*, Oxford: Oxford University Press.

Golland, Y., Bentin, S., Gelbard, H., Benjamini, Y., Heller, et al. (2007), "Extrinsic and Intrinsic Systems in the Posterior Cortex of the Human Brain Revealed during Natural Sensory Stimulation," *Cerebral Cortex*, 17 (4): 766–77. https://doi.org/10.1093/cercor/bhk030

Gopnik, A. (1993), "How We Know Our Minds: The Illusion of First-Person Knowledge of Intentionality," *Behavioral and Brain Sciences*, 16 (1): 1–14. https://doi.org/10.1017/S0140525X00028636

Gozzano, S. and Hill, C. S. (eds) (2012), *New Perspectives on Type Identity: The Mental and the Physical*, Cambridge: Cambridge University Press.

Gregory, R. (1998), "Brainy Mind," *British Medical Journal*, 317 (7174): 1693–5. https://doi.org/10.1136/bmj.317.7174.1693

Grosenick, L., Clement, T. S. and Fernald, R. D. (2007), "Fish Can Infer Social Rank by Observation Alone," *Nature*, 445: 419–32.

Gruber, R. P., Bach, M. and Block, R. A. (2015), "Perceiving Two Levels of the Flow of Time," *Journal of Consciousness Studies*, 22 (5–6): 7–22.

Grush, R. (2005), "Internal Models and the Construction of Time: Generalizing from State Estimation to Trajectory Estimation to Address Temporal Features of Perception, Including Temporal Illusions," *Journal of Neural Engineering*, 2 (3): 209–18.

Grush, R. (2016), "On the Temporal Character of Temporal Experience, Its Scale Non-Invariance, and Its Small Scale Structure," Creative Commons. https://doi.org/10.21224/P4WC73

Haggard, P., Clark, S. and Kalogeras, J. (2002), "Voluntary Action and Conscious Awareness," *Nature Neuroscience*, 5 (4): 382–5. https://doi.org/10.1038/nn827

Harmelech, T., Friedman, D. and Malach, R. (2015), "Differential Magnetic Resonance Neurofeedback Modulations across Extrinsic (Visual) and Intrinsic (Default-Mode)

Nodes of the Human Cortex," *Journal of Neuroscience*, 35 (6): 2588–95. https://doi.org/10.1523/JNEUROSCI.3098-14.2015

Hartogsohn, I. (2016), "Set and Setting, Psychedelics and the Placebo Response: An Extra-Pharmacological Perspective on Psychopharmacology," *Journal of Psychopharmacology*, 30 (12): 1259–67. https://doi.org/10.1177/0269881116677852

Hochner, B. (2012), "An Embodied View of Octopus Neurobiology," *Current Biology*, 22 (20): R887–R892. https://doi.org/10.1016/j.cub.2012.09.001

Hoerl, C. and McCormack, T. (2019), "Thinking in and about Time: A Dual Systems Perspective on Temporal Cognition," *Behavioral and Brain Sciences*, 42 (e244): 1–69. https://doi.org/10.1017/S0140525X18002157

Hohwy, J., Paton, B. and Palmer, C. (2016), "Distrusting the Present," *Phenomenology and the Cognitive Sciences*, 15 (3): 315–35. https://doi.org/10.1007/s11097-015-9439-6

Hume, D. (1739), *A Treatise of Human Nature*, ed. Jonathan Bennett, 2017, www.earlymoderntexts.com.

Humphrey, N. (1983), *Consciousness Regained*, Oxford: Oxford University Press.

Husserl, E. (1900), *Logical Investigations*, trans. J. N. Findlay, New York: Routledge 2001.

Husserl, E. (1905), *On the Phenomenology of the Consciousness of Internal Time (1893–1917)*, trans. J. B. Brough, Dordrecht: Kluwer Academic 1990.

Irvine, E. (2011), "Rich Experience and Sensory Memory," *Philosophical Psychology*, 24 (2): 159–76. https://doi.org/10.1080/09515089.2010.543415

James, W. (1890), *The Principles of Psychology, Vol. 1*, New York: Dover.

James, W. (1892), *Psychology*, New York: Henry Holt & Co.

James, W. (1902), *The Varieties of Religious Experience: A Study in Human Nature*, London: Collier Books 1961.

Jaynes, J. (1976), *The Origin of Consciousness in the Breakdown of the Bicameral Mind*, New York: Houghton Mifflin Harcourt.

Jennings, C. D. (2015), "Consciousness without Attention," *Journal of the American Philosophical Association*, 1 (2): 276–95. https://doi.org/10.1017/apa.2014.14

Kabat-Zinn, J. (2005), *Wherever You Go, There You Are: Mindfulness Meditation in Everyday Life*, New York: Hachette Books.

Kabat-Zinn, J. (2006), *Mindfulness for Beginners*, [CD] Sounds True.

Kanai, R., Chang, A., Yu, Y., Magrans De Abril, I., Biehl, M. and Guttenberg, N. (2019), "Information Generation as a Functional Basis of Consciousness," *Neuroscience of Consciousness*, 1 https://doi.org/10.1093/nc/niz016

Kang, M.-S. and Blake, R. (2011), "An Integrated Framework of Spatiotemporal Dynamics of Binocular Rivalry," *Frontiers in Human Neuroscience*, 5: 88. https://doi.org/10.3389/fnhum.2011.00088

Kanwal, J. S., Zhang, Z. and Feng, J. (2013), "Decision-Making and Socioemotional Vocal Behavior in Bats," in R. A. Adams, and S. C. Pedersen (eds), *Bat Evolution, Ecology, and Conservation*, New York: Springer Science & Business Media.

Kensinger, E. A. (2007), "Negative Emotion Enhances Memory Accuracy: Behavioral and Neuroimaging Evidence," *Current Directions in Psychological Science*, 16 (4): 213–18. https://doi.org/10.1111/j.1467-8721.2007.00506.x

Killingsworth, M. (2013), "Does Mind-Wandering Make You Unhappy?," 16 Julyhttp://greatergood.berkeley.edu/article/item/does_mind_wandering_make_you_unhappy (accessed February 23, 2016)

Kirk, R. (2017), *Robots, Zombies and Us: Understanding Consciousness*, London: Bloomsbury Academic.

Koch, C. (2004), *The Quest for Consciousness: A Neurobiological Approach*, Greenwood, CO: Roberts and Company.

Koch, C. (2012), *Consciousness: Confessions of a Romantic Reductionist*, Cambridge, MA: The MIT Press.

Koons, R. C. and Bealer, G. (2010), *The Waning of Materialism*, Oxford: Oxford University Press.

Kouider, S. and Dehaene, S. (2007), "Levels of Processing during Non-Conscious Perception: A Critical Review of Visual Masking," *Philosophical Transactions of the Royal Society B: Biological Sciences*, 362 (1481): 857–75. https://doi.org/10.1098/rstb.2007.2093

Kripke, S. A. (1982), *Wittgenstein on Rules and Private Language: An Elementary Exposition*, Cambridge, MA: Harvard University Press.

Kwan, D., Carson, N., Addis, D. R. and Rosenbaum, R. S. (2010), "Deficits in Past Remembering Extend to Future Imagining in a Case of Developmental Amnesia," *Neuropsychologia*, 48: 3179–86.

Lehrer, J. (2019), "The Mirror Neuron Revolution: Explaining What Makes Humans Social," https://www.scientificamerican.com/article/the-mirror-neuron-revolut/ (accessed June 10, 2019)

Levin, J. (2012), "Do Conceivability Arguments against Physicalism Beg the Question?" *Philosophical Topics*, 40 (2): 71–89.

Levine, J. (1997), "Recent Work on Consciousness," *American Philosophical Quarterly*, 34 (4): 379–404.

Libet, B., Gleason, C. A., Wright, E. W. and Pearl, D. K. (1983), "Time of Conscious Intention to Act in Relation to Onset of Cerebral Activity (Readiness-Potential)," *Brain*, 106 (3): 623–42. https://doi.org/10.1093/brain/106.3.623

Lichfield, G. (2015), "The Science of Near-Death Experiences," *The Atlantic*, 5 Aprilhttps://www.theatlantic.com/magazine/archive/2015/04/the-science-of-near-death-experiences/386231/ (accessed February 21, 2020)

Lin, Z. and He, S. (2009), "Seeing the Invisible: The Scope and Limits of Unconscious Processing in Binocular Rivalry," *Progress in Neurobiology*, 87 (4): 195–211. https://doi.org/10.1016/j.pneurobio.2008.09.002

Locke, J. (1689), *An Essay Concerning Human Understanding*, ed. P. H. Nidditch, Oxford: Oxford University Press 1979.

Lohr, S. (2018), "Facial Recognition Is Accurate, if You're a White Guy," *The New York Times*, 9 Februaryhttps://www.nytimes.com/2018/02/09/technology/facial-recognition-race-artificial-intelligence.html (accessed May 25, 2018)

Lycan, W. (1996), *Consciousness and Experience*, Cambridge, MA: MIT Press.

Lycan, W. (1998), "In Defense of the Representational Theory of Qualia," in J. E. Tomberlin (ed), *Philosophical Perspectives*, 479–87, Malden, MA: Blackwell Publishers.

Lyyra, P., Mäkelä, H., Hietanen, J. K. and Astikainen, P. (2014), "Implicit Binding of Facial Features during Change Blindness," *PLOS ONE*, 9 (1): e87682. https://doi.org/10.1371/journal.pone.0087682

Macpherson, F. and Dorsch, F. (eds) (2018), *Perceptual Imagination and Perceptual Memory*, Oxford: Oxford University Press.

Magee, B. and Elwood, R. W. (2013), "Shock Avoidance by Discrimination Learning in the Shore Crab (*Carcinus Maenas*) Is Consistent with a Key Criterion for Pain," *The Journal of Experimental Biology*, 216 (3): 353–8. https://doi.org/10.1242/jeb.072041

Maier, A., Panagiotaropoulos, T. I., Tsuchiya, N. and Keliris, G. A. (2012), "Introduction to Research Topic – Binocular Rivalry: A Gateway to Studying Consciousness," *Frontiers in Human Neuroscience*: 263. https://doi.org/10.3389/fnhum.2012.00263

Markman, A. (2012), "Can You Be Unconsciously Creative?" 5, October,http://www.psychologytoday.com/blog/ulterior-motives/201210/can-you-be-unconsciously-creative (accessed April 12, 2016)

Mashour, G. A., Roelfsema, P., Changeux, J.-P. and Dehaene, S. (2020), "Conscious Processing and the Global Neuronal Workspace Hypothesis," *Neuron*, 105 (5): 776–98. https://doi.org/10.1016/j.neuron.2020.01.026

Masters, M. (2018), "What Do Flies See Out of Their Compound Eye?" http://animals.mom.me/flies-see-out-compound-eye-5361.html (accessed April 28, 2018)

McClure, S. M., Li, J., Tomlin, D., Cypert, K. S., Montague, L. M. and Montague, P. R. (2004), "Neural Correlates of Behavioral Preference for Culturally Familiar Drinks," *Neuron*, 44 (2): 379–87. https://doi.org/10.1016/j.neuron.2004.09.019

McGreal, S. (2012), "Psilocybin and Personality," *Psychology Today*, http://www.psychologytoday.com/blog/unique-everybody-else/201209/psilocybin-and-personality (accessed March 20, 2021)

McInerny, R. and O'Callaghan, J. (2015), "Saint Thomas Aquinas," in E. N. Zalta (ed.), *The Stanford Encyclopedia of Philosophy*, Spring, Available Online: http://plato.stanford.edu/archives/spr2015/entries/aquinas/ (accessed March 14, 2016)

Mendl, M., Burman, O. H. P. and Paul, E. S. (2010), "An Integrative and Functional Framework for the Study of Animal Emotion and Mood," *Proceedings of the Royal Society B: Biological Sciences*, 277 (1696): 2895–904. https://doi.org/10.1098/rspb.2010.0303

Metzinger, T. (2004), *Being No One*, Cambridge, MA: MIT Press.

Metzinger, T. (2010), *The Ego Tunnel: The Science of the Mind and the Myth of the Self*, New York: Basic Books.

Metzinger, T. (2014), "First-Order Embodiment, Second-Order Embodiment, Third-Order Embodiment," in L. Shapiro (ed), *The Routledge Handbook of Embodied Cognition*, 272–86, New York: Routledge.

Michaelian, K. (2016), *Mental Time Travel: Episodic Memory and Our Knowledge of the Personal Past*, Cambridge, MA: MIT Press.

Michaelian, K. and Sutton, J. (2017), "Memory," in E. N. Zalta (ed), *The Stanford Encyclopedia of Philosophy*, Metaphysics Research Lab, Stanford University. https://plato.stanford.edu/archives/sum2017/entries/memory/ (Accessed February 20, 2019)

Michaelian, K., Debus, D. and Perrin, D. (eds) (2018), *New Directions in the Philosophy of Memory*, New York: Routledge.

Millikan, R. G. (1984), *Language, Thought, and Other Biological Categories*, Cambridge, MA: MIT Press.

Millikan, R. G. (1989a), "Biosemantics," *Journal of Philosophy*, 86 (6): 281–97.

Millikan, R. G. (1989b), "In Defense of Proper Functions," *Philosophy of Science*, 56 (2): 288–302.

Millikan, R. G. (1993), *White Queen Psychology and Other Essays for Alice*, Cambridge, MA: MIT Press.

Millikan, R. G. (2000), *On Clear and Confused Ideas*, Cambridge: Cambridge University Press.

Millikan, R. G. (2004), *Varieties of Meaning*, Cambridge, MA: MIT Press.

Millikan, R. G. (2017), *Beyond Concepts: Unicepts, Language, and Natural Information*, Oxford: Oxford University Press.

"'Mind Reading' Technology Decodes Complex Thoughts" (2017), 27 June https://neurosciencenews.com/machine-learning-thought-6974/ (accessed June 5, 2019)

Montague, P. R. (2008), "Free Will," *Current Biology*, 18 (14): R584–R585. https://doi.org/10.1016/j.cub.2008.04.053

Montemayor, C. and Haladjian, H. H. (2015), *Consciousness, Attention, and Conscious Attention*, Cambridge, MA: The MIT Press.

Montemayor, C. and Wittmann, M. (2014), "The Varieties of Presence: Hierarchical Levels of Temporal Integration," *Timing & Time Perception*, 2 (3): 325–38. https://doi.org/10.1163/22134468-00002030

Montgomery, S. (2016), *The Soul of an Octopus: A Surprising Exploration into the Wonder of Consciousness*, New York: Atria Books.

Nagel, T. (1974), "What Is It Like to Be a Bat?" *Philosophical Review*, 83 (4): 435–50.

Neisser, U. (1981), "John Dean's Memory: A Case Study," *Cognition*, 9 (1): 1–22.

Newell, B. R. and Shanks, D. R. (2014), "Unconscious Influences on Decision Making: A Critical Review," *Behavioral and Brain Sciences*, 37 (1): 1–19. https://doi.org/10.1017/S0140525X12003214

Newport, C., Wallis, G., Reshitnyk, Y. and Siebeck, U. E. (2016), "Discrimination of Human Faces by Archerfish (*Toxotes Chatareus*)," *Scientific Reports*, 6: 27523. https://doi.org/10.1038/srep27523

Noë, A. (ed) (2002), *Is the Visual World a Grand Illusion?* Thorverton: Imprint Academic.

Noë, A. (2004), *Action in Perception*, Cambridge, MA: MIT Press.

Noë, A. (2010), *Out of Our Heads: Why You Are Not Your Brain, and Other Lessons from the Biology of Consciousness*, New York: Hill and Wang.

Noë, A. (2012), *Varieties of Presence*, Cambridge, MA: Harvard University Press.

Nussbaum, M. C. (1999), *Sex and Social Justice*, Oxford: Oxford University Press.

O'Brien, G. and Opie, J. (1999), "A Connectionist Theory of Phenomenal Experience," *Behavioral and Brain Sciences*, 22: 127–96.

Oizumi, M., Albantakis, L. and Tononi, G. (2014), "From the Phenomenology to the Mechanisms of Consciousness: Integrated Information Theory 3.0," *PLoS Comput Biol*, 10 (5): e1003588. https://doi.org/10.1371/journal.pcbi.1003588

Oizumi, M., Tsuchiya, N. and Amari, S. (2016), "Unified Framework for Information Integration Based on Information Geometry," *Proceedings of the National Academy of Sciences*, 113 (51): 14817–22. https://doi.org/10.1073/pnas.1603583113

Overgaard, M. (2011), "Visual Experience and Blindsight: A Methodological Review," *Experimental Brain Research*, 209 (4): 473–9. https://doi.org/10.1007/s00221-011-2578-2

Pacherie, E. (2009), "Perception, Emotions, and Delusions: The Case of the Capgras Delusion," in T. Bayne, and J. Fernández (eds), *Delusion and Self-Deception: Affective and Motivational Influences on Belief Formation*, 107–26, East Sussex: Psychology Press.

Paley, W. (1802), *Natural Theology: Evidences of the Existence and Attributes of the Deity and Evidences of Christianity*, Oxford: Benediction Classics. 2017.

Papineau, D. (2002), *Thinking about Consciousness*, Oxford: Clarendon Press.

Parsons, B. D., Novich, S. D. and Eagleman, D. M. (2013), "Motor-sensory Recalibration Modulates Perceived Simultaneity of Cross-Modal Events at Different Distances," *Perception Science*, 4: 46. https://doi.org/10.3389/fpsyg.2013.00046

Pennartz, C. M. A., Farisco, M. and Evers, K. (2019), "Indicators and Criteria of Consciousness in Animals and Intelligent Machines: An Inside-Out Approach," *Frontiers in Systems Neuroscience*, 13. https://doi.org/10.3389/fnsys.2019.00025

Perry, J. (2001), *Knowledge, Possibility, and Consciousness*, Cambridge, MA: MIT Press.

Pessoa, L. (2017), "Do Intelligent Robots Need Emotion?" *Trends in Cognitive Sciences*, 21 (11): 817–19. https://doi.org/10.1016/j.tics.2017.06.010

Phillips, I. (2014), "Experience of and in Time," *Philosophy Compass*, 9 (2): 131–44.

Phillips, I. (ed) (2017), *The Routledge Handbook of Philosophy of Temporal Experience*, New York: Routledge.

Pieplow, N. (2009), "You Misidentified It Wrong – Earbirding," 1 December http://earbirding.com/blog/archives/1196 (accessed July 12, 2019)

Plato (375 AD), *Republic, Second Edition*, ed. C. D. C. Reeve, trans., G. M. A. Grube, Indianapolis: Hackett Publishing Company, Inc 1992.

Pöppel, E. (1988), *Mindworks: Time and Conscious Experience*, Boston: Harcourt.

Price, T. F. and Harmon-Jones, E. (2015), "Embodied Emotion: The Influence of Manipulated Facial and Bodily States on Emotive Responses," *Wiley Interdisciplinary Reviews. Cognitive Science*, 6 (6): 461–73. https://doi.org/10.1002/wcs.1370

Prinz, J. J. (2004), *Gut Reactions: A Perceptual Theory of Emotion*, Oxford: Oxford University Press.

Prinz, J. J. (2012a), *Beyond Human Nature: How Culture and Experience Shape the Human Mind*, New York: W. W. Norton & Company.

Prinz, J. J. (2012b), *The Conscious Brain: How Attention Engenders Experience*, Oxford: Oxford University Press.

Prosser, S. (2016), *Experiencing Time*, Oxford: Oxford University Press.

Proust, J. (2014), *The Philosophy of Metacognition: Mental Agency and Self-Awareness*, Oxford: Oxford University Press.

Proust, M. (1928), "Swann's Way," in *Remembrance of Things Past*, trans. C. K. S. Moncrieff, and T. Kilmartin, New York: Random House.

Rescorla, M. (2017), "The Computational Theory of Mind," in E. N. Zalta (ed), *The Stanford Encyclopedia of Philosophy*, Stanford: Metaphysics Research Lab, Stanford University. https://plato.stanford.edu/archives/spr2017/entries/computational-mind/ (accessed May 24, 2018)

Resnick, B. (2016), "Scientists Have Invented a Mind-Reading Machine. It Doesn't Work All That Well," 20 June https://www.vox.com/2016/6/20/11905500/scientists-invent-mind-reading-machine (accessed August 29, 2017)

Robinson, H. (2012), "Substance Dualism and Its Rationale," in R. Swinburne (ed), *Free Will and Modern Science*, Oxford: Oxford University Press.

Robinson, W. S. (2018), *Epiphenomenal Mind: An Integrated Outlook on Sensations, Beliefs, and Pleasure*, New York: Routledge.

Rodríguez, F., Durán, E., Gómez, A., Ocaña, F. M., Álvarez, E., Jiménez-Moya, et al. (2005), "Cognitive and Emotional Functions of the Teleost Fish Cerebellum," *Brain Research Bulletin*, 66 (4–6): 365–70. https://doi.org/10.1016/j.brainresbull.2004.11.026

Rosenthal, D. M. (1991), "The Independence of Consciousness and Sensory Quality," in E. Villanueva (ed), *Philosophical Issues: Consciousness*, 1:15–36, Atascadero, CA: Ridgeview Publishing.

Rosenthal, D. M. (1997), "A Theory of Consciousness," in N. Block, O. Flanagan, and G. Güzuldere (eds), *The Nature of Consciousness: Philosophical Debates*, 729–54, Cambridge, MA: MIT Press.

Rosenthal, D. M. (2004), "Varieties of Higher-Order Theory," in R. Gennaro (ed), *Higher-Order Theories of Consciousness*, 17–44, Amsterdam: John Benjamins.

Rosenthal, D. M. (2005), *Consciousness and Mind*, Oxford: Oxford University Press.

Rosenthal, D. M. (2008), "Consciousness and Its Function," *Consciousness and Perception: Insights and Hindsights A Festschrift in Honour of Larry Weiskrantz*, 46 (3): 829–40. https://doi.org/10.1016/j.neuropsychologia.2007.11.012

Ross, G. and Holderied, M. W. (2013), "Learning and Memory in Bats: A Case Study on Object Discrimination in Flower-Visiting Bats," in R. A. Adams, and S. C. Pedersen (eds), *Bat Evolution, Ecology, and Conservation*, 207–24, New York: Springer Science & Business Media.

Russell, B. (1921), *The Analysis of Mind*, Rockville, MD: Arc Manor.

Sacks, O. (1970), *The Man Who Mistook His Wife for a Hat and Other Clinical Tales*, New York: Harper Perennial.

Schwitzgebel, E. (2008), "The Unreliability of Naive Introspection," *The Philosophical Review*, 117 (2): 245–73. https://doi.org/10.1215/00318108-2007-037

Searle, J. R. (1980), "Minds, Brains, and Programs," *Behavioral and Brain Sciences*, 3 (3): 417–24. https://doi.org/10.1017/S0140525X00005756

Searle, J. (1983), *Intentionality: An Essay in the Philosophy of Mind*, Cambridge: Cambridge University Press.

Seth, A. (ed) (2014), *30-Second Brain*, London: Icon Books Ltd.

Seth, A. K. (2014), "A Predictive Processing Theory of Sensorimotor Contingencies: Explaining the Puzzle of Perceptual Presence and Its Absence in Synesthesia," *Cognitive Neuroscience*, 5 (2): 97–118. https://doi.org/10.1080/17588928.2013.877880

Seth, A. K. (2015), "Presence, Objecthood, and the Phenomenology of Predictive Perception," *Cognitive Neuroscience*, 6 (2-3): 111–17. https://doi.org/10.1080/175889 28.2015.1026888

Seth, A. K., Baars, B. J. and Edelman, D. B. (2005), "Criteria for Consciousness in Humans and Other Mammals," *Consciousness and Cognition*, 14: 119–39.

Shea, N. and Heyes, C. (2010), "Metamemory as Evidence of Animal Consciousness: The Type That Does the Trick," *Biology & Philosophy*, 25 (1): 95–110. https://doi. org/10.1007/s10539-009-9171-0

Siegel, S. (2010), *The Contents of Visual Experience*, Oxford: Oxford University Press.

Simons, D. J. and Chabris, C. F. (1999), "Gorillas in Our Midst: Sustained Inattentional Blindness for Dynamic Events," *Perception*, 28 (9): 1059–74.

"Sleep, Learning, and Memory" (2007) 17 December, http://healthysleep.med.harvard. edu/healthy/matters/benefits-of-sleep/learning-memory (accessed April 12, 2016)

Smilansky, S. (2000), *Free Will and Illusion*, Oxford: Oxford University Press.

Sneddon, L. U., Braithwaite, V. A. and Gentle, M. J. (2003), "Do Fishes Have Nociceptors? Evidence for the Evolution of a Vertebrate Sensory System," *Proceedings of the Royal Society of London. Series B: Biological Sciences*, 270 (1520): 1115–21. https://doi.org/10.1098/rspb.2003.2349

Sneddon, L. U., Elwood, R. W., Adamo, S. A. and Leach, M. C. (2014), "Defining and Assessing Animal Pain," *Animal Behaviour*, 97: 201–12. https://doi.org/10.1016/j. anbehav.2014.09.007

Sober, E. (2000), "Evolution and the Problem of Other Minds," *The Journal of Philosophy*, 97 (7): 365–86. https://doi.org/10.2307/2678410

Sperling, G. (1960), "The Information Available in Brief Visual Presentations," *Psychological Monographs: General and Applied*, 74 (11): 1–29. http://doi. org/10.1037/h0093759

Stetson, C., Cui, X., Montague, P. R. and Eagleman, D. M. (2006), "Motor-Sensory Recalibration Leads to an Illusory Reversal of Action and Sensation," *Neuron*, 51 (5): 651–9. https://doi.org/10.1016/j.neuron.2006.08.006

Stetson, C., Fiesta, M. P. and Eagleman, D. M. (2007), "Does Time Really Slow Down during a Frightening Event?" *PLoS ONE*, 2 (12): e1295. https://doi.org/10.1371/ journal.pone.0001295

Stewart, J., Gappene, O. and Di Paolo, E. A. (2011), *Enaction : Toward a New Paradigm for Cognitive Science*, Cambridge, MA: MIT Press.

Stoerig, P. (2006), "Blindsight, Conscious Vision, and the Role of Primary Visual Cortex," in S. Martinez-Conde, S. L. Macknik, J.-M. A. Martinez, and P. U. Tse (eds), *Visual Perception: Fundamentals of Awareness*, 155 (B): 217–34, Amsterdam: Elsevier. https://doi.org/10.1016/S0079-6123(06)55012-5

Tamietto, M., Castelli, L., Vighetti, S., Perozzo, P., Geminiani, G., Weiskrantz, L. and Gelder, B. de (2009), "Unseen Facial and Bodily Expressions Trigger Fast Emotional Reactions," *Proceedings of the National Academy of Sciences*, 106 (42): 17661–6. https://doi.org/10.1073/pnas.0908994106

Tebbich, S., Bshary, R. and Grutter, A. S. (2002), "Cleaner Fish *Labroides Dimidiatus* Recognise Familiar Clients," *Animal Cognition*, 5 (3): 139–45. https://doi.org/10.1007/s10071-002-0141-z

Thompson, E. (2007), *Mind in Life: Biology, Phenomenology and the Sciences of the Mind*, Cambridge, MA: Harvard University Press.

Thomson, E. (2009), "Consciousness (7): More Ambiguous Figures," 10 September http://neurochannels.blogspot.com/2009/09/consciousness-7-moreambiguous-figures.html (accessed April 16, 2016)

Thompson, E. and Stapleton, M. (2009), "Making Sense of Sense-Making: Reflections on Enactive and Extended Mind Theories," *Topoi*, 28 (1): 23–30. https://doi.org/10.1007/s11245-008-9043-2

Tillich, P. (1955), *Biblical Religion and the Search for Ultimate Reality*, Chicago: University of Chicago Press.

Timmermann, C., Roseman, L., Williams, L., Erritzoe, D., Martial, C., et al. (2018), "DMT Models the Near-Death Experience," *Frontiers in Psychology*, 9 https://doi.org/10.3389/fpsyg.2018.01424

Tisdall, C. (1979), *Joseph Beuys*, New York: Solomon R. Guggenheim Museum.

Tolle, E. (2004), *The Power of Now: A Guide to Spiritual Enlightenment*, Novato, CA: Namaste Publishing.

Tong, F., Meng, M. and Blake, R. (2006), "Neural Bases of Binocular Rivalry," *Trends in Cognitive Sciences*, 10 (11): 502–11. https://doi.org/10.1016/j.tics.2006.09.003

Tononi, G. (2004), "An Information Integration Theory of Consciousness," *BMC Neuroscience*, 5: 42.

Tononi, G. (2008), "Consciousness as Integrated Information: A Provisional Manifesto," *The Biological Bulletin*, 215 (3): 216–42. https://doi.org/10.2307/25470707

Tononi, G. (2012), *Phi: A Voyage from the Brain to the Soul*, New York: Pantheon.

Tononi, G. and Koch, C. (2015), "Consciousness: Here, There and Everywhere?" *Philosophical Transactions of the Royal Society of London B: Biological Sciences*, 370 (1668): 20140167. https://doi.org/10.1098/rstb.2014.0167

Tooley, M. D., Carmel, D., Chapman, A. and Grimshaw, G. M. (2017), "Dissociating the Physiological Components of Unconscious Emotional Responses," *Neuroscience of Consciousness*, 2017: 1 https://doi.org/10.1093/nc/nix021

Treisman, A. (1998), "Feature Binding, Attention and Object Perception," *Philosophical Transactions of the Royal Society B: Biological Sciences*, 353 (1373): 1295–306.

Tsuchiya, N., Wilke, M., Frässle, S. and Lamme, V. A. F. (2015), "No-Report Paradigms: Extracting the True Neural Correlates of Consciousness," *Trends in Cognitive Sciences*, 19 (12): 757–70. https://doi.org/10.1016/j.tics.2015.10.002

Tulving, E. (2005), "Episodic Memory and Autonoesis: Uniquely Human?" in H. S. Terrace, and J. Metcalfe (eds), *The Missing Link in Cognition*, 3–56, Oxford: Oxford University Press.

Tye, M. (2000), *Consciousness, Color, and Content*, Cambridge, MA: MIT Press.

Tye, M. (2003), *Consciousness and Persons: Unity and Identity*, Cambridge, MA: MIT Press.

Tye, M. (2016), *Tense Bees and Shell-Shocked Crabs: Are Animals Conscious?* Oxford: Oxford University Press.

Van Boxtel, J. J. A., Tsuchiya, N. and Koch, C. (2010), "Consciousness and Attention: On Sufficiency and Necessity," *Frontiers in Psychology*, 1 https://doi.org/10.3389/fpsyg.2010.00217

Van Ryckegham, A. (1998), "How Do Bats Echolocate and How Are They Adapted to This Activity?" 21 December https://www.scientificamerican.com/article/how-do-bats-echolocate-an/# (accessed May 22, 2017)

Vihvelin, K. (2015), "Arguments for Incompatibilism," in E. N. Zalta (ed), *The Stanford Encyclopedia of Philosophy*, Stanford: Metaphysics Research Lab, Stanford University. https://plato.stanford.edu/archives/fall2015/entries/incompatibilism-arguments/ (accessed July 13, 2017)

Waters, F., Allen, P., Aleman, A., Fernyhough, C., Woodward, T. S., Badcock, et al. (2012), "Auditory Hallucinations in Schizophrenia and Nonschizophrenia Populations: A Review and Integrated Model of Cognitive Mechanisms," *Schizophrenia Bulletin*, 38 (4): 683–93. https://doi.org/10.1093/schbul/sbs045

Wenke, D. and Haggard, P. (2009), "How Voluntary Actions Modulate Time Perception," *Experimental Brain Research. Experimentelle Hirnforschung. Experimentation Cerebrale*, 196 (3): 311–18. https://doi.org/10.1007/s00221-009-1848-8

Wilkes, K. V. (1988), "Yishi, Duh, Um, And Consciousness," in A. J. Marcel, and E. Bisiach (eds), *Consciousness in Contemporary Science*, 16–41, Oxford: Oxford University Press.

Wilson, N. (2015), "Why Termites Build Such Enormous Skyscrapers," 10 December http://www.bbc.com/earth/story/20151210-why-termites-build-such-enormous-skyscrapers (accessed August 4, 2018)

Windt, J. M. (2018), "Consciousness and Dreams: From Self-Simulation to the Simulation of a Social World," in R. J. Gennaro (ed), *The Routledge Handbook of Consciousness*, 420–35, Abingdon: Routledge. https://doi.org/10.4324/9781315676982

Wittgenstein, L. (1922), *Tractatus Logico-Philosophicus*, trans. C. K. Ogden, Routledge 1990.

Wittgenstein, L. (1953), *Philosophical Investigations*, 3rd edn, trans. G. E. M. Anscombe, New York: Macmillan 1968.

Wittmann, M. (2011), "Moments in Time," *Frontiers in Integrative Neuroscience*, 5: 66.
    https://doi.org/10.3389/fnint.2011.00066

Zimmer, C. (2019), "Scientists Created Bacteria with a Synthetic Genome. Is This
    Artificial Life?," *The New York Times* 21 May https://www.nytimes.com/2019/05/15/
    science/synthetic-genome-bacteria.html (accessed May 24, 2019)

# Index

www.ingramcontent.com/pod-product-compliance
Lightning Source LLC
Chambersburg PA
CBHW050421280326
41932CB00013BA/1952